Financial Literacy and Responsible Finance in the FinTech Era

A growing body of evidence suggests that financial literacy plays an important role in financial well-being, and that differences in financial knowledge acquired early in life can explain a significant part of financial and more general well-being in adult life. Financial technology (FinTech) is revolutionizing the financial services industry at an unrivalled pace. Views differ regarding the impact that FinTech is likely to have on personal financial planning, well-being and societal welfare. In an era of mounting student debt, increased (digital) financial inclusion and threats arising from instances of (online) financial fraud, financial education and enlightened financial advising are appropriate policy interventions that enhance financial and overall well-being.

Financial Literacy and Responsible Finance in the FinTech Era: Capabilities and Challenges engages in this important academic and policy agenda by presenting a set of seven chapters emanating from four parallel streams of literature related to financial literacy and responsible finance.

The chapters in this book were originally published as a special issue of *The European Journal of Finance*.

John O. S. Wilson is Professor of Banking & Finance and Director of the Centre for Responsible Banking & Finance at the University of St Andrews. His research focuses on financial institutions in Asia, Europe, and North America. He has published over 70 refereed journal articles. He is the author/co-author of numerous textbooks and monographs. He also co-edited the first, second and third editions of the Oxford Handbook of Banking.

Georgios A. Panos is Professor of Finance at the Adam Smith Business School of the University of Glasgow. He is working on issues of responsible finance and business and has been voted as a Poets & Quants Top 40 Under 40 MBA Professor for the year 2020. His early influential work on the behavioural determinants of business entry, performance and failure has been published at the *Journal of Financial Economics* and received prestigious awards for strengthening financial economic research and education. His most recent work on financial literacy received €1.6 million funding from the EU via the Horizon 2020 project "PROFIT: PROmoting FInancial awareness and sTability". His novel courses in responsible banking and development finance and his scholarly work on the educational curriculum in financial technology (FinTech) have led to the generation of new curricula and taught programmes at the Adam Smith Business School. He serves at the editorial teams of *The European Journal of Finance*, *Small Business Economics: An Entrepreneurship Journal* and the *Journal of General Management*.

Chris Adcock is Honorary Professor of Finance in Sheffield University Management School and visiting Professor at University College Dublin. He worked as Professor of Quantitative Finance at SOAS – University of London and as Professor of Financial Econometrics at the University of Sheffield. His research interests are in portfolio selection, asset pricing theory and development of quantitative techniques for portfolio management. He is also the founding editor of *The European Journal of Finance*.

Financial Literacy and Responsible Finance in the FinTech Era

Capabilities and Challenges

Edited by
John O. S. Wilson, Georgios A. Panos and Chris Adcock

LONDON AND NEW YORK

First published 2022
by Routledge
2 Park Square, Milton Park, Abingdon, Oxon OX14 4RN

and by Routledge
605 Third Avenue, New York, NY 10158

Routledge is an imprint of the Taylor & Francis Group, an informa business

British Library Cataloguing in Publication Data
A catalogue record for this book is available from the British Library

ISBN: 978-0-367-76977-2 (hbk)
ISBN: 978-0-367-76978-9 (pbk)
ISBN: 978-1-003-16919-2 (ebk)

Typeset in Minion Pro
by Newgen Publishing UK

Publisher's Note
The publisher accepts responsibility for any inconsistencies that may have arisen during the conversion of this book from journal articles to book chapters, namely the inclusion of journal terminology.

Disclaimer
Every effort has been made to contact copyright holders for their permission to reprint material in this book. The publishers would be grateful to hear from any copyright holder who is not here acknowledged and will undertake to rectify any errors or omissions in future editions of this book.

For
Alison, Kat and Libby
(John O. S. Wilson)

For
Magda and Lena
(Georgios Panos)

For
Judy, Mark, Ben and Tina
(Chris Adcock)

Contents

Citation Information

The chapters in this book were originally published in *The European Journal of Finance*, volume 26, issue 4–5 (2020). When citing this material, please use the original page numbering for each article, as follows:

For any permission-related enquiries please visit:
www.tandfonline.com/page/help/permissions

Notes on Contributors

Nikolaos Artavanis, Virginia Tech, Pamplin College of Business, Blacksburg, VA, USA.

Christos Avdoulas, Hellenic Financial Literacy Institute, Alimos, Greece; Interamerican part of achmea, Interamerican Research Center, Athens, Greece; Department of Accounting and Finance, Athens University of Economics and Business, Athens, Greece.

J. Michael Collins, Consumer Finance and Public Affairs, University of Wisconsin, Madison, WI, USA.

Christian Engels, Durham University Business School, Durham, UK.

Declan French, Queen's Management School, Queen's University Belfast, Belfast, UK.

Claudia Girardone, Essex Business School, University of Essex, Colchester, UK.

Soumya Karra, University of Massachusetts Amherst, Isenberg School of Management, Amherst, MA, USA.

Kamlesh Kumar, Durham University Business School, Durham, UK.

Donal McKillop, Queen's Management School, Queen's University Belfast, Belfast, UK.

Milena Migliavacca, Department of Economics and Business Administration, Faculty of Economics, Università Cattolica del Sacro Cuore, Milan, Italy.

Georgios A. Panos, Adam Smith Business School, University of Glasgow, Glasgow, UK.

Dennis Philip, Durham University Business School, Durham, UK.

Nikolaos D. Philippas, Department of Business Administration, University of Piraeus, Piraeus, Greece; Hellenic Financial Literacy Institute, Alimos, Greece; Interamerican part of achmea, Interamerican Research Center, Athens, Greece.

Anna Sarkisyan, Essex Business School, University of Essex, Colchester, UK.

Mais Sha'ban, Al-Zaytoonah University of Jordan, Amman, Jordan.

Elaine Stewart, Queen's Management School, Queen's University Belfast, Belfast, UK.

Carly Urban, Economics, Montana State University, Bozeman, MT, USA.

John O. S. Wilson, University of St. Andrews, Management School, St. Andrews, UK.

Introduction

Financial literacy and responsible finance in the FinTech era: capabilities and challenges

Georgios A. Panos ⓘ and John O. S. Wilson ⓘ

ABSTRACT

A growing body of evidence suggests that financial literacy plays an important role in financial well-being, and that differences in financial knowledge acquired early in life can explain a significant part of financial and more general well-being in adult life. Financial technology (FinTech) is revolutionising the financial services industry at an unrivalled pace. Views differ regarding the likely impact that FinTech is likely to have on personal financial planning, well-being and societal welfare. In an era of mounting student debt, increased (digital) financial inclusion, and threats arising from instances of (online) financial fraud, financial education and enlightened financial advising appropriate policy interventions that enhance financial and overall well-being. This special issue engages in this important academic and policy agenda by presenting a set of seven new papers emanating from four parallel streams of literature related to financial literacy and responsible finance.

A growing body of evidence suggests that financial literacy is among the most important determinants of financial well-being.[1] Informed financial decisions have been shown to be a key factor in making effective financial choices (Lusardi and Mitchell 2014). Differences in financial knowledge acquired early in life explain a significant part of wealth inequality during retirement (Lusardi, Michaud, and Mitchell 2017).

Financial technology (FinTech) is revolutionising the financial services industry at an unrivalled pace (Frost et al. 2019). From mobile payments, robo-advising, app-based investing platforms, to online banking solutions, FinTech developments have impacted upon financial planning, financial well-being and economic inequality (Frame, Wall, and White 2019). FinTech has the potential to enhance financial capability. Start-ups and platforms using technology to simplify personal finance and streamline financial planning processes are not only building the next generation of financial tools, but also encouraging and facilitating financial education. Improved financial and other (technological, political health, environmental) literacies enable individuals to better engage with artificial intelligence (Aun 2017). Moreover, the role of financial institutions, corporations and entrepreneurs is important for the formation of supply-side solutions that enhance financial literacy and reduce inequalities across demographic groups. Lusardi et al. (2015) argue that financial literacy research and practice should seek to understand how to make financial education more effective via improved design and delivery. In the wake of the FinTech era, visualisation and accessibility/user-friendliness are important for financial inclusion. Indeed, the presentation format of financial information has been shown to affect choices made by individuals with low financial literacy (Hastings and Tejeda-Ashton 2008; Hastings and Mitchell 2018).

FinTech developments may also damage financial well-being by triggering impulsive consumer behaviour when interacting with financial technologies and platforms. For example, mobile apps could attract impulsive and unsophisticated individuals, who lack the necessary skills to forecast future preferences. As such, mobile apps can lead to individuals making faulty decisions in 'hot' states or under sales pressure. In such cases, the reduced time between the purchase and ultimate consumption of financial services is likely to be detrimental to consumer welfare. Hundtofte and Gladstone (2017) provide evidence that mobile users are more likely to engage in impulsive purchasing behaviour and more likely to use payday loans. Mobile loan products are often *too accessible* and allow fleeting preferences to be acted upon. This suggests that mobile apps and platforms should be complemented by training. In a recent cross-country study, Panos and Karkkainen (2019) find that financial literacy is negatively related to cryptocurrency ownership. This suggests that less financially literate consumers have a limited understanding of the greater risk and reward trade-offs of cryptocurrencies relative to alternative asset classes. The domination of the market by largely unsophisticated investors is a likely factor driving the volatility of cryptocurrencies.

The papers in this special issue of the *European Journal of Finance* inform the current educational and policy agenda regarding developments in financial-literacy research, and the role of financial technology in enhancing financial capability within a responsible finance framework.[2] They cover four broad themes related to financial capability, namely FinTech apps and financial capability (McKillop, French, and Stewart 2020); financial inclusion and financial well-being (Shaban, Girardone, and Sarkisyan 2020; Urban and Collins 2020; Philippas and Avdoulas 2020); student financial literacy and financial outcomes (Philippas and Avdoulas 2020; Artavanis and Kara 2020); and knowledge, financial advice and fraud detection (Migliavacca 2020; Engels, Kamlesh, and Philip 2020).

In the first study in this issue, McKillop, French, and Stewart (2020) assess whether smartphone apps can be utilised to improve desirable financial capability. The authors provide four smartphone apps, (packaged together under the title 'Money Matters') to working age members (16–65 years) of the largest credit union in Northern Ireland. These comprise a loan interest comparison app; an expenditure comparison app; a cash calendar app; and a debt management app. In a randomised control trial, the authors find significant improvements in 'financial knowledge, understanding and basic skills' and 'attitudes and motivations' for the group of individuals that used the apps. Those using the apps were more likely to keep track of their income and expenditure and proved to be more resilient when faced with a financial shock.[3]

In the second study in this issue, Shaban, Girardone, and Sarkisyan (2020) use six indicators drawn from the International Monetary Fund Financial Access Survey to construct a multidimensional financial inclusion index across 95 countries. They present evidence for the period 2004–15, which suggests an overall increase in the access and use of financial services. At a macroeconomic level, the authors find that financial inclusion is positively associated with economic development, banking system conditions, human development, and internet usage and government integrity. Based upon these findings, the authors suggest that policies to boost financial capability should account for the level of economic development.[4]

In the third study in this issue, Urban and Collins (2020) assess the importance of financial well-being within overall well-being. Using a large US cross-sectional dataset, the authors find that a standardised financial well-being score generally tracks income, wealth, and participation in investment markets. However, financial well-being measures are distinct from general subjective well-being and financial literacy measures over the life course.[5]

In the fourth paper in this issue, Philippas and Avdoulas (2020) examine the relationship between financial literacy and financial well-being using a primary dataset of Greek university students who lived through the financial crisis.[6] The authors find that male students are more financially literate than female students. They also find a relationship between student financial literacy and parental education and income. Their findings suggest that students who are more financial literate are better equipped to cope with unexpected financial shocks. Overall, financial literacy is a key driver of financial well-being among Greek University students.

The fifth study in this issue by Artavanis and Kara (2020) engages in the theme of student debt by utilising a novel dataset of US students, from a major, land-grant, public university in Massachusetts. Here the authors examine the level of financial literacy of college students, and its implications on the repayment of student debt. They find low levels of financial literacy (39.5%), particularly among female (26%), minority (24%) and first-generation (33%) students. Moreover, students with a deficit in financial literacy are more likely to underestimate future student loan payments. Specifically, 38.2% of low-literacy students underestimate future annual payments by more than $1000. High financial literacy reduces the probability of significant payment underestimation by 17–18 percentage points. The authors also uncover a financial literacy wage gap; students with low financial literacy expect significantly lower starting salaries than their high-literacy counterparts. Consequently, low-literacy students are more vulnerable to unexpected, adverse shocks on their payment-to-income ratios, which in turn impairs future creditworthiness and ability to service debt post-graduation.

In the sixth study in this special issue, Migliavacca (2020) examines financial advice.[7] The author asserts that the readiness, effectiveness and impact of educational programmes aimed at increasing financial literacy are yet largely undocumented. Her findings suggest that financial advisors are an effective mediator of the increase in investors' financial awareness. She establishes this relationship using three measures of financial literacy (basic, advanced and overall), and also tests distinctive typologies of advisors. She finds that the presence of independent financial advisors tends to increase the 'advanced' financial literacy skills of their respective clients. Based on these findings, the author highlights the important role of enlightened financial advising as a complement to financial education programmes.

In the final study of this special issue, Engels, Kamlesh, and Philip (2020) examine financial fraud, which is likely to induce major losses in terms of consumer morale and the essential trust in financial institutions.[8] The authors find that more financially knowledgeable individuals have a higher propensity to detect fraud. A one standard deviation increase in financial knowledge increases the probability of detecting fraud by three percentage points. The result is not driven by higher financial product usage and is moderated by individual subjective well-being. Interestingly, prudent financial behaviour relating to basic money management is found to have negligible effects for detecting fraud. The findings confirm that fraud tactics are increasingly complex, and it is greater financial knowledge rather than basic money management skills that provides the degree of sophistication necessary to detect fraud. The paper draws policy implications for consumer education programmes to go beyond cultivating money management skills, and provide advanced financial knowledge necessary for tackling fraud.

Notes

1. The growing interest in this area is related to concerns that some financial institutions mis-sell products and services to their clients or engage in other negative practices that take advantage of uninformed (less financially literate) consumers.
2. The papers were presented at the 3rd International Workshop on the Internet for Financial Collective Awareness & Intelligence (http://ifin-workshop.iti.gr/), with the theme 'Financial Literacy and the FinTech Era: Capabilities and Challenges'. The two-day workshop was hosted by the Adam Smith Business School at the University of Glasgow on 12th–13th November 2018. The workshop was organised by the EU-funded PROFIT project (Promoting Financial Awareness and Stability: http://projectprofit.eu), as part of the events of the UK Talk Money Week 2018 (https://www.fincap.org.uk/fincap-week). The organisers and supporters of the workshop were: the Centre for Research & Technology, Hellas; the Adam Smith Business School and the Wards Trust Fund of the University of Glasgow; the Centre for Responsible Finance of the University of St. Andrews; the Democritus University of Thrace and the Hellenic Financial Literacy Institute in Greece. The host academics were Sotirios Diplaris (CERTH-ITI), Georgios A. Panos (University of Glasgow), John O.S. Wilson (University of St. Andrews) and Robert Wright (University of Strathclyde). The keynote address was delivered by Michael Haliassos (Goethe University, Frankfurt).
3. In a related inquiry, Carlin et al. (2018) examine how a new technology (which provides better access to financial information) changes financial behaviour. The authors exploit the introduction of a smartphone application for personal financial management as a source of exogenous variation in access to financial information. The find that FinTech adoption reduces financial fee payments and penalties, but differs cross-sectionally. After adopting the new technology, Millennials and members of Generation X incur fewer financial fees and penalties, whereas Baby Boomers do not benefit.
4. In a recent quasi-experimental study examining the impact of Congressional legislation inducing unintended differences in financial market development across Native-American reservations, Brown et al. (2019) show that, by increasing financial literacy and financial trust, early life exposure to local financial institutions increased household financial inclusion and induced long-term improvements in consumer credit outcomes.
5. van Praag et al. (2003) and van Praag and Ferrer-i-Carbonell (2004) find that health shocks impact more on individual well-being than financial shocks. Lusardi et al. (2017) suggests that differences in financial literacy can explain some 35–40% of retirement wealth inequality in the US. The ability of individuals to assess financial risk and make optimal financial decisions entails vast implications for the portfolio allocation, wealth accumulation (Behrman et al., 2012), and ultimately financial well-being.
6. Mueller and Yiannelis (2019) show that shifts in the composition of student loan borrowers and the collapse in house prices during the global financial crisis account for approximately 30% of the rise in student loan defaults in the US.
7. Low financial-literacy has been associated with mistaken perceptions and beliefs regarding the attributes of financial products and less willingness to accept financial advice (Anderson et al., 2017). Von Gaudecker (2015) posits that households that score high on financial literacy or rely on professionals or private contacts for advice achieve reasonable investment outcomes. Household investment mistakes are common and pose major threats in household finance. Portfolio under diversification ranks

among those mistakes that are potentially most costly. The author finds that households with below-median financial literacy that trust their own decision-making capabilities realize large losses in their investment portfolios and all group differences stem from the top of the loss distribution. Collins (2012) shows that financial literacy and financial advice are complementary rather than substitute. Evidence suggests that the more financially literate have access to better financial information and financial advisors (Calcagno and Monticone 2015; Stolper 2018).

8. Much financial fraud occurs in three ways: account takeovers, synthetic ID use, and business e-mail compromise, and the number of successful attempts has risen 34% from 2013 to 2016 (Hasham et al., 2018).

Acknowledgements

We thank colleagues at the 3rd International Workshop on the Internet for Financial Collective Awareness & Intelligence (http://ifin-workshop.iti.gr/), with the theme 'Financial Literacy and the FinTech Era: Capabilities and Challenges' for valuable comments.

Disclosure statement

No potential conflict of interest was reported by the authors.

Funding

Panos gratefully acknowledges funding from the PROFIT project. Project PROFIT has received funding from the European Union's Horizon 2020 Framework Programme for Research and Innovation under grant agreement no. 687895.

ORCID

Georgios A. Panos 🅘 http://orcid.org/0000-0003-2466-0444
John O. S. Wilson 🅘 http://orcid.org/0000-0002-9554-9332

References

Anderson, A., F. Baker, and D. Robinson. 2017. "Precautionary Savings, Retirement Planning and Misperceptions of Financial Literacy." *Journal of Financial Economics* 126: 383–398.

Artavanis, N., and S. Kara. 2020. "Financial Literacy and Student Debt." *European Journal of Finance* 26 (4–5): 382–401.

Aun, J. 2017. *Robot-Proof: Higher Education in the Age of Artificial Intelligence.* Boston, MA: MIT Press.

Behrman, J. R., O. S. Mitchell, C. K. Soo, and D. Bravo. 2012. "How Financial Literacy Affects Household Wealth Accumulation." *American Economic Review* 102 (3): 300–304.

Brown, J. R., J. A. Cookson, and R. Z. Heimer. 2019. "Growing Up Without Finance." *Journal of Financial Economics* 134: 591–616.

Calcagno, R., and C. Monticone. 2015. "Financial Literacy and the Demand for Financial Advice." *Journal of Banking and Finance* 50: 363–380.

Carlin, B., A. Olafsson, and M. Pagel. 2018. "FinTech and Consumer Well-being in the Information Age". Columbia GSB working paper.

Collins, J. M. 2012. "Financial Advice: A Substitute for Financial Literacy?" *Financial Services Review* 21 (4): 307–322.

Engels, C., K. Kamlesh, and D. Philip. 2020. "Financial Literacy and Fraud Detection." *European Journal of Finance* 26 (4–5): 420–442.

Frame, W. S., L. Wall, and L. J. White. 2019. "Technological Change and Financial Innovation in Banking: Some Implications for FinTech." In *Oxford Handbook of Banking*, 3rd ed., edited by A. Berger, P. Molyneux, and J. O. S. Wilson, 262–284. Oxford: Oxford University Press.

Frost, J., L. Gambacorta, Y. Huang, H. S. Shin, and P. Zbinden. 2019. "BigTech and the Changing Structure of Financial Intermediation," Bank of International Settlements Working Paper Number 779.

Hasham, S., Hayden, R., and R. Wavra. 2018. "Combating Payments Fraud and Enhancing Customer Experience". McKinsey & Company Report. https://www.mckinsey.com/industries/financial-services/our-insights/combating-payments-fraud-and-enhancingcustomer-experience.

Hastings, J., and O. S. Mitchell. 2018. "How Financial Literacy and Impatience Shape Retirement Wealth and Investment Behaviors". Wharton Pension Research Council Working Papers, Number 13.

Hastings, J., and L. Tejeda-Ashton. 2008. "Financial Literacy, Information, and Demand Elasticity: Survey and Experimental Evidence from Mexico". National Bureau of Economic Research Paper No. 14538.

Hundtofte, S., and J. Gladstone. 2017. "Who Uses a Smartphone for Financial Services? Evidence of a Selection for Impulsiveness from the Introduction of a Mobile FinTech App". Working Paper.

Lusardi, A., P. C. Michaud, and O. S. Mitchell. 2017. "Optimal Financial Knowledge and Wealth Inequality." *Journal of Political Economy* 127 (2): 431–477.

Lusardi, A., and O. S. Mitchell. 2014. "The Economic Importance of Financial Literacy: Theory and Evidence'." *Journal of Economic Literature* 52 (1): 5–44.

Lusardi, A., A. Samek, A. Kapteyn, and L. Glinert. 2015. "Visual Tools and Narratives: New Ways to Improve Financial Literacy." *Journal of Pension Economics and Finance* 16 (3): 1–27.

McKillop, D., D. French, and E. Stewart. 2020. "The Effectiveness of Smart Phone Apps in Improving Financial Capability." *European Journal of Finance* 26 (4–5): 302–318.

Migliavacca, M. 2020. "Keep Your Customer Knowledgeable: Financial Advisors as Educators." *European Journal of Finance* 26 (4–5): 402–419.

Mueller, H. M., and C. Yannelis. 2019. "The Rise in Student Loan Defaults." *Journal of Financial Economics* 131 (1): 1–19.

Panos, G. A., and T. Karkkainen. 2019. Financial Literacy and Attitudes to Cryptocurrencies. Working Paper.

Philippas, N., and C. Avdoulas. 2020. "Children of Crisis: Financial Literacy and Financial Well-being among Generation-Z Business-School Students in Greece." *European Journal of Finance* 26 (4–5): 360–381.

Shaban, M., C. Girardone, and A. Sarkisyan. 2020. "Cross-Country Variation in Financial Inclusion: A Global Perspective." *European Journal of Finance* 26 (4–5): 319–340.

Stolper, O. A. 2018. "It Takes Two to Tango: Households' Response to Financial Advice and the Role of Financial Literacy." *Journal of Banking and Finance* 92: 215–310.

Urban, C., and J. M. Collins. 2020. "Understanding Financial Well-Being Over the Lifecourse: An Exploration of Measures." *European Journal of Finance* 26 (4–5): 341–359.

van Praag, B. M. S., and A. Ferrer-i-Carbonell. 2004. *Happiness Quantified: A Satisfaction Calculus Approach.* Oxford: Oxford University Press.

van Praag, B. M. S., P. Frijters, and A. Ferrer-i-Carbonell. 2003. "The Anatomy of Subjective Well-being." *Journal of Economic Behavior & Organization* 51 (1): 29–49.

von Gaudecker, H. M. 2015. "How Does Household Portfolio Diversification Vary With Financial Sophistication and Advice?" *Journal of Finance* LXX (2): 489–507.

The effectiveness of smartphone apps in improving financial capability

Declan French, Donal McKillop and Elaine Stewart

ABSTRACT
This study is the first to assess whether smartphone apps can be utilised to improve financially capable behaviours. In this study four smartphone apps, packaged together under the title 'Money Matters', were provided to working-age members (16–65 years) of the largest credit union in Northern Ireland (Derry Credit Union). The smartphone apps consisted of a loan interest comparison app, an expenditure comparison app, a cash calendar app, and a debt management app. The assessment methodology used was a Randomised Control Trial (RCT) with the U.K. Financial Capability Outcome Frameworks used to set the context for the assessment. For those receiving the apps (the treatment group) statistically significant improvements were found in a number of measures designed to gauge 'financial knowledge, understanding and basic skills' and 'attitudes and motivations'. These improvements translated into better financially capable behaviours; those receiving the apps were more likely to keep track of their income and expenditure and proved to be more resilient when faced with a financial shock.

1. Introduction

Making good financial decisions is important for a person's economic and financial well-being (Money Advice Service 2013). Whether a person is in a position to make good financial decisions is, however, dependent upon their financial capability. The OECD defines financial capability as 'a combination of awareness, knowledge, skill, attitude and behaviour necessary to make sound financial decisions and ultimately achieve individual financial wellbeing' (OECD INFE 2011). This emphasises that financial capability is about not only having knowledge, understanding and skills but also the ability to apply these attributes in a way that results in positive financial outcomes (Spencer, Nieboer, and Elliott 2015). Financial capability does not necessarily follow from having knowledge, understanding and skills it is shaped also by the psychological motivations and biases that drive our behaviour (Hershfield et al. 2011).[1]

Increasing levels of financial capability in the U.K. population is a Government priority (Financial Capability Strategy for the UK 2015). Measurement of the financial capability of the U.K. population suggests that at best it is mediocre (Spencer, Nieboer, and Elliott 2015). Approximately 30% of the U.K. population do not make a budget. One in six have problems in identifying the balance on their bank statement. Almost 90% of U.K. adults do not read the full terms and conditions when taking out financial products and nearly half of U.K. adults admit falling into debt as a direct result of their social lives (Money Advice Service 2013). A survey undertaken by the Financial Services Authority (FSA) in 2005 found that those who scored well below average on all aspects of financial capability were young (average age 36), and included roughly equal numbers of single people and couples. Furthermore, their incomes and levels of product holding were lower than average, but not the lowest of all the groups surveyed (FSA 2006).[2]

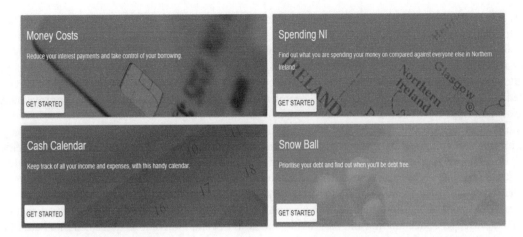

Figure 1. 'Money Matters' mobile app package.

Notes: Developed by the authors and a local web developing company, each app has been specifically designed to target, facilitate and improve different aspects of an individuals' financial capability. The first app (Money Costs) is a tool to enable participants to easily compare different types of borrowing using different amounts and time periods. The second (Spending NI) provides an indicator of how much a user spends against the Northern Ireland average household spend in various spending categories. The third (Cash Calendar) is a budgeting tool designed to help a user balance income and expenditure over time. This app was designed in light of recommendations by a particular Credit Union concerned about the impact of Universal Credit on its members' ability to avoid overdrafts. The fourth (Snowball) was developed for users with multiple debts and provides them with an optimal debt reduction strategy. All four apps are packaged together under the name 'Money Matters'.

The Financial Capability Strategy for the U.K., 2015 highlights the improvement of digital literacy as an important outcome in the advancement of financially capable behaviours ' . . . being able to use online banking services, to use mobile apps, and to compare financial services online is crucial for being able to keep track of your money and make informed decisions' (Bagwell et al. 2014, 22, Financial Capability Outcome Frameworks). Digital literacy is the ability to effectively and critically locate, evaluate and create information using a range of digital technologies (Spires and Bartlett 2012). There are five basic digital skills: managing information, communicating, problem solving, transacting and creating (Reedy and Goodfellow 2012). Attainment of these digital skills could save the average person in the U.K. £744 per annum (Lloyds Bank 2017). However, 1 in 10 U.K. adults (aged 16+) have never used the internet (ONS 2017), and 4.3 million people are thought to have none of the five basic digital skills (Lloyds Bank 2018).

In the U.K., 41 million 16–75-year-olds own a smartphone, with those aged 55–75 the fastest growing adopters (Deloitte 2017). While there is extensive research on the effectiveness of smartphone apps in the improvement of health outcomes and behaviours, there are no studies investigating the efficacy of smartphone apps as a means of improving financial capability.[3] Our study addresses this paucity of research by assessing whether four smartphone apps, packaged together under the title *Money Matters*, could improve financially capable behaviours of working-age members (16–65 years) of the largest credit union in Northern Ireland (Derry Credit Union).[4] The smartphone apps consisted of a loan interest comparison app (*Money Costs*), an expenditure comparison app (*Spend NI*), a cash calendar app (*Cash Calendar*), and a debt management app (*Snowball*). Further details about each app are provided in Figure 1.

We used a Randomised Control Trial (RCT) to assess the efficacy of the smartphone apps. The analysis was conducted based on intention to treat (ITT) where outcomes are compared between those receiving the smartphone apps (treatment group) and those not receiving the apps (control group). However, often in RCTs subjects do not comply with the treatment and in the case of high non-compliance, the intervention may be ineffective but may still be efficacious for those who adhere to the treatment. To accommodate for imperfect adherence we use the 'complier average casual effect' (CACE), developed by Imbens and Rubin (1997), and report results where outcomes are compared between compliers in the treatment group and those who would have complied in the control group.

The U.K. Financial Capability Outcome Frameworks provides the context for the RCT. The evaluation initially assessed whether access to the smartphone apps, improved financial knowledge, understanding and basic skills (i.e. loan confidence, financial literacy and digital literacy) as well as attitudes and motivations (i.e. the ability to effect change, resilience in the face of stressful events, spending behaviour and planning for the future). The evaluation then considered whether changes in ability and mindset translated into better financially capable behaviours (i.e. management of bills, keeping track of finances, maximising income and building financial resilience through regular saving). The assessment concluded by considering whether changes in behaviour resulted in improved financial well-being (i.e. keeping up with bills and credit commitments, improvements in financial planning).

A number of insights emerged from the investigation. First, those receiving the smartphone apps experienced improvements in financial knowledge, understanding and basic skills. They expressed greater confidence in their understanding of loan repayments and demonstrated improved financial literacy. Secondly, receiving the smartphone apps led to changes in attitudes and motivations. Those provided with the apps were more likely to prefer to plan for tomorrow, reported a greater sense of self-efficacy and a greater confidence in their ability to improve financial decision-making through engaging with technology. Thirdly, the identified changes in financial knowledge, understanding and basic skills, and attitudes and motivations translated into better financially capable behaviours. Those receiving the smartphone apps proved more resilient when subject to a financial shock and were more likely to keep track of their income and expenditure. Unfortunately, the improvements in financially capable behaviours did not result in improved financial well-being. Arguably, this was due to the RCT being conducted over a six-month period; too short a period for improvements in financial well-being to emerge.

This study is the first to demonstrate that digital technology, in the form of smartphone apps, can be utilised to improve financially capable behaviours. Four out of five U.K. adults now have a smartphone. It is, therefore, reasonable to suggest that our study has demonstrated an accessible and cost-effective means for the targeting of interventions to improve the financial capability of a significant proportion of the U.K. population. The remainder of the study is organised as follows. Section 2 provides a review of the literature, the methodological approach is detailed in Section 3 and the data described in Section 4. The empirical findings are presented in Section 5 with concluding comments reported in Section 6.

2. Literature review

In this section of the paper, we commence by drawing on the literature to define financial capability and distinguish between it and financial literacy. The discussion then considers literature pertaining to financial knowledge, understanding and basic financial skills, which arguably are the foundation stones upon which financially capable behaviours are built. Attitudes and motivations shape financially capable behaviours and we consider the importance of potential influences such as impulsiveness, optimism, confidence, resilience and susceptibility to peer effects. The overview concludes with consideration of the relationship between digitalisation and financial capability.

2.1. Financial capability

Being financially literate is a necessary although not sufficient condition for the achievement of financial capability (Lusardi 2011). Financial literacy reflects how much knowledge one has about various financial matters, whereas financial capability is the ability to apply that knowledge in a meaningful way resulting in positive financial outcomes (Spencer, Nieboer, and Elliott 2015).[5] Someone can be financially literate (in the sense that they have the knowledge, understanding and skills which would enable them to manage their personal finances well) without necessarily being financially capable, as demonstrated by their actual behaviour (Mundy 2011). Financial capability is determined in part by the psychological motivations and biases that drive our behaviour (Hershfield et al. 2011). These behavioural hurdles are not necessarily character flaws; they are in many instances natural aspects of human behaviour, holding us back from optimally managing our finances (Spencer, Nieboer, and Elliott 2015). The OECD defines financial capability as 'a combination of awareness, knowledge, skill, attitude and behaviour necessary to make sound financial decisions and ultimately achieve individual financial wellbeing' (OECD INFE 2011). In this context, 'knowledge' is the ability to understand personal and broader financial matters, 'skill' is the ability to apply that knowledge in everyday life, and 'attitude and behaviour' refers to having the self-confidence to make appropriate financial decisions (French and McKillop 2016).

Financially capable behaviour does not yet have a standard scale of measurement (Shephard et al. 2017). Rather, a range of measures are used to capture the behaviours that people exhibit or the actions they take, for example saving regularly, keeping track of their finances, working towards longer term goals, or how they use credit (Atkinson 2016; Money Advice Service 2016).

2.2. Financial knowledge, understanding and basic skills

Financial knowledge, understanding and basic financial skills, which many categorise as financial literacy (Lusardi and Mitchell 2007) are the foundation stones upon which financially capable behaviours are built. A significant body of research has established that those who are more financially literate have better economic outcomes. Poor understanding of interest rate calculations is associated with higher debt burdens, incurring greater fees, and defaults and delinquency (Campbell 2006; Bucks and Pence 2008; Gerardi, Goette, and Meier 2010; Disney and Gathergood 2013; Duca and Kumar 2014). Poor money management skills are a strong negative predictor of the tendency to overspend and to worry about financial affairs (Garðarsdóttir and Dittmar 2012). Financial literacy is positively correlated with planning for retirement, savings and wealth accumulation (Hastings and Mitchell 2011; Van Rooij, Lusardi, and Alessie 2012). Financial literacy is predictive of investment behaviours including stock market participation (Almenberg and Dreber 2011; Van Rooij, Lusardi, and Alessie 2011; Arrondel, Debbich, and Savignac 2012) and choosing a low fee investment portfolio (Choi, Laibson, and Madrian 2009).

Research has mainly used performance test questions to measure the various components of financial literacy (Lusardi and Mitchell 2007, 2011; Van Rooij, Lusardi, and Alessie 2011; Van Rooij, Lusardi, and Alessie 2012). These questions capture knowledge and understanding of elements considered important in making savings and investment decisions. This includes the capacity to do interest rate calculations, an understanding of inflation and an understanding of portfolio diversification. About one-third of studies also use self-assessment procedures in conjunction with performance tests questions to measure financial literacy (Hastings and Mitchell 2011). The literature finds that self-assessed financial capabilities and performance test based measures are positively correlated (Lusardi and Mitchell 2014).

2.3. Attitudes and motivations

Attitudes, motivations and biases shape financial capability behaviours (Shephard et al. 2017). The authors found that in the Netherlands psychological motivations and biases explained twice the variance in financial capability behaviour compared to the explanatory power of financial knowledge and spending attitudes alone. The important psychological constructs influencing financial capability behaviour were those of non-impulsiveness, optimism, confidence, goal orientation, and susceptibility to peer influences.

Those who are non-impulsive are better financial decision-makers than those who are not because they are able to delay gratification to benefit their overall financial well-being (Birkenmaier, Sherraden, and Curley 2013). Seeking instant gratification (present bias) over a larger potential reward in the future can result in impulse spending and undermine long-term planning and savings (Von Stumm, O'Creevy, and Furnham 2013).

In general, people tend to be optimistic about the future and overconfident about their abilities (Kenrick et al. 2009). Mild optimism correlates with a range of good financial behaviours, such as timely repayment of credit card balance and saving more (Puri and Robinson 2007). Another benefit of mild optimism is that it supports emotional resilience, which may be important in recovering from negative financial surprises (Kenrick et al. 2009; Kahneman, 2011). Those who are very optimistic, however, are found to have a shorter planning time horizon, are less likely to think that saving is a good thing and, on average, save less than people who are less optimistic (Puri and Robinson 2007).

Having confidence in your ability to manage your financial situation is key to improving financial well-being (Parker et al. 2012; Fernandes, Lynch, and Netemeyer 2014; Letkiewicz, Robinson, and Domian 2016). Those with a high sense of financial self-efficacy (confidence that one can effectively manage one's financial affairs) are considered to be less likely to perceive themselves being at risk for disrupted income, unforeseen expenses, and unsuccessful investments (Engelberg 2007). Overconfidence is, however, detrimental. When overconfidence is present, households may fail to seek financial advice, fail to save for retirement, or fail to insure themselves against the potential of loss (Campbell 2006; Lusardi and Mitchell 2007).

Susceptibility to peer influences may be either harmful or helpful to financial capability. If peer effects encourage excessive spending, it may limit the ability to maintain a budget. On the other hand, peer influences can encourage people to display positive financial behaviours such as taking out insurance or saving for their retirement (Spencer, Nieboer, and Elliott 2015). People are more likely to invest in the stock market if their family do (Chitegi and Stafford 1999; Hong, Kubik, and Stein 2004), or make a particular investment if other investors do (Bursztyn et al. 2014). Low-income children who receive encouragement and hands-on support from parents are more likely to save (Kempson, Atkinson, and Collard 2006).

2.4. Digitalisation and financial capability

Digital literacy is 'the ability to effectively and critically locate, evaluate and create information using a range of digital technologies' (Bagwell et al. 2014, 22, Financial Capability Outcome Frameworks). The improvement of digital literacy is an important outcome in the advancement of financially capable behaviours, 'budgeting and spending meters and financial goal trackers' can be used to enhance money management skills and control finances while 'interactive online/mobile games' can be used to improve personal financial confidence (OECD INFE 2018, 20). Digital technologies can also be used to nudge consumers into action through 'automated reminders to save or pay back a loan' and to enhance opportunities for financial behaviour changes 'through virtual price/product/offer comparison and just-in time reminders at the point of sale or immediately after' (OECD INFE 2018, 22).

In the U.K., 41 million 16–75-year-olds own a smartphone, with those aged 55–75 the fastest growing adopters (Deloitte 2017). Over 22 million adults in the U.K. regularly used mobile banking apps to access their accounts (UK Finance 2018). There is also evidence of an increase in the use of budgeting and saving mobile apps (Lloyds 2017). While there is extensive research on the effectiveness of smartphone apps in the improvement of health outcomes and behaviours there are no studies investigating the efficacy of smartphone apps as a means of improving financial capability behaviours.[6] However, two studies assess the effect of alternative forms of digitalisation on financial capability. Servon and Kaestner (2008), assessed whether access to an online financial demonstration programme, combined with financial literacy training could help low- and moderate-income individuals be more effective financial actors. A small number of qualitative improvements were identified. Piercy (2018) evaluated the efficacy of online assisted digital transactions (in the form of online training centres) as a way of improving financial capabilities. Digital assistance helped increase the confidence of individuals about their financial future through the building of financial skills.

3. Methodology

The standard approach in a randomised control trial (RCT) is to analyse on the basis of intention to treat (ITT) where outcomes are compared between the treatment and control groups. The ITT effect can be determined by a simple OLS regression

$$Y_j = \beta_0 + \beta_1 Z_j + \varepsilon_j \tag{1}$$

where Z_j is an indicator variable for whether subject j has been assigned to the treatment ($Z_j = 1$) or not ($Z_j = 0$).

But often in trials subjects do not comply with the treatment – either they do not take the treatment or they may take it partially. In the event of high non-compliance, the intervention will probably be ineffective but may still be efficacious for those who adhere to the treatment.

To deal with imperfect adherence, Imbens and Rubin (1997) developed the 'complier average casual effect' (CACE) where outcomes are compared between compliers in the treatment group and those who would have complied in the control group. They classified subjects into four categories of compliance. 'Compliers' will follow the treatment assignment and take the treatment if randomised to treatment or not take the

Randomized to Treatment (Z=1)		Randomized to Control (Z=0)	
Treatment taken (T=1)	Treatment not taken (T=0)	Treatment taken (T=1)	Treatment not taken (T=0)
Always-takers or Compliers	Never-takers or defiers	Always-takers or defiers	Never-takers or compliers

Figure 2. Compliance status.

treatment if randomised to the control group. 'Always-takers' (A) will always receive the treatment regardless of assignment. 'Never-takers' (N) will refuse the treatment regardless of assignment. 'Defiers' (D) will do the opposite of the randomisation assignment. Possible outcomes for these categories are summarised in Figure 2.

Assuming outcomes for any subject are unaffected by other subjects' assignment (the stable unit treatment value assumption (SUTVA)), the ITT effect can be decomposed:

$$\text{ITT} = \bar{Y}_1 - \bar{Y}_0 = (\bar{Y}_{1c} - \bar{Y}_{0c})\pi_c + (\bar{Y}_{1A} - \bar{Y}_{0A})\pi_A + (\bar{Y}_{1N} - \bar{Y}_{0N})\pi_N + (\bar{Y}_{1D} - \bar{Y}_{0D})\pi_D$$

where $\bar{Y}_{1i}$ ($\bar{Y}_{0i}$) is the mean outcome among those in category i in the treatment (control) group.

The SUTVA condition can be violated by spillover effects between participants or general equilibrium effects of the treatment (Heckman, LaLonde, and Smith 1999). The conventional solution of changing the unit of analysis to a higher level such as multiple credit unions in different localities was not available to us. Spillover was mitigated to an extent by only allowing one participant per household. General equilibrium effects although possible do not seem likely.

As the apps were password-protected, we expect the number of always-takers in the control group to be zero. Never-takers are assumed to have the same outcomes regardless of assignment (exclusion restriction). A violation of this condition would imply that randomisation affects financial outcomes through channels other than the apps (Angrist, Imbens, and Rubin 1996). We believe this restriction should hold as (i) participants could not have inferred assignment in advance and (ii) both trial arms were exposed to the same information about the purpose of the trial. It is, however, possible that other aspects of the intervention structure such as regular messaging could have had some effect on outcomes.

It is conventional to assume also that there are no defiers in the trial (monotonicity assumption). Defiance relies on taking the opposite treatment to assigned and therefore having a prior preference for the opposite treatment. This seems unlikely in our trial as participation in this trial was voluntary and participants knew in advance that the efficacy of financial phone apps was being tested.

The ITT effect then reduces to

$$\text{ITT} = (\bar{Y}_{1c} - \bar{Y}_{0c})\pi_c$$

or

$$\text{CACE} = \bar{Y}_{1c} - \bar{Y}_{0c} = \frac{\text{ITT}}{\pi_c}$$

This can be estimated using 2SLS with a first-stage regression of actual treatment (T) on treatment assignment (Z) and a second-stage regression of outcome Y on actual treatment (T) since

$$\text{CACE} = \frac{\text{ITT}}{\pi_c} = \frac{\bar{Y}_1 - \bar{Y}_0}{\pi_c} = \frac{\bar{Y}_1 - \bar{Y}_0}{\bar{T}_1 - \bar{T}_0} = (Z'T)^{-1}Z'Y \tag{2}$$

Table 1. Post-intervention response.

	Treatment			Control
	Downloaded app			
	Yes	No	Total	
Pre-intervention survey	176	64	240	260
Post-intervention survey	147	44	191	212
Response	84%	69%	80%	82%

The CACE estimates are therefore larger than ITT estimates by a factor reflecting the proportion of compliers π_c in the treatment group and CACE standard errors additionally take account of sampling variability in π_c.

4. Data

The sample participating in the trial were from the Derry city area and were members of Derry Credit Union, the largest Credit Union in NI. Recruitment for the trial ran from April to August 2017 by attracting participants through the Derry Credit Union account on Facebook, posters in the branch office and direct recruitment among customers attending the branch. All prospective participants registered their contact details online and the small number without an email address gave a family member's account. Our only exclusion criteria were that participants were over 18 years of age and only one participant was allowed per household.

A market research company carried out pre and post-intervention surveys, June–August 2017 and February–March 2018. From a sampling frame of 835 registered individuals, 500 respondents were interviewed in the pre-intervention survey. Of these, 403 people were surveyed post-intervention (81%) including 191 (80%) of those allocated the app (see Table 1).

The survey explored participants' financial circumstances, employment, income, attitudes to risk and household demographics. It featured questions from the (MAS) Adult Financial Capability Framework (Financial Capability Strategy for the UK 2015) and elements from previous work conducted with Northern Irish Credit Unions (French and McKillop 2016).

Participants were randomised to treatment using a random number-producing algorithm in Excel prior to surveyors going into the field. Surveyors preferred the assignment to be known in advance so that they could organize for the longer interviews where the app was downloaded. The only data available from registration for the purposes of stratification was gender. However, a simple randomisation schedule was preferred as substantial imbalances were not anticipated with the relatively large and relatively homogenous sample recruited. Randomisation was completed on participants in three tranches as recruitment progressed.

5. Results

Table 2 confirms that those in the treatment and control groups interviewed in the post-intervention survey are statistically the same for known factors associated with financial capability. The means for each variable are reported with a statistical test for differences. For every variable, the p-values are well above the conventional 5% or 10% levels of significance.

5.1. Usage

Figure 3 profiles the number of times the treatment group opened each of the applications during the trial. Initially usage is high but declines steadily between June and August 2017. Usage during this period reflects the initial download of the apps which were provided to participants on a rolling basis over the June to August period. Engagement and user retention are two of the most commonly identified problems in mobile application usage. For example Statista found that for 2017, approximately 24% of apps downloaded from Google Play were accessed only once during the first six months of ownership.[7] The Cash Calendar was found to be the most

Table 2. Comparison of treatment and control group for known confounders.

Variable	Control	Treatment	p-Value
Female	0.76	0.77	.715
Partner	0.47	0.54	.147
Employed	0.43	0.46	.589
Retired	0.08	0.06	.501
Education	0.60	0.64	.354
Age[a]	39.6	40.4	.547
Children[b]	1.0	1.0	.919

Notes: All other statistical tests of differences are tests on the equality of proportions. *Female* Proportion of female respondents *Partner* Proportion of respondents with partner *Employed* Proportion of respondents employed *Retired* Proportion of respondents retired *Education* Highest educational qualification obtained A-level or above *Age* Respondent age *Children* Number of children living in household. $p < .10* \ p < .05** \ p < .01***$.

[a] t-Tests of equality of means.

[b] Chi-square test of independence.

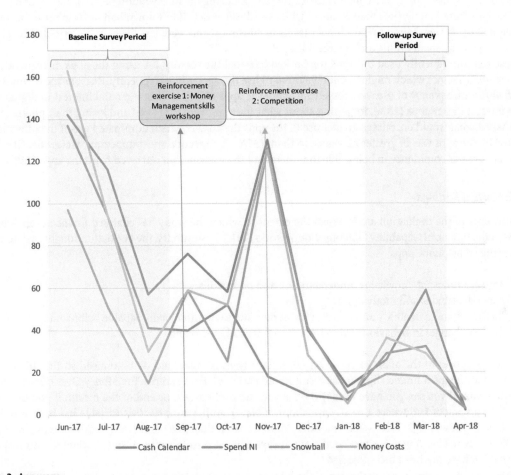

Figure 3. App usage.

popular application, making up 32% of the total usage, followed by Spend NI making up 28% with Snowball and Money Costs each making up 20% of total usage.

Throughout the RCT, use of the apps was promoted through weekly push notifications where information of various forms was sent to participants in the treatment group. In September 2017, the Project Team undertook a money management skills workshop to showcase the capabilities of the apps.[8] This reinforcement exercise resulted in a marginal increase in app usage with the increase in engagement probably due to both the promotion of the workshop (via Facebook, emails and push notifications) and the workshop itself.

A money skills competition was run over a two-week period in early December 2017. The competition took the form of seven problems and required participants to use either the Cash Calendar, Snowball or Money Costs applications to determine answers. The competition was promoted during November (by email and push notifications) with the deadline for submission of answers early December. There is a pronounced increase in the use of the Cash Calendar, Snowball and Money Costs applications during the promotion phase and over the two-week period in December that the competition was open. Usage of the Spending NI application which was not part of the competition did not experience any increase in use over the same period.

Figure 3 also highlights a further increase in app usage in February and March 2018. This coincided with the period over which the follow-up survey was undertaken. It may, therefore, be the case that the increase in usage was triggered by fresh communications from the Survey Team as they sought to set up suitable interview dates with participants.

Only 86 (45%) used the apps frequently (5 or more times during the intervention period). A further 61 (32%) used the apps infrequently (less than 5 times) while 44 (23%) either didn't download or didn't use the apps at all. Frequent users were found to have higher levels of education and were less likely to be retired. Age, gender and hours typically spent online did not affect usage.

Those that infrequently used the apps were asked to detail the reasons for using the apps infrequently and also to identify factors which might encourage them to use the apps more frequently. Reasons most commonly identified for infrequency of use were forgetting about the apps (25%), having a general interest in digital skills but no interest in our apps (13%), forgetting about what the apps were for (11%) and losing their phone (11%). When asked what would encourage greater use of the apps the answer which dominated was if the information provided by the apps was of greater relevance to them (35%). The second most important factor identified was if they had greater confidence in being able to understand the information retrieved from the apps (21%).

5.2. Empirical findings

The core aims of the evaluation are to assess the extent to which the study has changed financial capability as defined in the Financial Capability Outcome Frameworks, 2015. In summary, the evaluation sought to determine whether the smartphone apps:

(i)   Improved financial knowledge, understanding and basic skills;
(ii) Changed attitudes and motivations;
(iii) Whether changes in ability and mindset translated into better financially capable behaviours;
(iv) Whether changes in behaviour led to improved financial well-being.

For the purposes of the analysis, most variables have been recoded and dichotomised so that high values correspond to the most financially capable result for all variables. For example, the *Money Over* question asked 'How often would you say you have money over at the end of the week, or end of the month if you budget by month?' on a scale of 1–6 where 1 = Always and 6 = Never. In the analysis, this variable has been reordered so that 0 = {'1. Always', '2. Most weeks/months', '3. More often than not'} and 1 = {'4. Sometimes', '5. Hardly ever', '6. Never'}. This way a positive coefficient always equates to a 'positive' result. Variables with response scales of 0–10 have not been dichotomised.

The study group is not large enough for analysis by each app separately hence our findings show all outcomes for the apps as a package.

5.2.1. Financial knowledge, understanding and basic skills
In our first set of results, we examine the impact of using the apps on financial knowledge, understanding and basic skills (Table 3).[9] Our first variable is a measure of understanding of the amount to be prepaid on a financial product such as a loan or credit card. This skill is associated with lower use of high-cost borrowing, lower debt

Table 3. Estimates of treatment effect for financial knowledge, understanding and basic skills.

Theme	Variable	ITT		CACE	
		Coeff.	(s.e.)	Coeff.	(s.e.)
Self-confidence	Loan confidence	0.095**	0.047	0.172**	0.086
Financial literacy	Financial literacy	0.110***	0.042	0.199**	0.078
Digital literacy	Buying online	0.011	0.026	0.021	0.047
Digital literacy	Paying bills online	0.006	0.028	0.011	0.051
Digital literacy	Bank online	0.045	0.029	0.081	0.052
Digital literacy	Online comparisons	0.052	0.045	0.096	0.081
Digital literacy	Buying online improved	−0.048	0.050	−0.087	0.091
Digital literacy	Paying bills online improved	−0.035	0.050	−0.064	0.091
Digital literacy	Bank online improved	−0.011	0.050	−0.020	0.091
Digital literacy	Online comparisons improved	−0.008	0.050	−0.013	0.091

Notes: ITT – OLS regressions. CACE – 2SLS regression. *Loan confidence* 'When you are shown information about a financial product such as a loan, credit card or store card, how confident are you that you understand the total amount you need to repay?' (0 = '1. Not confident–3', 1 = '4–5. Very confident'). *Financial literacy* Three or more correct out of four financial literacy questions *Buying online* 'How would you rate your ability when using the internet for ... buying a product online?' (0 = 'Fair', 'Poor', 'Bad' 1 = 'Excellent', 'Good') *Paying bills online* ' ... for paying bills' (0 = 'Fair', 'Poor', 'Bad' 1 = 'Excellent', 'Good') *Bank online* ' ... using your bank's online services?' (0 = 'Fair', 'Poor', 'Bad' 1 = 'Excellent', 'Good') *Online comparisons* ' ... comparing financial products and services?' (0 = 'Fair', 'Poor', 'Bad' 1 = 'Excellent', 'Good'). *Buying online improved* 'Over the last 6 months, has your ability to use the internet for the following purposes improved? ... buying a product online?' ('Yes'/'No') *Paying bills online improved* ' ... for paying bills' ('Yes'/'No') *Bank online improved* ' ... using your bank's online services?' ('Yes'/'No') Online *comparisons improved* ' ... Comparing financial products and services?' ('Yes'/'No'). $p < .10* p < .05** p < .01***$.

and higher savings (Lusardi and Tufano 2015). As one of the apps was specifically designed to assist the understanding of the relative cost of borrowing we would expect a degree of increased understanding among those receiving the apps. The proportion of subjects in the treatment group expressing confidence in their understanding of loan repayments is almost 10% higher (ITT = 0.095) than in the control group. The CACE estimates indicate that the difference in proportions confident about loan repayments between the control group and those utilising the apps five or more times during the trial is larger again at 17.2%. Both results are statistically significant at the 5% level.

We measured financial literacy using a series of four simple questions on interpreting a bank statement, numeracy, understanding of inflation and risk diversification.[10] Financial literacy is associated with higher savings, stock market participation and retirement wealth (Lusardi and Mitchell 2007; Van Rooij, Lusardi, and Alessie 2011). The proportion of the treatment group answering three or more of these questions correctly is 11% higher than in the control group and almost 20% higher among those using the apps. The apps are designed to assist in more complex financial decision-making than captured by these financial literacy questions but their use has perhaps led to a greater confidence in the user's more general numeracy and problem-solving abilities.

The remaining questions in this set examine the subject's digital literacy. The ability to use online services such as internet banking and comparison sites in financial transactions was identified as being important for financial capability in the U.K. Financial Capability Outcome Frameworks (Bagwell et al. 2014). We find no evidence that using the apps led to higher self-rated ability to use the internet for commercial transactions or led to higher reports of improvements in these abilities over the duration of the trial. This is disappointing since two of the questions (*Online comparisons* and *Online comparisons improved*) specifically refer to using the internet for comparing financial products and services as in the Money Costs app.

5.2.2. Attitudes and motivations

In this section, we examine the fundamental economic preferences that underlie financial decision-making such as time discounting and consumption influences. Results are presented in Table 4.

The first measure is a hypothetical choice between £200 now and £400 in two months' time (AER 6400%) where the 'correct' answer is to wait. The following six measures also capture aspects of time discounting and attitudes to the future. The proportion of the treatment group stating they prefer to plan for tomorrow is 10.6 percentage points higher than in the control group while for those actually using the apps the difference is 19.3 percentage points. We also see that receiving the smartphone apps is strongly associated with what at first glance

Table 4. Estimates of treatment effect for attitudes and motivations.

Theme	Variable	ITT		CACE	
		Coeff.	(s.e.)	Coeff.	(s.e.)
Attitudes to future	Time discounting	0.009	0.043	0.017	0.078
Attitudes to future	Plan for tomorrow	0.106**	0.049	0.193**	0.089
Attitudes to future	Hate borrowing	−0.103**	0.042	−0.188**	0.077
Attitudes to future	Save for rainy day	0.008	0.024	0.015	0.044
Attitudes to future	Save for retirement	0.041	0.045	0.074	0.081
Attitudes to future	Buy on impulse	−0.060	0.344	−0.110	0.623
Attitudes to future	Shop around	0.004	0.024	0.007	0.043
Ability to effect change	Self-efficacy	0.086**	0.042	0.156**	0.077
Ability to effect change	Anxiety about finances	0.013	0.050	0.023	0.091
Ability to effect change	Keeping track of finances	0.041**	0.019	0.074**	0.034
Ability to effect change	Money management confidence	−0.145	0.186	−0.264	0.338
Ability to effect change	Seek advice	0.014	0.035	0.025	0.063
Ability to effect change	Happy to use tech	0.111***	0.041	0.201***	0.075
Consumption influences	Spend like friends	−0.004	0.263	−0.008	0.476
Consumption influences	Spend on children	0.405	0.390	0.737	0.710
Resilience	Bounce back	0.006	0.034	0.011	0.062
Resilience	Surviving stressful events	−0.018	0.048	−0.033	0.087
Resilience	Recovering from stressful events	0.068	0.046	0.123	0.083
Resilience	Snapping back	−0.026	0.047	−0.046	0.085
Resilience	Coming through difficulties	0.049	0.046	0.088	0.083
Resilience	Getting over setbacks	0.001	0.042	0.001	0.076

Notes: ITT – OLS regressions. CACE – 2SLS regression. *Time discounting* Would take £400 in two months and not £200 now. *Plan for tomorrow* 'When it comes to money I prefer to live for today rather than plan for tomorrow' ('Strongly disagree', 'Disagree'). *Hate borrowing* 'I hate to borrow – I would much rather save up in advance' ('Strongly agree', 'Agree'). *Save for rainy day* 'How important, if at all, do you think it is to save money for a rainy day' ('Very important', 'Fairly important'). *Save for retirement* 'How important, if at all, do you think it is to put aside money for your retirement' ('Very important', 'Fairly important'). *Buy on impulse* 'I often buy things on impulse' (0–10) *Shop around* 'How important, if at all, do you think it is shop around in order to make your money go further' ('Very important', 'Fairly important'). *Self-efficacy* 'Nothing I will do will make much difference to my financial situation' ('Strongly disagree', 'Disagree'). *Anxiety about finances* 'Thinking about my financial situation makes me anxious' ('Strongly disagree', 'Disagree'). *Keep track of finances* 'How important, if at all, do you think it is to keep track of your and your partner/spouse's income and expenditure' ('Very important', 'Fairly important'). *Money management confidence* 'How confident do you feel managing your money?' (0–10). *Seek advice* If in financial difficulty 'Seek advice from family and friends' or 'Seek advice from a money advice service'. *Happy to use tech* 'I would be happy to use technology to help me in my day to day financial decision-making' ('Strongly agree', 'Agree'). *Spend like friends* 'I feel under pressure to spend like my friends even when I can't afford it' (0–10). *Spend on children* 'I feel under pressure to spend money on my children even when I can't afford it' (0–10). *Bounce back* 'I tend to bounce back quickly after hard times' ('Strongly agree', 'Agree'). *Surviving stressful events* 'I have a hard time making it through stressful events' ('Strongly disagree', 'Disagree'). *Recovering from stressful events* 'It does not take me long to recover from a stressful event' ('Strongly agree', 'Agree'). *Snapping back,* 'It is hard for me to snap back when something bad happens' ('Strongly disagree', 'Disagree'). *Coming through difficulties* 'I usually come through difficult times with little trouble' ('Strongly agree', 'Agree'). *Getting over setbacks* 'I tend to take a long time to get over setbacks in my life' ('Strongly disagree', 'Disagree'). $p < .10*$ $p < .05** p < .01***$.

seems like a counterintuitive reduction in hatred of borrowing (ITT = −0.103; CACE = −0.188). result. However, we should not be surprised if smartphone apps which have been designed to aid borrowing comparisons and which have been shown above to improve confidence about loans also reduce antipathy towards borrowing. There is no statistically significant difference on the other indicators.

The next four measures capture the individual's confidence in their ability to determine their financial situation. Confidence is associated with better financial planning, budgeting and saving (Neymotin 2010) and a sense of control is an important determinant for seeking professional financial planning help (Letkiewicz, Robinson, and Domian 2016). The proportion of the treatment group reporting a sense of self-efficacy is 8.6 percentage points higher than in the control group (CACE = 0.156). Those receiving the apps are also more likely to report that it is important to keep track of income and expenditure (ITT = 0.041; CACE = 0.074). The next two measures also capture the individual's ability to effect change by proactively seeking advice or engaging with technology to improve decision-making. The treatment group are no more likely to seek advice from family, friends or a money advice service but they are considerably more willing to use technology for day-to-day financial decisions (ITT = 0.111; CACE = 0.201).

There are no significant effects of using the apps for the remaining indicators reflecting the degree to which individuals are influenced by others in their consumption and their degree of resilience to shocks.

Table 5. Estimates of treatment effect on financially capable behaviours.

Theme	Variable	ITT		CACE	
		Coeff.	(s.e.)	Coeff.	(s.e.)
Managing bill payment	Unexpected expense	0.121***	0.046	0.221***	0.084
Keeping track	Check account	0.062*	0.033	0.113*	0.060
Keeping track	Know balance	−0.038	0.047	−0.069	0.086
Keeping track	Tracking finances	0.002	0.026	0.003	0.048
Keeping track	Keeping track	0.022	0.042	0.040	0.077
Keeping track	Personal budget	0.030	0.051	0.054	0.093
Maximising income	Get deal on financial products	0.022	0.045	0.040	0.082
Maximising income	Get deal on utilities	−0.017	0.050	−0.032	0.091
Maximising income	Get other deal	0.022	0.050	0.040	0.090
Build resilience	Save monthly	0.012	0.039	0.023	0.070

Notes: ITT – OLS regressions. CACE – 2SLS regression. *Unexpected expense* Pay an unexpected bill of £300 with own money, dipping into savings or cutting back on essentials. *Check account* Check how much money in current account 'every day' or 'at least once a week'. *Know balance* Know balance on current account 'within a pound or two' or 'within £10'. *Tracking finances* 'Do you keep track of your personal income and expenditure?' (Y/N). *Keeping track* Regularly check incomings and outgoings. *Personal budget* 'Do you set a personal budget of how much you spend?' (Y/N). *Get deal on financial products* 'In the last 6 months, have you tried to get a better deal on . . . financial products (for example: current account/credit union account, credit card, savings account, home buildings/content insurance)' (Y/N). *Get deal on utilities* ' . . . Household utilities (for example: gas, electricity)' (Y/N). *Get other deal* ' . . . other (for example mobile, internet)'. *Save monthly* 'Do you currently save some money each month?' (Y/N). $p < .10*p < .05**p < .01***$.

5.2.3. Financially capable behaviours

An individual's financial behaviour is determined by their financial knowledge, understanding and basic skills as well as their attitudes and motivations. We have seen in the previous two subsections that the apps improved ability and mindset to an extent and in this subsection we examine whether these effects translated into better financially capable behaviours. Results are presented in Table 5.

The first indicator elicits the individual's likely actions in the event of an unexpected bill of £300 to be paid in seven days' time where the financially capable response is relying on own resources (savings or reducing consumption) and not resorting to credit (loan, credit card, overdraft or borrowing from family and friends) or selling assets. Lusardi, Schneider, and Tufano (2011) found widespread fragility to financial shocks in the U.S. and these households were more likely to cut back on essential spending such as healthcare. The treatment group are seen to be more resilient being more likely to report they would rely on their own resources to deal with an unexpected bill (ITT = 0.121; CACE = 0.221).

The next five measures cover behaviours to track income and expenditure. The treatment group were more likely to regularly check their current account (ITT = 0.062; CACE = 0.113) but this effect is only statistically significant at the 10% level. On all other measures there is no effect of using the apps.

There was no effect on the remaining indicators relating to shopping round to maximize income as well as saving regularly. The latter result is surprising given that the treatment group appears more resilient to financial shocks.

5.2.4. Financial well-being

Financial well-being reflects the overall financial position of the household. Financially capable behaviour should lead to greater financial well-being but is obviously limited by the resources available to the household as well as unanticipated shocks. Results for a number of mainly subjective measures of financial well-being including debt levels, arrears, ability to make ends meet and satisfaction with their financial situation are given in Table 6. There is no evidence that the apps have improved the household financial situation on any of these measures. We can only speculate as to how improvements in ability and mindset have not led to an improvement in financial well-being. The window of the trial could have been too short to see better financial decisions translating into meaningful changes in the household financial situation. Also, members of credit unions tend to be from lower income backgrounds and as such have limited means and are more susceptible to economic shocks. Improvements in financial capability can do little to alter the types of work available to the household to generate income or their vulnerability to ill health, crime and unemployment.

Table 6. Estimates of treatment effect on financial well-being.

	ITT		CACE	
Variable	Coeff.	(s.e.)	Coeff.	(s.e.)
Financial satisfaction	0.041	0.205	0.075	0.372
Debt trouble	−0.023	0.027	−0.042	0.048
Money over	0.014	0.050	0.026	0.091
Managing financially	−0.038	0.041	−0.069	0.075
Bills and credit burden	−0.037	0.050	−0.068	0.091
Bills and credit arrears	0.006	0.028	0.011	0.051
Tracking approach works	−0.217	0.157	−0.394	0.284
Keeping up with bills	0.023	0.032	0.041	0.058
Total owed	0.372	0.295	0.682	0.532

Notes: ITT – OLS regressions. CACE – 2SLS regression. *Financial satisfaction* 'How satisfied are you with your overall financial circumstances?' (1–10). *Debt trouble* Trouble with debts 'only sometimes' or 'never'. *Money over* Money over at the end of the week/month? 'Always', 'Most weeks/months' or 'More often than not'. *Managing financially* 'Manage very well' or 'Manage quite well'. *Bills and credit burden* Keeping up with your bills and credit commitments is 'not a burden at all'. *Bills and credit arrears* 'In the last 6 months, have you fallen behind on, or missed any payments for credit commitments or domestic bills for 3 or more months?' ('No' = 1). *Tracking approach works* 'Thinking overall about yours and your partner/spouse's approach to keeping track of income and expenditure, how well do you think this approach works?' (0–10). *Keeping up with bills* Keeping up with your bills and credit commitments 'without any difficulties' or 'Keeping up but it is a struggle from time to time'. *Total owed* Sum of balances on credit cards, store cards, personal loans, hire purchase, car finance and student loans. $p < .10* p < .05** p < .01***$.

5.2.5. Improving the technology

Participants in the treatment group were asked to assess the quality of the apps. In general, the quality of the apps was viewed positively with on average 59% of those that downloaded the apps considering them as either very good or good. The Spend NI app was viewed as best (64% rated it as either very good or good) while the least popular was the Snowball app (50% rated it as either very good or good). Only a small percentage of participants (3–5%) indicated that they did not like the apps.

Participants in the treatment group were then asked to identify what they most liked about each of the apps. *Ease of use* was the feature that was most liked across all four apps (28% on average) followed by *content* (12%) and then *functionality* (8%) while *speed of use* was seldom selected as the most liked feature (3%). Participants were also asked to identify what they least liked about each of the apps but more than half reported they did not know.

A number of questions were asked to assess changes in attitude to digital technology. One-quarter of participants receiving the intervention reported that their attitude towards the use of digital technology had changed as a consequence of using the smartphone apps. They suggested that they now think more about how online money advice and guidance could help them; they now see the importance of timing in repayments and interest charges; they see the importance of setting financial goals for the short to medium and longer term; and they recognise the importance of thinking about future financial needs.

6. Conclusion

In this study four smartphone apps, packaged together under the title 'Money Matters', were provided to working-age members of the largest credit union in Northern Ireland. The apps were designed to enhance financially capable behaviours. An RCT was used to evaluate the apps with the U.K. Financial Capability Outcome Frameworks providing context for the evaluation.

The assessment of the impact of the apps on financial knowledge, understanding and basic skills revealed that those receiving the apps expressed greater confidence in their understanding of loan repayments with loan confidence most pronounced for those utilising the apps more frequently. Financial literacy also improved and again was strongest for those using the apps more frequently. In the assessment of whether the apps led to changes in attitudes and motivations, it was established that those receiving the apps were more likely to prefer to plan for tomorrow with this effect greater for those using the apps more frequently. Those receiving the apps also reported a greater sense of self-efficacy and a greater confidence in their ability to improve financial decision-making through engaging with technology.

Importantly, the changes in financial knowledge, understanding and basic skills, and attitudes and motivations, were found to translate into better financially capable behaviours. In particular, those receiving the apps were more resilient when faced with a financial shock in the form of an unexpected bill. They were also more likely to keep track of their income and expenditure through regularly checking their current account. These improvements in financially capable behaviours did not however result in an improvement in the financial situation of the household. This may have been due to the fact that the RCT was conducted over a six-month period, too short a time frame for improvements in financial well-being to emerge.

As part of the study, we also assessed whether changes emerged in attitudes to digital technology. One-quarter of those receiving the smartphone apps reported that they now think more about how money advice and guidance could help them. They also reported a better awareness of their future financial needs and of the importance in setting financial goals. They also found use of the apps to have improved their understanding of interest charges and the importance of timing in bill and loan repayments.

There is extensive research documenting the effectiveness of smartphone apps in the improvement of health outcomes and behaviours. Our study is, however, the first to establish the efficacy of smartphone apps as a means of improving financially capable behaviours. As four out of five U.K. adults now have a smartphone, our study demonstrates that smartphone apps offer money advice providers and related bodies an accessible, cost-effective and credible means for the targeting of interventions to improve the financial capability of their client base. Our study was neither targeted at a particularly segment of the population nor at a particular problem faced by the cohort involved in the trial. The relevance and applicability of a particular app depended on the stage in the financial journey that a trial participant was at and their financial circumstances at that time. Research suggests that the most effective financial programmes are those targeted at a specific audience faced with an explicit area of financial concern (Martin 2007; Lusardi and Mitchell 2014). The next stage in this research programme will be the targeting of the apps towards a specific cohort and a particular problem for example those from a low-income background struggling with high-cost debts.

Notes

1. These psychological motivations and biases include, non-impulsiveness (Birkenmaier, Sherraden, and Curley 2013), optimism (Puri and Robinson 2007; Kahneman, 2011; Kenrick et al. 2009), confidence (Parker et al. 2012; Fernandes, Lynch, and Netemeyer 2014; Letkiewicz, Robinson, and Domian 2016) and peer influences (Chitegi and Stafford 1999; Hong, Kubik, and Stein 2004; Kempson, Atkinson, and Collard 2006).
2. The FSA (2006) noted that there is no single indicator of financial capability; rather it encompasses four domains – 'managing money', 'planning ahead', 'choosing products' and 'staying informed'.
3. A majority of this research has focused on primary outcomes (any objective measure of health or health service delivery) with assessment of the effectiveness of smartphone apps on secondary (self-reported) outcomes less prevalent (Ali, Chew, and Yap 2016; Haskins et al. 2017).
4. The development cost of the smartphone apps was £50,000. Funding support for the development and testing of the apps was provided by the ESRC and the Money Advice Service (What Works Fund).
5. Taylor (2011) provides a slightly more nuanced definition, referring to financial capability as the combination of knowledge, attitudes, and behaviours that enable a person to navigate successfully their economic life.
6. Currently there are in excess of 260,000 health apps on the market (Peiris, Miranda, and Mohr 2018). Smartphone app interventions have been demonstrated to be effective in promoting physical activity, weight management, the reduction of alcohol consumption and in the management of diabetes, depression and asthma (Watts et al. 2013; Glynn et al. 2014; Smith et al. 2014; Chan et al. 2018). Smartphones are more appealing than other intervention methods such as websites, face-to-face counselling and group sessions because apps have the facility to provide information and advice, real-time self-monitoring, feedback, reinforcement, social support, and rewards 'on the go' (Schoeppe et al. 2016). Features that increase app usage include, ease of use, not having too many features, being developed by credential experts, enabling self-monitoring, providing advice on how to change behaviour, including positively framed alerts/reminders/push notifications (but not too frequent), providing accurate tracking functions and incorporating adequate privacy (O'Reilly and Spruijt-Metz 2013; Peng et al. 2016).
7. https://www.statista.com/statistics/271628/percentage-of-apps-used-once-in-the-us/.
8. 'A recurring insight from research on behavioural finance is that simple interventions that account for or remove psychological constraints, such as social nudges and reminders, can go a long way toward improving financial behaviour' (World Bank 2015, 119.)
9. We anticipated that participants may only use one app from the package as each app was designed for a particular type of financial decision and analysing the apps separately would have effectively reduced our 'treated' group.

10. The first question asked how much money was in the account of the sample Derry Credit Union statement at the end of the month. The remaining three questions were taken from Lusardi and Mitchell (2011) and have been used in many international surveys. (Question 2) Suppose you had £100 in a savings account and the interest rate was 2% per year. After 5 years, how much do you think you would have in the account if you left the money to grow? (1. More than £102 2. Exactly £102 3. Less than £102 4. Do not know). (Question 3) Imagine that the interest rate on your savings account was 1 percent per year and inflation was 2 percent per year. After 1 year, would you be able to buy: 1. More than today 2. Exactly the same as today 3. Less than today 4. Do not know. (Question 4) Do you think that the following statement is true or false? 'Buying a single company stock usually provides a safer return than a stock mutual fund.'

Disclosure statement

No potential conflict of interest was reported by the authors.

Funding

This work was supported by Economic and Social Research Council [Development of web-based tools to enhance the financial capability of credit union members]; Money Advice Service (What Works Fund) [Financial Capability Tools: Assessment Framework].

References

Ali, E. E., L. Chew, and K. Y. Yap. 2016. "Evolution and Current Status of Mhealth Research: A Systematic Review." *BMJ Innovations* 2: 33–40.

Almenberg, J., and A. Dreber. 2011. "Gender, Stock Market Participation and Financial Literacy." Working Paper Series in Economics and Finance, Stockholm School of Economics.

Angrist, J. D., G. W. Imbens, and D. B. Rubin. 1996. "Identification of Causal Effects Using Instrumental Variables." *Journal of the American Statistical Association* 91 (434): 444–455.

Arrondel, L., M. Debbich, and F. Savignac. 2012. "Stockholding and Financial Literacy in the French Population." *International Journal of Social Sciences and Humanity Studies* 4 (2): 1309–8063.

Atkinson, A. 2016. *International Survey of Adult Financial Literacy Competencies*. Paris: OECD.

Bagwell, S., C. Hestbaek, E. Harries, and A. Kail. 2014. "Financial Capability Outcomes Framework." www.fincap.org.uk/uk_strategy.

Birkenmaier, J., M. Sherraden, and J. Curley. 2013. *Financial Capability and Asset Development: Research, Education, Policy and Practice*. Oxford: Oxford University Press.

Bucks, B., and K. Pence. 2008. "Do Borrowers Know Their Mortgage Terms?" *Journal of Urban Economics* 64: 218–233.

Bursztyn, L., F. Ederer, B. Ferman, and N. Yuchtman. 2014. "Understanding Mechanisms Underlying Peer Effects: Evidence From a Field Experiment on Financial Decisions." *Econometrica* 82 (4): 1273–1301.

Campbell, J. 2006. "Household Finance." *The Journal of Finance* 61: 1553–1604.

Chan, Y., B. Bot, M. Zweig, N. Tignor, W. Ma, C. Suver, R. Cedeno, et al. 2018. "The Asthma Mobile Health Study, Smartphone Data Collected Using ResearchKit." *Scientific Data* 5: 1–11.

Chitegi, N. S., and F. P. Stafford. 1999. "Portfolio Choices of Parents and Their Children as Young Adults: Asset Accumulation by African-American Families." *American Economic Review* 89 (2): 377–380.

Choi, J. J., D. Laibson, and B. C. Madrian. 2009. "Mental Accounting in Portfolio Choice: Evidence From a Flypaper Effect." *American Economic Review* 99 (5): 2085–2095.

Deloitte. 2017. "State of the Smart: Consumer and Business Usage Patterns." http://www.deloitte.co.uk/mobileuk/assets/img/download/global-mobile-consumer-survey-2017_uk-cut.pdf.

Disney, R., and J. Gathergood. 2013. "Financial Literacy and Consumer Credit Portfolios." *Journal of Banking and Finance* 37: 2246–2254.

Duca, J. V., and A. Kumar. 2014. "Financial Literacy and Mortgage Equity Withdrawals." *Journal of Urban Economics* 80: 62–75.

Engelberg, E. 2007. "The Perception of Self-Efficacy in Coping with Economic Risks among Young Adults: An Application of Psychological Theory and Research." *International Journal of Consumer Studies* 31: 95–101.

Fernandes, D., J. G. Lynch Jr., and R. G. Netemeyer. 2014. "Financial Literacy, Financial Education and Downstream Financial Behaviors." *Management Science* 60: 1861–1883.

Financial Capability Strategy for the UK. 2015. "Evidence and Analysis."

Financial Services Authority. 2006. *Financial Capability in the UK: Establishing a Baseline*. London: Financial Services Authority.

French, D., and D. G. McKillop. 2016. "Financial Literacy and Over-Indebtedness in Low-Income Households." *International Review of Financial Analysis* 48: 1–11.

Garðarsdóttir, R. B., and H. Dittmar. 2012. "The Relationship of Materialism to Debt and Financial Well-Being: The Case of Iceland's Perceived Prosperity." *Journal of Economic Psychology* 33 (3): 471–481.

Gerardi, K., L. Goette, and S. Meier. 2010. "Financial Literacy and Subprime Mortgage Delinquency: Evidence from a Survey Matched to Administrative Data." Working Paper, Federal Reserve Bank of Atlanta.

Glynn, L. G., P. S. Hayes, M. Casey, F. Glynn, A. Alvarez-Iglesias, J. Newell, G. ÓLaighin, D. Heaney, M. O'Donnell, and A. W. Murphy. 2014. "Effectiveness of a Smartphone Application to Promote Physical Activity in Primary Care: The SMART MOVE Randomised Controlled Trial." *British Journal of General Practice* 64 (624): e384–e391.

Haskins, B. L., D. Lesperance, P. Gibbons, and E. D. Boudreaux. 2017. "A Systematic Review of Smartphone Applications for Smoking Cessation." *Society of Behavioural Medicine* 7: 292–299.

Hastings, J., and O. S. Mitchell. 2011. "How Financial Literacy and Impatience Shape Retirement Wealth and Investment Behaviours." Working Paper 16740, National Bureau of Economic Research.

Heckman, J. J., R. J. LaLonde, and J. A. Smith. 1999. "The Economics and Econometrics of Active Labor Market Programs." *Handbook of Labor Economics* 3: 1865–2097.

Hershfield, H. E., D. G. Goldstein, W. F. Sharpe, J. Fox, L. Yeykelis, L. L. Carstensen, and J. N. Bailenson. 2011. "Increasing Saving Behavior Through Age-Progressed Renderings of the Future Self." *Journal of Marketing Research* 48: S23–S37.

Hong, H., J. D. Kubik, and J. C. Stein. 2004. "Social Interaction and Stock-Market Participation." *The Journal of Finance* 59 (1): 137–163.

Imbens, G. W., and D. B. Rubin. 1997. "Estimating Outcome Distributions for Compliers in Instrumental Variables Models." *The Review of Economic Studies* 64 (4): 555–574.

Kahneman, D. 2011. *Thinking, Fast and Slow.* New York: Macmillan.

Kempson, E., A. Atkinson, and S. Collard. 2006. *Saving for Children: A Baseline Survey at the Inception of the Child Trust Fund.* HM Revenue and Customs Research Report 18. London: HMRC.

Kenrick, D. T., V. Griskevicius, J. M. Sundie, N. P. Li, Y. J. Li, and S. L. Neuberg. 2009. "Deep Rationality: The Evolutionary Economics of Decision Making." *Social Cognition* 27 (5): 764.

Letkiewicz, J., C. Robinson, and D. Domian. 2016. "Behavioral and Wealth Considerations for Seeking Professional Financial Planning Help." *Financial Services Review* 25 (2): 105–126.

Lloyds Bank 2017 Consumer Digital Index. 2017. https://www.lloydsbank.com/banking-with-us/whats-happening/consumer-digital-index.asp.

Lloyds Bank 2018 Consumer Digital Index. 2018. https://www.lloydsbank.com/banking-with-us/whats-happening/consumer-digital-index.asp.

Lusardi, A. 2011. "Americans' Financial Capability." Working Paper 17103, National Bureau of Economic Research.

Lusardi, A., and O. S. Mitchell. 2007. "Baby Boomer Retirement Security: The Roles of Planning, Financial Literacy, and Housing Wealth." *Journal of Monetary Economics* 54 (1): 205–224.

Lusardi, A., and O. S. Mitchell. 2011. "Financial Literacy and Planning: Implications for Retirement Wellbeing." In *Financial Literacy: Implications for Retirement Security and the Financial Marketplace*, edited by O. S. Mitchell and A. Lusardi, 17–39. Oxford: Oxford University Press.

Lusardi, A., and O. S. Mitchell. 2014. "The Economic Importance of Financial Literacy: Theory and Evidence." *Journal of Economic Literature* 52 (1): 5–44.

Lusardi, A., D. J. Schneider, and P. Tufano. 2011. "Financially Fragile Households: Evidence and Implications." Working Paper 17072, National Bureau of Economic Research.

Lusardi, A., and P. Tufano. 2015. "Debt Literacy, Financial Experiences, and Overindebtedness." *Journal of Pension Economics and Finance* 14 (4): 332–368.

Martin, M. 2007. "A Literature Review on the Effectiveness of Financial Education." Working Paper, Federal Reserve Bank of Richmond.

Money Advice Service. 2013. *The Financial Capability of the UK.* Report. London: Money Advice Service.

Money Advice Service. 2016. *Measuring Financial Capability – Identifying the Building Blocks.* November. London: Money Advice Service.

Mundy, S. 2011. "Financial Capability: Why Is It Important and How Can It Be Improved? Perspective Report." CFBT Education Trust.

Neymotin, F. 2010. "Linking Self-Esteem with the Tendency to Engage in Financial Planning." *Journal of Economic Psychology* 31 (6): 996–1007.

OECD INFE. 2011. *Measuring Financial Literacy: Core Questionnaire in Measuring Financial Literacy: Questionnaire and Guidance Notes for Conducting an Internationally Comparable Survey of Financial Literacy.* Paris: Organization for Economic Co-Operation and Development.

OECD INFE Policy Guidance. 2018. "Digitalisation and Financial Literacy." http://www.oecd.org/finance/G20-OECD-INFE-Policy-Guidance-Digitalisation-Financial-Literacy-2018.pdf.

Office for National Statistics. 2017. "Labour Force Survey." https://www.ons.gov.uk/businessindustryandtrade/itandinternetindustry/bulletins/internetusers/2017.

O'Reilly, G. A., and D. Spruijt-Metz. 2013. "Current Mhealth Technologies for Physical Activity Assessment and Promotion." *American Journal of Preventive Medicine* 45 (4): 501–507.

Parker, A. M., W. B. Bruin, J. Yoong, and R. Willis. 2012. "Inappropriate Confidence and Retirement Planning: Four Studies with a National Sample." *Journal of Behavioral Decision Making* 25: 382–389.

Peiris, D., J. J. Miranda, and D. Mohr. 2018. "Going Beyond Killer Apps: Building a Better Mhealth Evidence Base." *BMJ Global Health* 3: 1–3.

Peng, W., S. Kanthawala, S. Yuan, and S. Hussain. 2016. "A Qualitative Study of User Perceptions of Mobile Health Apps." *BMC Public Health* 16: 1–11.

Piercy, L. 2018. "Changing Behaviour Around Online Transactions." https://www.fincap.org.uk/document/WqgSUSoAACoA4glR/changing-behaviour-around-online-transactions.

Puri, M., and D. T. Robinson. 2007. "Optimism and Economic Choice." *Journal of Financial Economics* 86 (1): 71–99.

Reedy, K., and R. Goodfellow. 2012. "Digital and Information Literacy Framework." Open University, November.

Schoeppe, S., S. Alley, W. Van Lippevelde, N. Bray, S. Williams, M. Duncan, and C. Vandelanotte. 2016. "Efficacy of Interventions That Use Apps to Improve Diet, Physical Activity and Sedentary Behaviour: A Systematic Review." *International Journal of Behavioral Nutrition and Physical Activity* 13: 1–26.

Servon, L. J., and R. Kaestner. 2008. "Consumer Financial Literacy and the Impact of Online Banking on the Financial Behavior of Lower-Income Bank Customers." *Journal of Consumer Affairs* 42 (2): 271–305.

Shephard, D., J. M. Contreras, J. Mueris, A. te Kaat, S. Bailey, A. Custers, and N. Spencer. 2017. "Beyond Financial Literacy: The Psychological Dimensions of Financial Capability." Technical Report. Think Forward Initiative. http://www.thinkforwardinitiative.com/research/the-psychological-dimensions-of-financialcapability.

Smith, J. J., P. J. Morgan, R. C. Plotnikoff, K. A. Dally, J. Salmon, A. D. Okely, T. L. Finn, and D. R. Lubans. 2014. "Smart-Phone Obesity Prevention Trial for Adolescent Boys in Low-Income Communities: The ATLAS RCT." *Pediatrics* 134 (3): e723–e731.

Spencer, N., J. Nieboer, and A. Elliott. 2015. *Wired for Imprudence*. London: RSA.

Spires, H., and M. Bartlett. 2012. "Digital Literacies and Learning: Designing a Path Forward." Friday Institute White Paper Series. NC State University.

Taylor, M. 2011. "Measuring Financial Capability and Its Determinants Using Survey Data." *Social Indicators Research* 102 (2): 297–314.

UK Finance. 2018. "The Way We Bank Now." https://www.ukfinance.org.uk/wp-content/uploads/2018/05/WWBN-FINAL-Digital.pdf.

Van Rooij, M., A. Lusardi, and R. Alessie. 2011. "Financial Literacy and Stock Market Participation." *Journal of Financial Economics* 101 (2): 449–472.

Van Rooij, M., A. Lusardi, and R. Alessie. 2012. "Financial Literacy, Retirement Planning and Household Wealth." *The Economic Journal* 122: 449–478.

Von Stumm, S., M. F. O'Creevy, and A. Furnham. 2013. "Financial Capability, Money Attitudes and Socioeconomic Status: Risks for Experiencing Adverse Financial Events." *Personality and Individual Differences* 54 (3): 344–349.

Watts, S., A. Mackenzie, C. Thomas, A. Griskaitis, L. Mewton, A. Williams, and G. Andrews. 2013. "CBT for Depression: A Pilot RCT Comparing Mobile Phone vs. Computer." *BMC Psychiatry* 13 (1): 1–9.

World Bank. 2015. *World Development Report 2015: Mind, Society and Behaviour*. Washington, DC: World Bank.

Cross-country variation in financial inclusion: a global perspective

Mais Sha'ban, Claudia Girardone and Anna Sarkisyan

ABSTRACT
Recent years have witnessed a global commitment to advancing financial inclusion as a key enabler for promoting equal opportunity and reducing poverty. In this paper, we use the IMF's Financial Access Survey data and two different approaches to construct a multidimensional financial inclusion index for a global sample of 95 countries over 2004-15. Results reveal an overall progress in financial inclusion over the period under study, most markedly in the use and access dimensions. Financial inclusion appears to be positively and significantly associated with GDP per capita, employment, bank competition, human development, government integrity, and internet usage. Our evidence also points to the importance of considering the level of national income when designing policies to boost financial inclusion.

1. Introduction

Access to financial services is recognised globally as a key factor for economic and social development. Individuals and businesses excluded from mainstream financial services are prone to different types of risk, such as social exclusion and missed opportunities for business. Empirical studies have emphasised the importance of financial inclusion and the role it plays in achieving high levels of well-being and development through lowering income inequality, reducing poverty, and smoothing consumption (Aslan et al. 2017; Burgess and Pande 2005; Gertler, Levine, and Moretti 2009). Despite the global commitment and the accelerated efforts to boost more inclusive financial systems in both developed and developing countries, the research in this area remains somewhat limited. One of the difficulties relates to the identification of suitable measurement methods.

This paper contributes to the existing literature on financial inclusion in several ways. First, we construct a multidimensional financial inclusion index using the IMF's Financial Access Survey data that incorporates three main dimensions – use, access, and depth of financial services. We employ both a non-parametric and a parametric approach, namely, a standard geometric mean and a more sophisticated principal component analysis that limits the problem of assigning exogenous or equal weights to components (Camara and Tuesta 2014; Park and Mercado 2018a).

Second, we expand the time span of the existing research on financial inclusion. Specifically, we focus on a sample of 95 economies over a relatively long time period (2004-15) that enables us to analyse trends and perform regression analysis. Our financial inclusion index shows an overall progress over the 12 years under investigation, most markedly in the use and access dimensions and to a lesser extent in the depth dimension. We also find high variation in financial inclusion among countries and across macro regions. Although financial inclusion is a universal goal, there have been initiatives focusing on countries located in specific macro regions characterised by high level of financial exclusion, such as Sub-Saharan Africa and Middle East and North Africa. Regional trends in our financial inclusion index reveal improvements in most regions over the sample period, particularly in Sub-Saharan Africa and South Asia; however, European countries significantly over-rank other regions and the Sub-Saharan African region ranks the lowest. These variations motivate the need to investigate factors that can help explain the level of financial inclusion. A number of studies document the importance of macroeconomic conditions, social development, technological advancements, and institutional quality in advancing financial inclusion (Honohan 2008; Rojas-Suarez 2010; Allen et al. 2016; Demirgüç-Kunt and Klapper 2013). Therefore, the third contribution of our study to the extant literature is that we assess a comprehensive set of factors in their relation to financial inclusion, including banking system conditions.

Finally, we test whether the relation between these factors and financial inclusion varies across countries with different income level. The World Bank reports that there has been a significant improvement in financial inclusion globally as the share of adults owning an account increased from 51 per cent in 2011 to 62 per cent in 2014 and reached 69 per cent in 2017. This progress has been mainly driven by government policies and the use of technology (that is, mobile phones and the internet). However, the variation across countries with different income levels is still considerably high; as of 2017, 94 per cent of adults have an account in high income countries, compared to 65 per cent in middle income countries and only 35 per cent in low income countries (Demirguc-Kunt et al. 2018). Investigating how factors that associate with financial inclusion differ across high and low income countries is therefore particularly important. While in some economies (for example, the Sub-Saharan African region) considerable progress has been achieved mainly through new mobile accounts, other emerging economies such as India have progressed significantly in increasing the account ownership through financial institutions. High income economies, such as the European Union countries, have more inclusive financial systems not only in terms of having a bank account but also in terms of using different financial services including savings and borrowings. In fact, financial inclusion is not only about having an account; the actual usage of the account is what matters for achieving the benefits of financial inclusion.

Our main findings reveal that financial inclusion is positively and significantly associated with GDP per capita, employment, competition in the banking system, human development, government integrity, and internet usage. The results are robust across the parametric and non-parametric approaches used to construct the financial inclusion index. We find that the relevance of the factors varies with the level of national income, whereby bank competition and internet usage appear to be more important for enabling financial inclusion in low income countries. This is a useful set of results in relation to the factors that should be prioritised to achieve greater financial inclusion.

The remainder of the paper is structured as follows. Section 2 presents a review of the relevant literature. Section 3 details the data and the empirical approach that we follow to measure financial inclusion and to test its determinants. Section 4 presents the empirical results. Section 5 concludes.

2. Selected literature review

In this section, we first review how existing empirical research captures financial inclusion, including single and composite measures. In the second part, we discuss the studies that examine the determinants of financial inclusion.

2.1. Measuring financial inclusion

The existing research on financial inclusion has suggested various approaches to measuring its extent. One strand of the literature focuses on single measures of financial inclusion. The most widely used is the proportion of adults that have an account (including transactions, savings, or loan accounts) at a bank or other formal financial intermediary (Allen et al. 2016; Honohan 2008; Rojas-Suarez 2010; Demirgüç-Kunt and Klapper 2013; Beck, Demirguc-Kunt, and Martínez-Pería 2007; Owen and Pereira 2018). Another single measure of financial inclusion is account 'usage' that captures the frequency or the volume of account use (Allen et al. 2016; Demirguc-Kunt, Klapper, and Singer 2013). Beyond account-related measures, branch penetration and mobile money have been used to proxy the extent of financial inclusion (Ardic, Heimann, and Mylenko 2011; Demirgüç-Kunt and Klapper 2013).

A second strand of literature proposes composite indices of financial inclusion capturing its multidimensional and complex nature. Studies in this strand typically combine at least the following two dimensions of financial inclusion – (i) the *use*, captured by the size of 'banked' population, that is, the proportion of people with an account at a formal financial institution; and (ii) the *access*, captured by the presence of physical points of financial services, that is, the number of branches and ATMs (Mialou, Amidzic, and Massara 2017; Park and Mercado 2018a, 2018b; Sarma 2012; Chakravarty and Pal 2013; Camara and Tuesta 2014). Some studies also incorporate a third dimension – most commonly, the *depth,* that is proxied by the extent of the utilisation of financial services by the population, that is, the volume of loans and deposits (Sarma 2012; Chakravarty and Pal 2013; Park and Mercado 2018a). Barriers to financial inclusion in the form of distance, affordability, and lack of trust in the financial system, have also been included in the financial inclusion index as a third dimension (Camara and Tuesta 2014).[1] When constructing a composite index of financial inclusion, two approaches have been alternatively used in the literature: a non-parametric approach where the weights for the components of the financial inclusion index are assigned exogenously, based on a judgement element (Sarma 2008, 2012; Chakravarty and Pal 2013); and a parametric approach that allows for the weights to be assigned endogenously, based on the information structure of the data (Camara and Tuesta 2014; De Sousa 2015; Park and Mercado 2018a).

2.2. *Financial inclusion determinants*

The literature on the determinants of financial inclusion has examined both the individual- and country-level characteristics. This section reviews studies that focus on country-level determinants of financial inclusion as these are directly relevant to the current research.[2]

Among the first studies that explore the driving forces behind cross-country variation in financial inclusion, Beck, Demirguc-Kunt, and Martínez-Pería (2007) find that factors such as the level of the economic development, the quality of the institutional environment, the strength of the informational environment of credit markets, and the development of the physical banking infrastructure are positively associated with financial outreach (that is, access to and use of financial services) and depth. At the same time, the association is found to be negative for the cost of contract enforcement and the degree of government ownership of the banking sector. The research that followed has provided further evidence on the importance of benign economic conditions (Ardic, Heimann, and Mylenko 2011; Demirgüç-Kunt and Klapper 2013; Park and Mercado 2018b; Rojas-Suarez 2010), social development (Rojas-Suarez 2010; Park and Mercado 2018b; Honohan 2008), institutional quality (Allen et al. 2016; Rojas-Suarez 2010; Park and Mercado 2018b; Honohan 2008; Owen and Pereira 2018), and technological infrastructure (Honohan 2008; Arun and Kamath 2015) for enhancing financial inclusion.

There is also a consensus in the literature on the existence of an important relationship between a country's financial architecture and financial inclusion (Allen et al. 2016). One of the channels through which this relationship can exist is competition. Higher competitive pressures can incentivise innovation and expansion of financial services, lower their cost, and expand the risk spectrum of customers, thereby fostering financial inclusion (Love and Martínez Pería 2015; Owen and Pereira 2018). Another channel is bank concentration; however, the empirical evidence on its association with financial inclusion is mixed. Some studies suggest that high level of bank concentration may deter the incentives for banks to provide financial services to smaller businesses and riskier individuals (Ardic, Heimann, and Mylenko 2011; Demirgüç-Kunt and Klapper 2013). Other studies find evidence to suggest that larger banks in concentrated markets can be more efficient through economies of scale which in turn can incentivise them to provide financial services to households and small enterprises (Owen and Pereira 2018). Empirical evidence also suggests that restrictions on banking activities and capital stringency can limit the creation of new financial products and services and the use of innovative financial instruments, thereby impairing financial inclusion (De Sousa 2015; Rojas-Suarez 2010).

To conclude, while the country-level characteristics discussed above have been found to be important factors for fostering financial inclusion, the literature also suggests that it is not sufficient to develop only one factor, nor it is always necessary to develop all factors to reach financial inclusion, and that combinations of certain factors might be the optimal solution (Kabakova and Plaksenkov 2018).

3. Data and methodology

3.1. Data

To examine the determinants of financial inclusion, we compile a cross-country dataset for the period 2004–15 using several sources. The data for constructing the financial inclusion index are drawn from the IMF's Financial Access Survey (FAS) that contains supply-side annual data and covers the use and access dimensions; for the depth dimension, we use the Global Financial Development Database (GFDD). The data on the macroeconomic and technological factors are obtained from the World Bank Development Indicators (WDI). Banking conditions data are drawn from the Global Financial Development Database, Heritage Foundation, and World Bank Surveys on Bank Regulation (Barth, Caprio Jr, and Levine 2013).[3] The socioeconomic data are obtained from the UN Human Development Reports and the institutional environment data from the Heritage Foundation. Appendix B summarises the data sources.

When compiling the dataset, we start with all the 189 countries included in the Financial Access Survey. We first exclude countries with population lower than 100,000 adults.[4] We then drop observations with missing values for any of the variables used to construct the financial inclusion index. This selection procedure results in a sample of 95 countries covering the 2004–15 period. To mitigate the influence of outliers, all variables are winsorised at the top and bottom 1 per cent of the distribution.

3.2. Variables

3.2.1. Financial inclusion index

In this study we combine in one index three dimensions of financial inclusion: use, access, and depth. The use dimension reflects the outreach of financial services to adults, which we capture employing two indicators: the number of deposit accounts and the number of loan accounts, both per 1,000 adults. For the access dimension, we consider the demographic outreach of banks' physical outlets using two indicators: the number of branches and the number of ATMs, both per 100,000 adults. The depth dimension refers to the actual usage of financial services and is captured by two indicators: bank deposits and domestic credit to private sector by banks, both scaled by GDP.

To construct the financial inclusion index, we use a three-step procedure commonly followed in the literature, for example, in the context of well-being indices such as the Human Development Index, financial development indices (Svirydzenka 2016), and financial inclusion indices (Park and Mercado 2018a).

We employ a non-parametric approach to derive an equally-weighted composite index. Specifically, in the first step, we normalise the six indicators of financial inclusion using empirical normalisation to arrive at a common scale ranging from 0 to 1:

$$I^n_{(i,t,c)} = \frac{I_{i,t,c} - Min\,(I_i)}{Max\,(I_i) - Min\,(I_i)} \qquad (1)$$

where $I_{i,t,c}$ is the value of financial inclusion indicator i in period t for country c; $Min\,(I_i)$ and $Max\,(I_i)$ are the minimum and maximum value, respectively, for indicator i over the sample period for all sample countries. Therefore, the normalised value represents the indicator's deviation from the minimum and maximum limits across the sample, that is, it relates a country's extent of financial inclusion to the global minimum and maximum across all countries and years. A higher value of $I_{i,t,c}$ within the [0; 1] range indicates greater financial inclusion.

In the second step, the six normalised indicators are used to calculate three dimensional indices – use index, access index, and depth index. Each dimensional index is derived by taking the arithmetic mean of the two corresponding indicators. In the final third step, the three dimensional indices are aggregated into the composite financial inclusion index using the geometric mean as follows:

$$\text{Financial inclusion index} = (\text{Use index} \times \text{Access index} \times \text{Depth index})^{(1/3)} \qquad (2)$$

The construction of the financial inclusion index is summarised in Appendix A.

3.2.2. Determinants of financial inclusion

We examine five categories of factors in their relation to financial inclusion at the country level: (i) macroeconomic factors, (ii) banking system conditions, (iii) institutional environment, (iv) socioeconomic factors, and (v) technological factors.

Within the first category, we use GDP per capita in logarithm form, *GDP per capita*, as a measure of country income. We expect this variable to be positively associated with financial inclusion, as people in countries with a higher level of income tend to be more integrated into the financial system (Ardic, Heimann, and Mylenko 2011; Owen and Pereira 2018). We next include the level of unemployment in the country, *Unemployment*, measured as the share of total labour force without work and actively seeking employment. We expect a negative association between this variable and financial inclusion, as the unemployed population is less likely to be included or motivated to participate in the financial system, whereas formally employed individuals might be required to have a bank account to receive salary (Allen et al. 2016). We also include the level of general inflation in the economy, *Inflation*, captured by the GDP deflator. To the extent that inflation creates uncertainty in the economy and hence may adversely affect both the demand for and supply of financial services, we expect this variable to be negatively associated with financial inclusion (Rojas-Suarez 2010; Allen et al. 2014).

Turning to the second category, we add a set of factors that reflect a country's banking system conditions. These factors include the competitive conditions in the banking sector, *Boone indicator*, captured by the Boone indicator that measures the degree of competition as the elasticity of profits to marginal costs (Leuvensteijn et al. 2013; Schaeck and Cihák 2014). We expect this variable to be negatively related to financial inclusion as higher competitive pressures (lower Boone indicator) can incentivise banks to innovate and expand their financial services, to lower the cost of their financial services, and to reach out to relatively riskier borrowers (Love and Martínez Pería 2015; Owen and Pereira 2018). We also consider a structural measure that is the banking system concentration, *Bank concentration*, calculated as the share of deposits of the five largest banks in total banking system deposits. The literature provides mixed evidence in terms of the relationship between concentration and financial inclusion. High levels of concentration in the banking sector can be negatively related to financial inclusion if banks become less motivated to assess the quality of potential borrowers and subsequently lend to relatively riskier ones due to the lack of competitive incentives (Demirgüç-Kunt and Klapper 2013). On the other hand, banks in a highly concentrated banking sector can achieve higher efficiency through economies of scale and thus be more inclined to invest in information acquisition thereby providing more opportunities for riskier borrowers (Owen and Pereira 2018; Petersen and Rajan 1995). Besides concentration and competition, we examine international differences in the stringency of bank capital regulation and the extent of financial freedom. For the former, we use a capital regulatory index, *Capital regulation*, which is a summary measure of capital stringency derived as the sum of initial capital stringency and overall capital stringency. On the one hand, it can be expected that higher capital stringency can increase banks' costs and hence discourage them from investing in riskier / smaller customers, subsequently leading to lower financial inclusion (De Sousa 2015). On the other hand, it can be argued that better capitalised banks have access to cheaper funding and hence more resources for their customers. Additionally, capital stringency can be considered as an indicator of banks' soundness which in turn might encourage customers to engage in the financial system (Rahman 2014). To capture the extent of an economy's financial freedom, we use a composite index, *Financial freedom*, that draws on the degree of government regulation of financial services, state intervention in financial institutions through direct and indirect ownership, financial and capital market development, government influence on the allocation of credit, and openness to foreign competition. We expect this variable to have a positive association with financial inclusion as government control can deter the ease of access to and provision of financial services (Beck, Demirguc-Kunt, and Martínez-Pería 2007; Rojas-Suarez 2010).

Our third category of financial inclusion determinants captures the institutional environment in the form of government integrity. We use an indicator, *Government integrity*, based on the perceived levels of public sector corruption. We expect this variable to be positively associated with financial inclusion, as low corruption in a country can facilitate the development of the financial system and strengthen confidence in public institutions (Beck, Demirguc-Kunt, and Martínez-Pería 2007; Rojas-Suarez 2010; Demirgüç-Kunt and Klapper 2013; Honohan 2008; Clausen, Kraay, and Nyiri 2011). Similarly, more financial inclusion can mitigate corruption, as suggested by Rajan (2014) in relation to the Indian case.

In the fourth category, we broadly capture the socioeconomic environment using the human development index, *HDI*, which is a composite of the three key dimensions of human development – health, education, and standard of living. We expect this variable to be positively associated with financial inclusion (Kabakova and Plaksenkov 2018). For example, the education component of the human development index can be linked to financial literacy that has been shown to improve the ability of consumers to make informed financial decisions (Klapper, Lusardi, and Panos 2013).

In the fifth category we introduce technological factors. Our proxy for technology is the percentage of population using the internet, *Individuals using internet*. We expect this variable to have a positive association with financial inclusion (Kabakova and Plaksenkov 2018; Honohan 2008; Park and Mercado 2018a). Diffusion of the internet to deliver financial services in both developed and developing countries can deepen financial inclusion by improving access to credit and deposit facilities, providing more efficient allocation of credit, and facilitating financial transfers and other financial services, such as insurance products. This can ultimately result in more opportunities for the unbanked population to participate in the formal financial sector (Kpodar and Andrianaivo 2011).

The construction of the variables is summarised in Appendix B.

3.3. Model specification

To examine the association between financial inclusion and the country-level factors, we use the following model in a panel setup:

$$
\begin{aligned}
Financial\ inclusion_{c,t} = {} & a + \beta_1 GDP\ per\ capita_{c,t-1} + \beta_2 Unemployment_{c,t-1} \\
& + \beta_3 Inflation_{c,t-1} + \beta_4 Boone\ indicator_{c,t-1} + \beta_5 Bank\ concentration_{c,t-1} \\
& + \beta_6 Capital\ regulation_{c,t-1} \\
& + \beta_7 Financial\ freedom_{c,t-1} + \beta_8 Government\ integrity_{c,t-1} + \beta_9 HDI_{c,t-1} \\
& + \beta_{10} Individual\ using\ internet_{c,t-1} + c_c + c_t + u_{c,t}
\end{aligned}
\tag{3}
$$

where the dependent variable, *Financial inclusion*$_{c,t}$, is the financial inclusion index of country c at time t; c_c and c_t are country and time fixed effects, respectively; and $u_{c,t}$ is the error term. The model is estimated using ordinary least squares. The independent variables are lagged by one period to control for potential endogeneity issues. Standard errors are clustered at the country level to control for serial correlation of errors and heteroscedasticity (Petersen 2009). The correlation matrix for the variables used in the main specification is provided in Appendix C.

4. Results

4.1. Summary statistics

Table 1, Panel A, reports the descriptive statistics for the variables used in the baseline regression analysis. Looking at financial inclusion, the mean number of deposit accounts (1,092 per 1,000 adults) is substantially higher than that of loan accounts (294 per 1,000 adults). In terms of volumes, bank deposits total around 50 per cent of GDP, whereas domestic credit to the private sector around 45 per cent. The mean number of branches and ATMs across sample countries is approximately 17 and 35 per 100,000 adults, respectively. The data show a high variation in the level of financial inclusion across the sample countries, most noticeably in the number of deposit accounts where the minimum is 13 (Cameroon, Rwanda, and Central African Republic) and the maximum is 7,211 (Japan) per 1,000 adults. The mean of the composite financial inclusion index is 0.20, which is relatively low compared to the maximum of 0.68 (Spain).[5]

Panel B of Table 1 reports the statistics on financial inclusion distinguishing between high and upper-middle income countries (referred to as high income countries hereafter) and low and lower-middle income countries (referred to as low income countries hereafter). As expected, the data show that high income countries are more

Table 1. Descriptive statistics.

Panel A: Full sample

Variable	Obs	Mean	Std. Dev.	Min	Max
Deposit accounts with commercial banks (per 1,000 adults)	779	1092.14	1148.59	13.23	7211.21
Loan accounts with commercial banks (per 1,000 adults)	779	293.77	295.57	1.30	1275.83
Branches of commercial banks (per 100,000 adults)	779	16.77	17.81	0.61	99.24
ATMs (per 100,000 adults)	779	34.65	35.05	0.05	157.36
Bank deposits (% of GDP)	779	49.82	38.83	5.07	217.53
Domestic credit to private sector by banks (% of GDP)	779	44.54	33.40	2.63	156.12
Financial inclusion index	773	0.20	0.16	0.00	0.68
GDP per capita	779	8.24	1.30	5.45	10.81
Unemployment	508	9.49	7.09	0.50	32.20
Inflation	779	5.45	6.15	−15.71	29.05
Boone indicator	688	−0.06	0.11	−0.65	0.24
Bank concentration	524	74.24	19.05	37.01	100.00
Capital regulation	583	6.64	2.11	1.00	10.00
Financial freedom	721	50.79	15.66	20.00	90.00
Government integrity	727	36.67	16.01	10.00	87.00
HDI	771	0.66	0.14	0.34	0.91
Individuals using internet	770	29.54	24.22	0.51	89.63

Panel B: Income groups

	High income group		Low income group		Difference in means (%)
	Obs	Mean	Obs	Mean	
Deposit accounts with commercial banks (per 1,000 adults)	425	1629.66	354	446.82	256***
Loan accounts with commercial banks (per 1,000 adults)	425	455.55	354	99.56	358***
Branches of commercial banks (per 100,000 adults)	425	23.69	354	8.46	180***
ATMs (per 100,000 adults)	425	53.94	354	11.49	370***
Bank deposits (% of GDP)	425	63.95	354	32.86	95***
Domestic credit to private sector by banks (% of GDP)	425	60.44	354	25.46	137***
Financial inclusion index	425	0.29	348	0.09	239***

Note: The table reports descriptive statistics. Panel A reports summary statistics for variables used in the analysis for the full sample of 95 countries over the period 2004-15. Panel B reports the comparison of financial inclusion variables between the sub-samples of high (and upper middle) income and low (and lower middle) income countries, with the t-test for the equality of means reported in the last column. *, **, *** indicate significance at 10, 5, and 1 percent levels, respectively. Definitions of the variables are provided in Appendix B.

financially inclusive across all the indicators, with the most significant difference observed in the number of ATMs and loan accounts.

Table 2 reports the time trend for the financial inclusion indicators used in the construction of the composite index over the sample period. On average, we observe a stable growth in financial inclusion, except for the years 2008–12 when the financial inclusion indicators remain stable or decline. The latter can be a consequence of the global financial crisis, the Euro sovereign debt crisis, and, for some countries, a greater focus on unconventional monetary policies. The highest growth over the sample period is observed in the number of loan accounts and ATMs, whereas the lowest in the depth indicators. The growth is also slow in the number of branches which can be linked to cost-cutting strategies, particularly in the recession period, and most importantly to the diffusion of internet banking and the move towards cashless transactions, particularly in developed countries (Demirguc-Kunt et al. 2018).

Figure 1 shows the time trend for the composite and dimensional indices of financial inclusion. The progress appears most prominent in the use and access dimensions and to a lesser extent in the depth dimension.

Figures 2 and 3 present the time trend for the composite financial inclusion index for the sample countries by income group and macro region, respectively. As expected, the data show that high income countries, on average, over-rank low income countries. The growth in financial inclusion over time is however more pronounced in low income countries. At the macro-regional level, European countries, on average, over-rank other regions and the Sub-Saharan African region ranks the lowest. However, Sub-Saharan Africa and South Asia show substantial improvement in financial inclusion over time, while other regions show moderate progress.[6]

Table 2. Financial inclusion indicators – Time trend.

Dimension	Year	2004	2005	2006	2007	2008	2009	2010	2011	2012	2013	2014	2015
Use	Deposit accounts with commercial banks (per 1,000 adults)	912.20	992.43	1015.43	1094.93	1043.59	1066.27	1088.62	1081.86	1080.49	1110.39	1168.11	1201.31
	Loan accounts with commercial banks (per 1,000 adults)	135.82	188.38	210.23	289.25	300.54	316.84	308.57	305.62	314.25	309.95	313.82	318.75
Access	Branches of commercial banks (per 100,000 adults)	12.55	15.73	15.92	17.72	16.97	18.28	17.68	16.60	16.55	16.50	16.78	16.85
	ATMs (per 100,000 adults)	19.76	21.83	23.90	30.94	30.83	36.42	36.48	36.02	36.57	37.28	38.78	40.71
Depth	Bank deposits (% of GDP)	45.49	50.21	48.36	51.06	49.07	51.54	49.45	48.41	48.20	48.25	51.11	53.79
	Domestic credit to private sector by banks (% of GDP)	36.94	40.49	42.21	47.79	44.27	47.05	45.68	44.20	43.83	43.40	44.89	46.92

Note: The table reports the mean values for financial inclusion indicators used in the study by year over the period 2004-15. Definitions of the variables are provided in Appendix B.

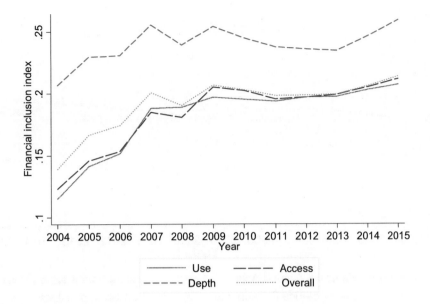

Figure 1. Financial inclusion index – Time trend.

Note: The graph plots the trend of financial inclusion overall and by dimension over the period 2004-15. The financial inclusion dimensions are use, access, and depth.

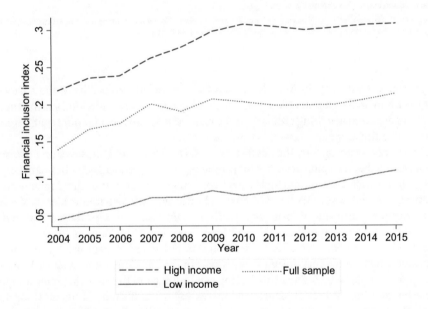

Figure 2. Financial inclusion index – Time trend by income group.

Note: The graph plots the trend of financial inclusion by income region over the period 2004-15. The sample countries are grouped into high (and upper-middle) income region and low (and lower-middle) income region.

4.2. Baseline regression analysis

To examine the link between financial inclusion and country-level characteristics we estimate our baseline model in Equation (3). Results are reported in Table 3. In Model (1), we test macroeconomic factors including GDP per capita, unemployment, and inflation. In Model (2), we introduce banking system conditions related to the competition, structure, capital regulation, and financial freedom. In Model (3), we add institutional environment

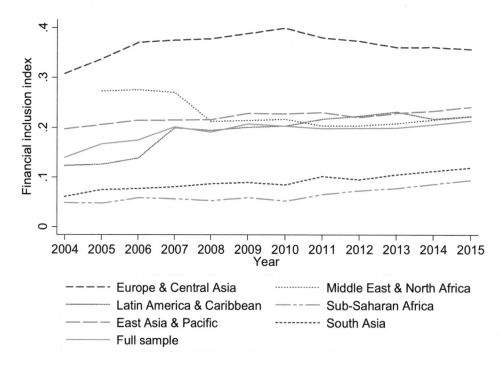

Figure 3. Financial inclusion index – Time trend by macro region.

Note: The graph plots the trend of financial inclusion by macro region over the period 2004-15. The sample countries are grouped into Europe & Central Asia, Middle East & North Africa, Latin America & Caribbean, Sub-Saharan Africa, East Asia & Pacific, and South Asia.

measured by government integrity. In Models (4) and (5), we include, respectively, the socioeconomic factors captured by the human development index and technology proxied by individuals using the internet.[7] All model specifications are estimated using ordinary least squares (OLS) and include country and time fixed effects. Standard errors in all estimations are clustered at the country level.

Among the macroeconomic factors, the coefficient on GDP per capita is positive and statistically significant, thereby suggesting that the countries' level of income is positively associated with financial inclusion. The negative and significant coefficient on unemployment confirms the expectation that higher employment in a country is positively associated with the level of financial inclusion. We also find evidence of a negative association between inflation and financial inclusion, which is in line with the expectation that high and volatile inflation rates could be detrimental to financial inclusion (Allen et al. 2014; Yetman 2018).

Focusing on the banking system conditions, we find a negative and statistically significant coefficient on the Boone indicator, which shows that greater competition in the banking sector (a lower Boone indicator) is associated with greater financial inclusion. This finding can be linked to the view that high competition fosters access to finance by lowering the cost of finance and increasing the availability of financial services (Love and Martínez Pería 2015; Owen and Pereira 2018). As to the concentration, the coefficient is positive and statistically significant. This supports the argument that banks operating in more concentrated banking sectors are more inclined to invest in information acquisition and hence provide more opportunities for riskier borrowers (Owen and Pereira 2018; Petersen and Rajan 1995). Further, we find some evidence of a positive association between bank capital regulation and financial inclusion. This is in line with the view that greater capital stringency lowers banks' cost of funding and enhances customers' confidence in banks' soundness, thereby fostering financial inclusion (Rahman 2014). We also find evidence of the expected positive relationship between financial freedom and financial inclusion. Taken together, the latter two findings suggest that financial inclusion can be fostered through stringent regulation but without limiting the freedom of financial institutions in their provision of financial services.

Table 3. Baseline regression analysis.

	Model (1)	Model (2)	Model (3)	Model (4)	Model (5)
GDP per capita$_{t-1}$	0.1168**	0.0987**			
	(3.99)	(5.08)			
Unemployment$_{t-1}$	−0.0005	−0.0015**	−0.0033**	−0.0029**	−0.0033**
	(−0.61)	(−2.07)	(−3.23)	(−2.64)	(−2.96)
Inflation$_{t-1}$	−0.0007**	−0.0009**	−0.0003	−0.0004	−0.0004
	(−2.13)	(−2.86)	(−1.08)	(−1.24)	(−1.10)
Boone indicator$_{t-1}$		−0.0583**	−0.0435**	−0.0433**	−0.0330**
		(−3.24)	(−3.34)	(−2.92)	(−2.62)
Bank concentration$_{t-1}$		0.0009**	0.0012**	0.0010**	0.0009**
		(2.16)	(2.35)	(2.09)	(2.08)
Capital regulation$_{t-1}$		0.0025	0.0028	0.0031	0.0042**
		(1.16)	(1.25)	(1.41)	(2.03)
Financial freedom$_{t-1}$		0.0006	0.0008	0.0005	0.0012**
		(1.26)	(1.56)	(0.97)	(2.37)
Government integrity$_{t-1}$			0.0012**		
			(2.14)		
HDI$_{t-1}$				1.1572**	
				(3.92)	
Individuals using internet$_{t-1}$					0.0019**
					(3.36)
Constant	−0.7453**	−0.6886**	0.1096	−0.6633**	0.0797
	(−2.91)	(−3.63)	(1.52)	(−2.92)	(1.39)
Country fixed effects	Yes	Yes	Yes	Yes	Yes
Time fixed effects	Yes	Yes	Yes	Yes	Yes
Clustering	Yes	Yes	Yes	Yes	Yes
Observations	449	343	343	342	343
Adjusted R-squared (within)	0.267	0.309	0.208	0.233	0.272

Note: The table reports the regression results of estimating the relation between financial inclusion and country-level characteristics. The dependent variable is financial inclusion index. The independent variables are macroeconomic, banking system, institutional, socioeconomic, and technological characteristics (all lagged by one year). The regressions are run on the full sample of 95 countries covering the period 2004-15. The t-statistics reported in parentheses are based on standard errors clustered at the country level. *, **,*** indicate significance at 10, 5, and 1 percent levels, respectively. Definitions of the variables are provided in Appendix B.

Turning to the institutional environment, the coefficient on government integrity is positive and statistically significant. This indicates that lower perceived public sector corruption (higher government integrity) is associated with greater financial inclusion. As to the socioeconomic environment, the coefficient on the human development index is positive and significant and shows the highest magnitude. This suggests that, as expected, human development in terms of health, education, and standard of living has a strong positive association with financial inclusion.

Finally, with regard to the technological factors, we find a positive and significant coefficient for individuals using the internet, which provides evidence of a positive association between technology and financial inclusion.

4.3. Principal component analysis

To further corroborate the baseline findings, we re-construct the financial inclusion index using a two-stage principal component analysis (PCA). This parametric approach avoids the assignment of exogenous or equal weights to the components and has been applied in the construction of financial inclusion and development indices (Camara and Tuesta 2014; De Sousa 2015; Svirydzenka 2016; Park and Mercado 2018a).

In the first step, in line with our main approach where we use the geometric mean, we normalise the six indicators of financial inclusion (Equation (1)). In the second step, we use a principal component analysis to assign weights to the normalised indicators in their respective dimensional indices (the first stage of the PCA). We then estimate each dimensional index as a weighted average of the two corresponding indicators using the assigned weights. In the third step, we apply the above procedures to the derived dimensional indices (the second

Table 4. Principal component analysis.

Indices	Indicators	Normalised weights
Use	Deposit accounts with commercial banks (per 1,000 adults)	0.633
	Loan accounts with commercial banks (per 1,000 adults)	0.367
Access	Branches of commercial banks (per 100,000 adults)	0.591
	ATMs (per 100,000 adults)	0.409
Depth	Bank deposits (% of GDP)	0.574
	Domestic credit to private sector by banks (% of GDP)	0.426
Aggregate	Use	0.298
	Access	0.293
	Depth	0.408

Note: The table reports the weights of (i) financial inclusion indicators in the respective dimensional indices and (ii) dimensional indices in the aggregate financial inclusion index, both obtained from principal component analysis. Definitions of the variables are provided in Appendix B.

stage of the PCA) to construct the aggregate financial inclusion index as follows:

$$Financial\ inclusion\ index = w_1 \times Use\ index + w_2 \times Access\ index + w_3 \times Depth\ index \qquad (4)$$

where w is the weight assigned to a dimensional index in the principal component analysis. Finally, we normalise the derived financial inclusion index using Equation (1).

Table 4 reports the weights assigned by the PCA in both stages. In the use index, the weight assigned to the number of deposit accounts is 63 per cent compared to 37 per cent assigned to the number of loan accounts. In the access dimension, the number of branches outweighs (59 per cent) the number of ATMs (41 per cent); and deposits to GDP have a greater weight (57 per cent) in the depth index than domestic credit to GDP (43 per cent). Looking at the aggregate financial inclusion index, the largest weight of 41 per cent is assigned to the depth dimension, followed by roughly equal weights (around 29 per cent) for the use and access dimensions.

We next re-estimate the baseline regressions with the financial inclusion index constructed using the PCA as dependent variable. Results are reported in Table 5 and largely confirm the baseline findings. Specifically, we find that financial inclusion is positively related to GDP per capita, bank concentration, capital regulation, financial freedom, government integrity, human development index, and individuals using the internet. In contrast, financial inclusion is negatively related to unemployment, inflation, and Boone indicator.

4.4. Country income level

In this section we examine whether the association between financial inclusion and the country-level factors varies across countries with different income levels. To do so, we first re-construct the financial inclusion index separately for the two sub-samples: high (and upper-middle) income countries and low (and lower-middle) income countries. We use the three-step procedure described in Section 3.2.1; however in this case the minimum and maximum values used in the normalisation of the six financial inclusion indicators (that is, $Min(I_i)$ and $Max(I_i)$ in Equation (1)) represent the minimum and maximum values over the sample period across countries in the respective sub-sample.

We next verify our baseline findings by estimating Equation (3) with the re-constructed financial inclusion index as dependent variable. The results are reported in Table 6, Models (1)–(3), and are consistent with the main results (Table 3, Models (3)–(5)).

We then proceed to test whether the results vary with the country's income level. In so doing, we augment Equation (3) with interaction terms between the country-level determinants of financial inclusion and a low income group dummy, *Low income group*, which takes the value of one for the countries with low (and lower-middle) income. The results are reported in Table 6, Models (4)–(6).

We find that, while the negative association between unemployment and financial inclusion holds in both income groups, it is weaker in low income countries as indicated by the positive and significant coefficient on the interaction term between unemployment and low income. On the contrary, the insignificant coefficient on inflation and the negative and significant coefficient on its interaction with low income (Model (4)) provide

Table 5. Baseline regression analysis – PCA.

	Model (1)	Model (2)	Model (3)	Model (4)	Model (5)
GDP per capita$_{t-1}$	0.1426**	0.1183**			
	(3.46)	(4.54)			
Unemployment$_{t-1}$	−0.001	−0.0025**	−0.0047**	−0.0044**	−0.0047**
	(−0.82)	(−2.33)	(−3.10)	(−2.64)	(−2.89)
Inflation$_{t-1}$	−0.0008*	−0.0010**	−0.0004	−0.0004	−0.0005
	(−1.95)	(−2.56)	(−0.98)	(−1.08)	(−1.05)
Boone indicator$_{t-1}$		−0.0874**	−0.0697**	−0.0697**	−0.0549**
		(−3.41)	(−3.58)	(−3.21)	(−2.94)
Bank concentration$_{t-1}$		0.0012*	0.0015**	0.0014*	0.0011*
		(1.98)	(2.28)	(1.99)	(2.01)
Capital regulation$_{t-1}$		0.0029	0.0033	0.0036	0.0052*
		(1.07)	(1.14)	(1.28)	(1.98)
Financial freedom$_{t-1}$		0.0007	0.0009	0.0006	0.0014**
		(1.19)	(1.51)	(0.96)	(2.53)
Government integrity$_{t-1}$			0.0016**		
			(2.19)		
HDI$_{t-1}$				1.2000**	
				(3.22)	
Individuals using internet$_{t-1}$					0.0027**
					(3.54)
Constant	−0.8553**	−0.7651**	0.1853**	−0.5991**	0.1366*
	(−2.37)	(−3.07)	(2.17)	(−2.17)	(1.81)
Country fixed effects	Yes	Yes	Yes	Yes	Yes
Time fixed effects	Yes	Yes	Yes	Yes	Yes
Clustering	Yes	Yes	Yes	Yes	Yes
Observations	449	343	343	342	343
Adjusted R-squared (within)	0.237	0.289	0.21	0.218	0.285

Note: The table reports the regression results of estimating the relation between financial inclusion and country-level characteristics. The dependent variable is financial inclusion index constructed using principal component analysis. The independent variables are macroeconomic, banking system, institutional, socioeconomic, and technological characteristics (all lagged by one year). The regressions are run on the full sample of 95 countries covering the period 2004-15. The t-statistics reported in parentheses are based on standard errors clustered at the country level. *,**,*** indicate significance at 10, 5, and 1 percent levels, respectively. Definitions of the variables are provided in Appendix B.

evidence to suggest that the negative association between inflation and financial inclusion holds only in low income countries.

Our evidence also reveals that the estimated positive association between competition and financial inclusion tends to be driven mainly by low income countries, as suggested by the insignificant coefficient on the Boone indicator and the negative and significant coefficient on its interaction with low income (Model (6)). Finally, we find a positive and significant coefficient both on individuals using the internet and its interaction with low income. This indicates that while the positive association between technology and financial inclusion holds in high income countries, it is significantly stronger in low income countries. This finding supports the use of technology for expanding financial access, especially in developing countries such as the introduction of mobile accounts in Kenya (Demirguc-Kunt et al. 2015) and the use of biometric identification in India that helped individuals that lack proof of identity to own a bank account (Demirguc-Kunt et al. 2018).

We find no variation in the association between financial inclusion and the remaining banking system conditions, institutional environment, and socioeconomic factors across the two groups of countries, as suggested by the insignificant coefficients on the corresponding interaction terms.

Taken together, the results of this test imply that, when designing policies to enhance financial inclusion, the level of national income should be taken into account, as the most important factors enabling financial inclusion and hence to be supported and promoted tend to vary across countries with different income level.

4.5. Robustness tests

We conduct a number of tests that allow us verify whether our main results are robust to changes in the index construction and sample period.

Table 6. Country income level.

	Panel A			Panel B		
	Model (1)	Model (2)	Model (3)	Model (4)	Model (5)	Model (6)
Unemployment$_{t-1}$	−0.0039**	−0.0034**	−0.0040**	−0.0047**	−0.0042**	−0.0044**
	(−3.71)	(−2.97)	(−3.29)	(−4.07)	(−3.53)	(−3.97)
Unemployment$_{t-1}$* Low income group$_{t-1}$				0.0033**	0.0034**	0.0038**
				(2.1)	(2.11)	(2.83)
Inflation$_{t-1}$	−0.0006	−0.0007	−0.0007	−0.0003	−0.0004	−0.0005
	(−1.38)	(−1.55)	(−1.29)	(−0.80)	(−1.17)	(−0.96)
Inflation$_{t-1}$ * Low income group$_{t-1}$				−0.0014*	−0.0009	−0.0008
				(−1.77)	(−1.07)	(−0.89)
Boone indicator$_{t-1}$	−0.0569**	−0.0559**	−0.0462**	−0.028	−0.016	−0.0002
	(−3.57)	(−3.10)	(−2.85)	(−0.99)	(−0.55)	(−0.01)
Boone indicator$_{t-1}$ * Low income group$_{t-1}$				−0.0131	−0.054	−0.0690**
				(−0.40)	(−1.50)	(−2.14)
Bank concentration$_{t-1}$	0.0011*	0.0009	0.0007	0.0012**	0.0010*	0.0010**
	(1.85)	(1.56)	(1.42)	(2.17)	(1.96)	(2.08)
Bank concentration$_{t-1}$ * Low income group$_{t-1}$				−0.0009	−0.0001	0.0007
				(−0.26)	(−0.02)	(0.66)
Capital regulation$_{t-1}$	0.0031	0.0035	0.0046**	0.0022	0.003	0.0039
	(1.27)	(1.48)	(2.1)	(0.79)	(1.16)	(1.64)
Capital regulation$_{t-1}$ * Low income group$_{t-1}$				0.0048	−0.0013	0.0025
				(0.68)	(−0.17)	(0.45)
Financial freedom$_{t-1}$	0.0011**	0.0007	0.0015**	0.0008	0.0006	0.0011*
	(2.04)	(1.33)	(2.71)	(1.53)	(1.06)	(2.00)
Financial freedom$_{t-1}$ * Low income group$_{t-1}$				0.0016	0.0008	0.0013
				(1.6)	(0.68)	(1.18)
Government integrity$_{t-1}$	0.0020**			0.0013*		
	(2.13)			(1.74)		
Government integrity$_{t-1}$ * Low income group$_{t-1}$				0.0035		
				(1.16)		
HDI$_{t-1}$		1.4840**			1.0578**	
		(3.77)			(2.27)	
HDI$_{t-1}$ * Low income group$_{t-1}$					1.0327	
					(1.61)	
Individuals using internet$_{t-1}$			0.0019*			0.0016**
			(1.95)			(2.71)
Individuals using internet$_{t-1}$ * Low income group$_{t-1}$						0.0058**
						(8.92)
Constant	0.1114	−0.8610**	0.1188**	0.1205	−0.7096**	0.0845
	(1.2)	(−2.81)	(2.05)	(1.22)	(−2.15)	(1.39)
Country fixed effects	Yes	Yes	Yes	Yes	Yes	Yes
Time fixed effects	Yes	Yes	Yes	Yes	Yes	Yes
Clustering	Yes	Yes	Yes	Yes	Yes	Yes
Observations	343	342	343	343	342	343
Adjusted R-squared (within)	0.191	0.207	0.214	0.216	0.234	0.402

Note: The table reports the regression results of estimating the relation between financial inclusion and country-level characteristics while controlling for the country income level. The dependent variable is financial inclusion index constructed separately for high (and upper middle) and low (and lower middle) income sub-samples. In Panel A, the independent variables are macroeconomic, banking system, institutional, socioeconomic, and technological characteristics (all lagged by one year). In Panel B, the independent variables additionally include interaction terms between the country characteristics and the low income group dummy (all lagged by one year). The regressions are run on the full sample of 95 countries covering the period 2004-15. The t-statistics reported in parentheses are based on standard errors clustered at the country level. *, **,*** indicate significance at 10 percent, 5 per cent, and 1 percent levels, respectively. Definitions of the variables are provided in Appendix B.

First, we follow the methodology used in the construction of the human development indices in setting the minimum and maximum values for our six financial inclusion indicators as the 'natural zeros' and 'aspirational targets', respectively.[8] For the minimum values we use zeros for all the indicators. As for the maximum values, in the use dimension, we intuitively set the aspirational target for the number of deposit accounts and the number of loan accounts to one respective account per adult (or 1,000 accounts per 1,000 adults given the scale of the indicators). In the access dimension, we set the aspirational target for the number of branches and the number

Table 7. Robustness test – 'Natural zeros' and 'aspirational targets' for financial inclusion.

	Model (1)	Model (2)	Model (3)	Model (4)	Model (5)
GDP per capita$_{t-1}$	0.2164**	0.1668**			
	(3.97)	(3.99)			
Unemployment$_{t-1}$	0.0018	0.0000	−0.0031**	−0.0021*	−0.0032**
	(1.29)	(0.02)	(−2.33)	(−1.83)	(−2.35)
Inflation$_{t-1}$	−0.0015**	−0.0018**	−0.0009*	−0.0010**	−0.0010*
	(−2.79)	(−3.72)	(−1.93)	(−2.22)	(−1.74)
Boone indicator$_{t-1}$		−0.0725**	−0.0475**	−0.0470*	−0.0331
		(−2.15)	(−2.10)	(−1.86)	(−1.47)
Bank concentration$_{t-1}$		0.0009*	0.0014**	0.0011*	0.0009*
		(1.88)	(2.27)	(2.00)	(1.91)
Capital regulation$_{t-1}$		0.0006	0.0012	0.0016	0.0032
		(0.18)	(0.32)	(0.48)	(0.89)
Financial freedom$_{t-1}$		0.0005	0.0008	0.0001	0.0013*
		(0.74)	(1.06)	(0.08)	(1.68)
Government integrity$_{t-1}$			0.0022*		
			(1.96)		
HDI$_{t-1}$				2.5234**	
				(3.88)	
Individuals using internet$_{t-1}$					0.0026**
					(2.59)
Constant	−1.3449**	−0.9826**	0.3645**	−1.3491**	0.3464**
	(−2.80)	(−2.60)	(3.73)	(−2.73)	(4.87)
Country fixed effects	Yes	Yes	Yes	Yes	Yes
Time fixed effects	Yes	Yes	Yes	Yes	Yes
Clustering	Yes	Yes	Yes	Yes	Yes
Observations	449	343	343	342	343
Adjusted R-squared (within)	0.285	0.239	0.102	0.173	0.149

Note: The table reports the regression results of estimating the relation between financial inclusion and country-level characteristics while setting 'natural zeros' and 'aspirational targets' for financial inclusion. The dependent variable is financial inclusion index constructed with imposed minimum and maximum values for financial inclusion indicators. The independent variables are macroeconomic, banking system, institutional, socioeconomic, and technological characteristics (all lagged by one year). The regressions are run on the full sample of 95 countries covering the period 2004-15. The t-statistics reported in parentheses are based on standard errors clustered at the country level. *,**,*** indicate significance at 10, 5, and 1 percent levels, respectively. Definitions of the variables are provided in Appendix B.

of ATMs equal to the 90th percentile of the distribution of the respective indicator. For the depth dimension, we set the aspirational target for credit to the private sector to GDP as 100 per cent, based on the evidence that the positive effect of financial depth on economic growth vanishes when credit to the private sector reaches that level (Arcand, Berkes, and Panizza 2015); for the bank deposits to GDP we use the 90th percentile of the distribution of the indicator as the target level.

We next re-construct the financial inclusion index following the three-step procedure described in Section 3.2.1 and using the set natural zeros and aspirational targets as the minimum and maximum values in the normalisation of the six financial inclusion indicators (that is, $Min(I_i)$ and $Max(I_i)$ in Equation (1)). We then re-estimate the baseline model (Equation (3)) using the re-constructed index. Results are reported in Table 7 and are consistent with our baseline findings.

Finally, we conduct a number of untabulated tests to further ensure the robustness of our findings. We set the maximum values for all the six indicators of financial inclusion as the 90th percentile of their distribution, respectively. We also control for the potential impact of the financial crisis and the ensuing unconventional monetary policy on financial inclusion by dropping the crisis years 2008–09 from our sample.[9] The results of the tests are largely consistent with our baseline findings.

5. Conclusions

Increasing financial inclusion is essential to drive development and can bring many associated benefits in reducing poverty and promoting prosperity. Hence, it is important to adopt a measure of financial inclusion that is comparable across economies and time to be able to monitor progress. In this study we use the IMF's Financial

Access Survey data and two different approaches (the geometric mean and the more sophisticated principal component analysis) to construct a multidimensional financial inclusion index for a global sample of 95 countries over 12 years (2004-15).

Our results suggest considerable progress in financial inclusion over the period under investigation, most markedly in the use and access dimensions. At the macro-regional level, Sub-Saharan Africa and South Asia show substantial improvement in financial inclusion over time; however, countries in the Sub-Saharan African region are still lagging behind and the gap remains significant.

We examine the link between financial inclusion and a comprehensive set of country-level characteristics. Our findings indicate that financial inclusion is positively and significantly associated with GDP per capita, employment, bank competition, human development, government integrity, and internet usage. Our evidence also highlights the importance of considering the level of national income when designing policies to boost financial inclusion.

There are several policy implications that can be drawn from the findings of this study. There is no doubt that to enhance financial inclusion considerable improvements are needed in a number of country-level characteristics and economic factors. Our study clearly points to the importance of banking system conditions and digital technology. Policy-makers worldwide should consider taking more action, particularly in countries with lower income, to improve the environment to stimulate bank competition and the use of technology in conjunction to greater financial inclusion. We contend that the benefits from pursuing these objectives at the same time are potentially substantial: from more efficient allocation of credit resources to greater use of the formal and regulated financial sector, as well as more access to a wide variety of financial products and services at a reasonable cost.

We observe in our study that financial inclusion is not only about having an account; the actual *usage* of financial services that are made available matters greatly for achieving the benefits of financial inclusion. It follows that, in addition to the focus on the supply side, policy-makers at a global level should continue to have high in their agendas targeted programmes, aimed at improving financial education. In addition, given the clear indication from our findings of the importance of technology for financial inclusion, we recommend that authorities work together to design ways to narrow the digital gaps in our modern societies. This would certainly have wide benefits including facilitating financial inclusion. Ideally, financial literacy programmes should also include basic technology skills for facilitating greater digital literacy.

Notes

1. The literature on financial inclusions uses different terms for the dimensions. For example, the proportion of people with a financial account has also been classified as *access*; whereas the number of branches and ATMs as *availability* or *outreach* (Sarma 2012; Mialou, Amidzic, and Massara 2017; Park and Mercado 2018a).
2. Studies examining individual-level factors that influence financial inclusion show that the most important determinants are employment, income, housing tenure, marital status, age, gender, and education (Devlin 2005; Demirguc-Kunt, Klapper, and Randall 2013). Also, geographic research on financial exclusion suggests that neighbourhood dynamics and location play an important role in determining financial access. For instance, disenfranchised areas and areas with increased number of minorities and immigrants tend to be neglected by banks (Graves 2003; Joassart-Marcelli and Stephens 2010).
3. The World Bank Surveys on Bank Regulation were conducted in 1999, 2003, 2007, and 2011; therefore, we fill in the remaining years during our sample period with data from the preceding surveys.
4. These countries include Palau, San Marino, St. Kitts and Ne, Marshall Islands, Dominica, Seychelles, Antigua and Barb, Aruba, Kiribati.
5. Appendix D reports the list of the sampled countries ranked by the financial inclusion index.
6. We acknowledge that mobile money played an important role in improving account ownership in Sub-Saharan Africa and can be used to improve financial inclusion in developing economies, rural areas, and conflict-affected areas. However, we do not include this indicator in our analysis due to limited data availability, in addition to our focus on banks (formal sector) that are regulated and monitored.
7. In Models (3)-(5), we alternatively add government integrity, the human development index, and number of individuals using the internet and omit GDP per capita to avoid multicollinearity due to high correlation among these variables. The correlation matrix is reported in Appendix C.
8. While we winsorise all variables at the top and bottom 1 per cent of the distribution, this test also provides an additional control for the potential effect of outliers in distorting the scale of the index (Sarma 2012).

9. This is a crucial exercise because during a crisis changes in deposits may stem from various factors including 'flight to quality' of capital from troubled countries to safer ones. This occurred for example during the eurozone crisis when capital fled from the eurozone to Japan (Azis and Shin 2014). In other cases deposits may have reduced because investors shifted to non-bank investments products, such as money market mutual funds.

Acknowledgement

We would like to thank the Editor Chris Adcock, the Guest Editors Georgios Panos and John O. S. Wilson, and two anonymous referees for their useful comments and suggestions. We also thank without implication Panayiotis Andreou, Thankom Arun, Rym Ayadi, Barbara Casu, Jose Linares-Zegarra, Rogelio Mercado Jr, Milena Migliavacca, and Andrea Presbitero, and participants at the 3rd International Workshop on the Internet for Financial Collective Awareness & Intelligence (University of Glasgow), the 2nd Forum on Economic and Social Policy (Central Bank of Cyprus), and Essex Finance Centre (EFiC) seminar series. We gratefully acknowledge financial support from UGC-UKIERI grant on 'Mainstreaming' of the Financial Inclusion Agenda in India' (IND/CONT/G/16-17/67).

Disclosure statement

No potential conflict of interest was reported by the authors.

Funding

We gratefully acknowledge financial support from UGC-UKIERI grant on 'Mainstreaming' of the Financial Inclusion Agenda in India' (IND/CONT/G/16-17/67).

References

Allen, F., E. Carletti, R. Cull, J. Q. Qian, L. Senbet, and P. Valenzuela. 2014. "The African Financial Development and Financial Inclusion Gaps." *Journal of African Economies* 23 (5): 614–642.

Allen, F., A. Demirguc-Kunt, L. Klapper, and M. S. Martinez Peria. 2016. "The Foundations of Financial Inclusion: Understanding Ownership and use of Formal Accounts." *Journal of Financial Intermediation* 27 (C): 1–30.

Arcand, J. L., E. Berkes, and U. Panizza. 2015. "Too Much Finance?" *Journal of Economic Growth* 20 (2): 105–148.

Ardic, O. P., M. Heimann, and N. Mylenko. 2011. *Access to Financial Services and the Financial Inclusion Agenda Around the World: A Cross-Country Analysis with a New Data Set.* The World Bank working paper No. 5537.

Arun, T., and R. Kamath. 2015. "Financial Inclusion: Policies and Practices." *IIMB Management Review* 27 (4): 267–287.

Aslan, G., C. Deléchat, M. M. Newiak, and M. F. Yang. 2017. Inequality in Financial Inclusion and Income Inequality. International Monetary Fund WP/17/236.

Azis, I. J., and H. S. Shin, eds. 2014. *Global Shock, Risks, and Asian Financial Reform.* Chelthenam: Edward Elgar.

Barth, J. R., G. Caprio Jr, and R. Levine. 2013. "Bank Regulation and Supervision in 180 Countries From 1999 to 2011." *Journal of Financial Economic Policy* 5 (2): 111–219.

Beck, T., A. Demirguc-Kunt, and M. S. Martínez-Pería. 2007. "Reaching out: Access to and use of Banking Services Across Countries." *Journal of Financial Economics* 85 (1): 234–266.

Burgess, R., and R. Pande. 2005. "Do Rural Banks Matter? Evidence From the Indian Social Banking Experiment." *American Economic Review* 95 (3): 780–795.

Camara, N., and D. Tuesta. 2014. Measuring Financial Inclusion: A Muldimensional index. *BBVA Research Paper*, (14/26).

Chakravarty, S. R., and R. Pal. 2013. "Financial Inclusion in India: An Axiomatic Approach." *Journal of Policy Modeling* 35 (5): 813–837.

Clausen, B., A. Kraay, and Z. Nyiri. 2011. "Corruption and Confidence in Public Institutions: Evidence From a Global Survey." *The World Bank Economic Review* 25 (2): 212–249.

Demirgüç-Kunt, A., and L. Klapper. 2013. "Measuring Financial Inclusion: Explaining Variation in Use of Financial Services Across and Within Countries." *Brookings Papers on Economic Activity* 2013 (1): 279–340. Brookings Institution Press. Retrieved June 29, 2019, from Project MUSE database.

Demirguc-Kunt, A., L. Klapper, and D. Randall. 2013. *Islamic Finance and Financial Inclusion: Measuring use of and Demand for Formal Financial Services Among Muslim Adults.* The World Bank working paper No. 6642.

Demirguc-Kunt, A., L. Klapper, and D. Singer. 2013. *Financial Inclusion and Legal Discrimination Against Women: Evidence from Developing Countries.* The World Bank working paper No. 6416.

Demirguc-Kunt, A., L. Klapper, D. Singer, S. Ansar, and J. Hess. 2018. *The Global Findex Database 2017: Measuring Financial Inclusion and the Fintech Revolution.* The World Bank.

Demirguc-Kunt, A., L. Klapper, D. Singer, and P. Van Oudheusden. 2015. *The Global Findex Database 2014: Measuring Financial Inclusion Around the World.* The World Bank working paper No. 7255.

De Sousa, M. M. 2015. Financial Inclusion and Global Regulatory Standards: An Empirical Study Across Developing Economies. CIGI working paper No 7.

Devlin, J. F. 2005. "A Detailed Study of Financial Exclusion in the UK." *Journal of Consumer Policy* 28 (1): 75–108.

Gertler, P., D. I. Levine, and E. Moretti. 2009. "Do Microfinance Programs Help Families Insure Consumption Against Illness?" *Health Economics* 18 (3): 257–273.

Graves, S. M. 2003. "Landscapes of Predation, Landscapes of Neglect: A Location Analysis of Payday Lenders and Banks." *The Professional Geographer* 55 (3): 303–317.

Honohan, P. 2008. "Cross-country Variation in Household Access to Financial Services." *Journal of Banking & Finance* 32 (11): 2493–2500.

Joassart-Marcelli, P., and P. Stephens. 2010. "Immigrant Banking and Financial Exclusion in Greater Boston." *Journal of Economic Geography* 10 (6): 883–912.

Kabakova, O., and E. Plaksenkov. 2018. "Analysis of Factors Affecting Financial Inclusion: Ecosystem View." *Journal of Business Research* 89: 198–205.

Klapper, L., A. Lusardi, and G. A. Panos. 2013. "Financial Literacy and its Consequences: Evidence From Russia During the Financial Crisis." *Journal of Banking & Finance* 37 (10): 3904–3923.

Kpodar, K., and M. Andrianaivo. 2011. *ICT, Financial Inclusion, and Growth Evidence from African Countries*. International Monetary Fund working paper No. 11-73.

Leuvensteijn, M., C. K. Sørensen, J. A. Bikker, and A. A. Van Rixtel. 2013. "Impact of Bank Competition on the Interest Rate Pass-Through in the Euro Area." *Applied Economics* 45 (11): 1359–1380.

Love, I., and M. S. Martínez Pería. 2015. "How Bank Competition Affects Firms' Access to Finance." *The World Bank Economic Review* 29 (3): 413–448.

Mialou, A., G. Amidzic, and A. Massara. 2017. "Assessing Countries' Financial Inclusion Standing - A New Composite Index." *Journal of Banking and Financial Economics* 2 (8): 105–126.

Owen, A. L., and J. M. Pereira. 2018. "Bank Concentration, Competition, and Financial Inclusion." *Review of Development Finance* 8 (1): 1–17.

Park, C. Y., and R. Mercado Jr. 2018a. Financial Inclusion: New Measurement and Cross-Country Impact Assessment. ADB Economics working paper No. 539.

Park, C. Y., and R. Mercado Jr. 2018b. "Financial Inclusion, Poverty, and Income Inequality." *The Singapore Economic Review* 63 (01): 185–206.

Petersen, M. A. 2009. "Estimating Standard Errors in Finance Panel Data Sets: Comparing Approaches." *The Review of Financial Studies* 22 (1): 435–480.

Petersen, M. A., and R. G. Rajan. 1995. "The Effect of Credit Market Competition on Lending Relationships." *The Quarterly Journal of Economics* 110 (2): 407–443.

Rahman, A. 2014. The Mutually-Supportive Relationship Between Financial Inclusion and Financial Stability, Issue: 1 (Report by the Alliance for Financial Inclusion; AFI). https://www.afi-global.org/sites/default/files/publications/afivp1-11.pdf.

Rajan, R. 2014. Finance and Opportunity in India, 20th Lalith Doshi Memorial Lecture, Mumbai, BIS Central Bankers Speeches, 11 August.

Rojas-Suarez, L. 2010. *Access to Financial Services in Emerging Powers: Facts, Obstacles and Recommendations*. Perspectives on Global Development 2010: Shifting Wealth, OECD, March 2010.

Sarma, M. 2008. *Index of Financial Inclusion*, Indian Council for Research on International Economics Relations working paper No. 215. New Delhi.

Sarma, M. 2012. Index of Financial Inclusion–A Measure of Financial Sector Inclusiveness. *Berlin (GE): Berlin Working Papers on Money, Finance, Trade and development, working paper No. 07/2012*.

Schaeck, K., and M. Cihák. 2014. "Competition, Efficiency, and Stability in Banking." *Financial Management* 43 (1): 215–241.

Svirydzenka, K. 2016. *Introducing a New Broad-Based Index of Financial Development*. International Monetary Fund working paper No. WP/16/5.

Yetman, J. 2018. Adapting Monetary Policy to Increasing Financial Inclusion. IFC Bulletins chapters, 47.

Appendix A: Financial inclusion index

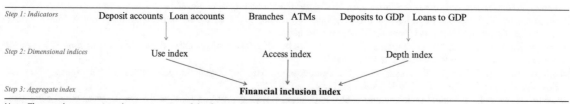

Note: The graph summarises the construction of the financial inclusion index used in the study.

Appendix B. Variables definitions and data sources

Variables	Definition	Source
Financial inclusion		
Financial inclusion index	An aggregate financial inclusion indicator at a country level based on three dimensions: use, access, and depth. It ranges from 0 to 1, with a higher value indicating greater financial inclusion.	Authors' calculations
Use	Deposit accounts with commercial banks (per 1,000 adults).	FAS
	Loan accounts with commercial banks (per 1,000 adults).	FAS
Access	Branches of commercial banks (per 100,000 adults).	FAS
	ATMs (per 100,000 adults).	FAS
Depth	Bank deposits (% of GDP).	GFDD
	Domestic credit to private sector by banks (% of GDP).	GFDD
Macroeconomic factors		
GDP per capita	Gross domestic product divided by mid-year population (log).	WDI
Unemployment	Share of the total labour force that is without work but available for and seeking employment (%).	WDI
Inflation	Inflation measured as the annual growth rate of the GDP implicit deflator. The GDP implicit deflator is the ratio of GDP in current local currency to GDP in constant local currency.	WDI
Banking system conditions		
Boone indicator	A measure of degree of competition based on profit-efficiency in the banking market. It is calculated as the elasticity of profits to marginal costs. A higher value of the Boone indicator implies a lower level of competition.	GFDD
Bank concentration	The degree of concentration of deposits in the 5 largest banks.	Bank Regulation Surveys (Barth et al., 2012)
Capital regulation	Sum of overall capital stringency and initial capital stringency. It ranges between 0-10, where a higher value indicates a higher level of capital stringency.	Bank Regulation Surveys (Barth et al., 2012)
Financial freedom	An indicator of banking efficiency as well as a measure of independence from government control and interference in the financial sector. It ranges between 0-100, where a higher value indicates a higher level of financial freedom.	Heritage Foundation
Institutional environment		
Government integrity	Derived by averaging scores for the following factors, all of which are weighted equally: public trust in politicians, irregular payments and bribes, transparency of government policymaking, absence of corruption, perceptions of corruption, and governmental and civil service transparency. It ranges between 0-100, where a higher value indicates a higher level of government integrity.	Heritage Foundation
Socioeconomic factors		
HDI (Human development index)	Summary measure of average achievement in key dimensions of human development: health, education, and standard of living. It ranges between 0-1, where a higher value indicates a higher level of human development.	UN Human Developments Reports
Technological factors		
Individuals using internet	Internet users are individuals who have used the internet (from any location) in the last 3 months (% of population). The internet can be used via a computer, mobile phone, personal digital assistant, games machine, digital TV, etc.	WDI

Note: The table defines the variables used in the analysis and data sources.

Appendix C: Correlation matrix

	Financial inclusion index	GDP per capita	Unemployment	Inflation	Boone indicator	Bank concentration	Capital regulation	Financial freedom	Government integrity	HDI
Financial inclusion index	1.000									
GDP per capita	0.810***	1.000								
Unemployment	0.119***	0.104**	1.000							
Inflation	-0.351***	-0.306***	-0.040	1.000						
Boone indicator	-0.131***	-0.137***	-0.118***	-0.015	1.000					
Bank concentration	-0.184***	-0.044	0.060	-0.026	0.264***	1.000				
Capital regulation	0.029	-0.017	-0.023	0.000	0.011	-0.006	1.000			
Financial freedom	0.564***	0.516***	0.123***	-0.168***	-0.118***	0.060	0.024	1.000		
Government integrity	0.754***	0.692***	0.008	-0.264***	-0.071*	0.044	-0.003	0.553***	1.000	
HDI	0.827***	0.912***	0.141***	-0.293***	-0.090**	-0.073*	0.097***	0.550***	0.686***	1.000
Individuals using internet	0.822***	0.824***	0.172***	-0.335***	-0.101***	-0.023	0.101***	0.524***	0.718***	0.841***

Note: The table reports key correlations for the variables used in our main empirical analysis. Definitions of the variables are provided in Appendix B.

Appendix D: Country ranking by financial inclusion index

Rank	Country	Financial inclusion index
1	Spain	0.632
2	Japan	0.632
3	Portugal	0.629
4	Malta	0.506
5	Greece	0.504
6	Belgium	0.458
7	Italy	0.443
8	The Bahamas	0.420
9	Netherlands	0.415
10	Estonia	0.392
11	Bulgaria	0.384
12	Malaysia	0.369
13	Lebanon	0.365
14	Poland	0.355
15	Brazil	0.352
16	Brunei Darussalam	0.350
17	Montenegro	0.341
18	Latvia	0.335
19	Mauritius	0.323
20	Thailand	0.313
21	Chile	0.307
22	Panama	0.307
23	Macedonia	0.297
24	Hungary	0.288
25	South Africa	0.286
26	Bosnia and Herzegovina	0.271
27	Costa Rica	0.261
28	Colombia	0.250
29	Belize	0.234
30	Trinidad and Tobago	0.226
31	Vanuatu	0.215
32	Guatemala	0.213
33	El Salvador	0.198
34	Suriname	0.198
35	Jordan	0.195
36	Georgia	0.192
37	Namibia	0.192
38	Saudi Arabia	0.190
39	Republic of Armenia	0.182
40	Fiji	0.176
41	Republic of Kosovo	0.176
42	Honduras	0.172
43	Paraguay	0.165
44	Botswana	0.164
45	Samoa	0.163
46	Sao Tome and Principe	0.159
47	Moldova	0.154
48	Maldives	0.153
49	Tonga	0.151
50	Dominican Republic	0.149
51	West Bank and Gaza	0.142
52	Ecuador	0.140
53	Argentina	0.135
54	India	0.135
55	Jamaica	0.135
56	Bolivia	0.133
57	Peru	0.130
58	Indonesia	0.124

(*continued*).

Rank	Country	Financial inclusion index
59	Bhutan	0.123
60	Guyana	0.113
61	Kenya	0.101
62	Nicaragua	0.101
63	Nepal	0.101
64	Swaziland	0.100
65	Federated States of Micronesia	0.096
66	Egypt	0.092
67	Angola	0.086
68	Bangladesh	0.083
69	Algeria	0.065
70	Nigeria	0.064
71	Pakistan	0.059
72	Solomon Islands	0.059
73	Djibouti	0.057
74	Cambodia	0.057
75	Lesotho	0.056
76	Gabon	0.045
77	Zambia	0.041
78	Haiti	0.035
79	Tanzania	0.034
80	Malawi	0.034
81	Uganda	0.031
82	Comoros	0.030
83	Rwanda	0.030
84	Liberia	0.027
85	Myanmar	0.024
86	Cameroon	0.019
87	Equatorial Guinea	0.016
88	Madagascar	0.016
89	Islamic Republic of Afghanistan	0.015
90	Burundi	0.013
91	Guinea	0.010
92	Chad	0.008
93	Central African Republic	0.007
94	South Sudan	0.005
95	Democratic Republic of Congo	0.004

Note: The table reports the average value of the financial inclusion index over the period 2004–15 by country for the full sample of 95 countries. The countries are ranked from the most financially inclusive (highest index score) to the least financially inclusive (lowest index score).

Measuring financial well-being over the lifecourse

J. Michael Collins ⓘ and Carly Urban ⓘ

ABSTRACT

Financial well-being is a relatively new construct that attempts to measure subjective financial status and perceived future financial trajectory. Using a large public cross-sectional dataset, we find that a standardized financial well-being score generally tracks income, wealth, and participation in investment markets, as well as markers of positive and negative financial behavior. However, financial well-being measures attributes that are distinct from general subjective well-being and financial literacy measures, especially over the life course. Financial well-being can be a useful construct to include in new surveys but can also be proxied in existing public datasets, as we demonstrate using separate survey data.

1. Introduction

The financial status of families is typically expressed using a measure such as income – families are labeled well-off if income levels are well above the median and poor if well below. These measures do not capture how well people are managing financial resources or how much financial strain they feel. Most readers can reflect on people who have relatively little income, yet appear to be financially secure, as well as those with relatively robust incomes who are financially stressed. Yet, in the household finance literature, financial well-being is generally not well measured, in part because there is a lack of standardized instruments to use in research. While prior studies attempt to proxy for financial well-being with measures ranging from assets or debt levels, to financial knowledge (or literacy), to the incidence of hardships, these are indirect indicators of how financially-healthy people perceive their situation. Understanding the financial well-being of households requires more holistic measures than account balances or paystubs can capture. This study explores a relatively new, subjective measure of financial perceptions called the Financial Well-Being (FWB) scale. We demonstrate how this broader measure of financial well-being can offer insights beyond traditional measures and how subjective financial well-being can potentially deepen our understanding of households' financial health.

Economists consider utility as a prime measure of individual's relative satisfaction from the consumption of goods and services. Seminal work by Angus Deaton points to subjective well-being as a measure of individual happiness (Deaton 2008). This work is also reflected in social psychology, where subjective well-being is often the focus of happiness and life satisfaction research, including at the population level (Diener 1984; Diener et al. 1999). Across fields, however, there is a consistent finding that while income and wealth are correlated with subjective well-being, there is still variation that economic resources do not explain (Diener and Biswas-Diener 2002). This begs the question of what contributes to financial well-being over and above general subjective well-being.

In 2015, the federal Consumer Financial Protection Bureau (CFPB) in the United States released a new FWB scale. This new measure was designed to capture the subjective well-being people express related to their financial status developed from extensive consumer interviews and surveys. The scale is based on a definition of FWB that has four basic elements: (1) having control of day-to-day and month-to-month finances; (2) having capacity to absorb a financial shock; (3) being on track to meet financial goals; and (4) having the freedom to make choices that allow enjoyment of life.

To understand how this FWB scale score differs from other common measures of financial status, we use a cross-sectional dataset collected by the CFPB from more than 6000 US households to estimate how demographic and a range of financial measures are related to FWB, as well as patterns of FWB at various ages. We also use another dataset to reproduce a pseudo-FWB scale measure, showing that the FWB construct can be proxied even with surveys that do not include the specific FWB scale question items.

This study contributes to the literature in three ways. First, few prior studies have used a standardized scale to measure financial well-being. We are able to compare the FWB scale to general subjective well-being, as well as levels of income, wealth, financial literacy, and financial perceptions. Second, we show how levels of the FWB scale vary over the life course and that FWB captures attributes not well measured in financial measures alone. Third, we create a proxy for FWB to show how researchers can use measures that are already in existing datasets to construct a measure of financial well-being with similar performance characteristics.

2. Overview of concepts and measures

Studies in household financial research tend to use a handful of measures to indicate how financially secure people are – measures like relative income, net wealth or levels of consumption. These measures can capture some aspects of household financial conditions, but there are always anecdotes of wealthy people on the brink of financial collapse, as well as thrifty low-income people who are financially independent and secure. Previous work generally uses a variety of measures of financial conditions. We summarize some key aspects of each below, in part to define the differences across measures and illustrate the need for a distinct financial well-being measure.

Financial status is among the most commonly measured financial attribute used in many household surveys, including measures of assets, debt, and income. One data source with these measures is the Federal Reserve Survey of Consumer Finances, which has provided detailed estimates of household finances dating back to the 1980s (and earlier in some cases) (Bricker et al. 2017). These data are useful for describing patterns and changes in financial status of cohorts of households over time. For example, Poterba, Venti, and Wise (1994) examine retirement account balances, and Bergstresser and Poterba (2004) study the types of accounts people hold. There are hundreds of surveys that include related measures of income and wealth, although there remains variation in how these items are measured.

Financial inclusion is a newer concept drawn from development economics where access to basic banking services is viewed as a critical infrastructure for developing economies (Demirguc-Kunt et al. 2018). In the US, inclusion focuses more on access to banking and lending services. For example, Rhine, Greene, and Toussaint-Comeau (2006) study the ownership of basic transactional bank accounts (checking accounts). The US Federal Deposit Insurance Corporation (FDIC) 'Unbanked Supplement' to the US Census Current Population survey was developed to track the rate of the population being banked or has access to financial services (Rhine and Greene 2013). In developed countries, financial inclusion may also be broadened to include participation in stock, bond, and mutual fund markets (Lusardi, van Rooij, and Alessie 2011).

Another domain of measures in household finance are related to material hardship (Short 2005). Material hardships are measures of consumption; a lack of consumption of items considered a necessity is defined as a hardship (Bhattacharya, Currie, and Haider 2004). Hardship measures are often related to the cost and quality of food or housing (Desmond and Gershenson 2016). Material deprivation measures are somewhat broader and include access to durable goods or other consumption (Beverly 2001), such as basic health care (Lyons and Yilmazer 2005). For example, Mayer and Jencks (1989) show that income thresholds mask the fact that some households have higher incomes but experience material hardships, while other households have incomes below poverty thresholds and face few or no hardships.

Financial capability is another newer construct. Capability measures focus on people's ability to take actions to manage their finances (Atkinson et al. 2007). Financial capability measures are more diffused, including measures of financial behavior, confidence and satisfaction (Taylor 2011; Xiao, Chen, and Chen 2014). Financial capability may also include aspects of financial inclusion to capture the ability of people to make financial decisions (Johnson and Sherraden 2007). Financial capability is one of the newer incarnations of measures of consumers in financial contexts and in part reflects the need for measures that better capture financial well-being.

Other aspects of household financial capability can be captured in scales related to financial knowledge or 'literacy' (Hung, Parker, and Yoong 2009). Financial literacy is measured through either perceived financial knowledge or actual factual knowledge, often using questions about topics like inflation, compound interest or investment types. Correct responses to objective items in financial knowledge tend to be associated with better financial behaviors (Lusardi and Mitchell 2007; Knoll and Houts 2012; Taft, Hosein, and Mehrizi 2013; Lusardi and Mitchell 2014).

3. Financial well-being

Financial well-being is a relatively new concept in household or consumer finances. The concept is grounded by the literature on subjective well being, the subject of much study in psychology and economics over the last few decades, including pathbreaking work by Diener (1984) and Kahneman and Krueger (2006). For example, Kobau et al. (2010) developed the five-item Satisfaction With Life Scale.[1] Income or wealth levels are often included in studies of subjective well-being, where well-being and economic resources are only weakly correlated (Diener and Biswas-Diener 2002; Dolan, Peasgood, and White 2008). However, subjective well-being encompasses a wide range of non-financial factors like health, family situation and social influences. Only a subset of overall subjective well-being is related to finances and financial management.

The FWB scale was developed based on a consumer-defined meaning of financial well-being. Researchers conducted qualitative interviews and focus groups to define what is included in financial well-being and to draft and test survey items. This definition of financial well-being is measured at the individual level and is based on reports of feelings of (1) control over day-to-day, month-to-month finances; (2) the capacity to absorb a financial shock; (3) being on track to meet financial goals; and (4) having the financial freedom to make the choices that allow for the enjoyment of life. Being in control includes being able to pay bills on time, not having unmanageable debt, and being able to make ends meet. Absorbing a shock includes resilience by having a financial cushion, savings, health insurance, access to credit, or friends and family for financial assistance. Financial goals, which can vary based on the individual and his or her needs, are related to resource planning and being confident to make financial decisions. Financial freedom includes aspects of autonomy, where a lack of financial resources can limit basic life choices. This includes simple forms of discretionary consumption, such as being able to eat a meal out of home with family members.

The FWB scale was then tested to establish scoring procedures based on a 10-question scale with 5-point likert scales, as well as a scoring formula.[2] The FWB scale question items are displayed in Table 1. These 10 items are not simply summed from 0 to 50, as might be standard in a classical scale method of adding up raw score points. Instead the FWB scale uses item response theory (IRT) modeling where each response has a different meaning. Each question item and item response does not have equal weighting and may contribute in different ways to the scale. The use of IRT some question responses to provide a stronger (or weaker) indication of overall financial well-being. The IRT model estimates parameters for each response item to calculate a combined score (Edelen and Reeve 2007).[3] The FWB score is transformed into a roughly 100 point score, ranging from about 20 to 90. The FWB score IRT procedure is weighted separately for people in working ages (18–61) and those who are retired or close to retiring from work (62 and older). Older people respond to the same set of questions, but the relative weighting of questions shifts as people are out of the workforce, spending down savings, and on relatively fixed incomes with reduced discretionary consumption, a pattern commonly shown in prior studies of the economics of the household (Browning and Crossley 2001; Gerrans, Speelman, and Campitelli 2014).

The FWB scale questions have only been available for a few years, but are already being included in a growing number of studies in the US, including future editions of the FINRA Investor Education Foundation's National Financial Capability Study (NFCS) and the Federal Reserve Board Survey of Household Economic Decisionmaking (SHED).

Table 1. The CFPB financial well-being scale.

This statement describes me . . .					
1. I could handle a major unexpected expense.	Completely 5	Very well 4	Somewhat 3	Very little 2	Not at all 1
2. I am securing my financial future.	Completely 5	Very well 4	Somewhat 3	Very little 2	Not at all 1
3. Because of my money situation, I feel like I will never have the things I want in life.**	Completely 1	Very well 2	Somewhat 3	Very little 4	Not at all 5
4. I can enjoy life because of the way I'm managing my money.	Completely 5	Very well 4	Somewhat 3	Very little 2	Not at all 1
5. I am just getting by financially.**	Completely 1	Very well 2	Somewhat 3	Very little 4	Not at all 5
6. I am concerned that the money I have or will save won't last.**	Completely 1	Very well 2	Somewhat 3	Very little 4	Not at all 5
How often would you say . . .					
7. Giving a gift for a wedding, birthday or other occasion would put a strain on my finances for the month.	Always 5	Often 4	Sometimes 3	Rarely 2	Never 1
8. I have money left over at the end of the month.**	Always 1	Often 2	Sometimes 3	Rarely 3	Never 4
9. I am behind with my finances.	Always 5	Often 4	Sometimes 3	Rarely 2	Never 1
10. My finances control my life.**	Always 1	Often 2	Sometimes 3	Rarely 3	Never 4

Note: ** reverse scored as shown.

4. Data

This analysis uses the 2016 CFPB National Financial Well-being Survey. These data are nationally representative and the first to collect such a sample of financial well-being for respondents in the US. The dataset represents a large public investment and was carried out in partnership with the nonprofit organization Prosperity Now, as well as researchers from Abt Associates, Vector Psychometric Group, and the University of Wisconsin-Madison's Center for Financial Security. More background on this survey is available in the Appendix.

In addition to the FWB scale, there are other attributes that make this dataset useful, such as a variety of measures to capture individuals' financial situation, ranging from subjective perceptions to objective responses on financial status. There are no administrative data linked to individual responses to validate self-reports of financial well-being in the data, however. The survey is cross sectional for 2016 with no plans for another survey. As a result, we try to show the constructs of the FWB scale relative to other measures, as well as patterns of the scale relative to the what we would predict from standard economic life cycle theories in economics.

Table 2 shows the means, standard deviations and range for each of the key variables we use in this study. Our main focus is the FWB scale, which has a mean of 54, ranges from 14 to 95, and has a standard deviation of 13. We also tabulate a FWB score without using the IRT, simply summing the score and adding 25 to center the distribution similarly to the IRT score. The the summation score has a mean of 57, a standard deviation of 6.7, and ranges from 39 to 71. This distribution is similar to the scale, but the IRT-scored scale expands the distribution, especially at the tails. Figure 1 shows the distribution of the FWB scale with IRT scoring, where lower scores imply lower financial well-being. The pattern generally displays a normal distribution.

The financial literacy (Fin Lit) score is based on a 9-item quiz using multiple choice options covering (1) long-term investment returns, (2) volatility of investments, (3) benefits of diversification, (4) stock markets prices, (5) the role of life insurance, (6) housing values, (7) how credit card payments work, (8) bonds prices and interest rates, and (9) the relationship between mortgage term length and interest costs. The survey also has a 3-item scale by Lusardi, van Rooij, and Alessie (2011); both scales perform similarly but we use the richer 9-item scale with more gradation in scores. The score is the number correct as a percentage in round numbers (0–100). The mean is 67, meaning on average respondents answered 67 percent of the items correctly.

The subjective well-being (SWB) scale is based on three commonly used survey items used in prior studies (Kahneman and Krueger 2006). The items ask the respondent to agree or disagree with (1) I am satisfied with my life; (2) I am optimistic about my future; and (3) If I work hard today, I will be more successful in the future. Each question has a 7-point likert scale of levels of agreement or disagreement. In order to be able to compare FWB scales and SWB scales in our figures, we score the SWB scale in the same method as the FWB scale, using an IRT graded response model, transformed to center around 50. The mean is 52 with a standard deviation of 13, a minimum of 14, and maximum of 74.

Table 2. Summary statistics, national financial well-being survey.

	mean	sd	min	max
FWB score	54.25	(13.74)	14.00	95.00
FWB sum	57.12	(6.74)	39.00	71.00
Financial literacy score	67.37	(20.81)	0.00	100.00
Subjective wellbeing	52.53	(13.34)	14.00	74.00
Savings level	3.42	(2.33)	0.00	7.00
Own financial investments	0.26	(0.44)	0.00	1.00
Material hardship	0.34	(0.47)	0.00	1.00
Victim of fin fraud	0.24	(0.43)	0.00	1.00
Banked	0.82	(0.38)	0.00	1.00
Own fin investments	0.26	(0.44)	0.00	1.00
Debt in collections	0.15	(0.35)	0.00	1.00
Food assistance	0.12	(0.32)	0.00	1.00
Owns home	0.59	(0.49)	0.00	1.00
Income level	5.38	(2.78)	1.00	9.00
Know: find advice	0.50	(0.50)	0.00	1.00
Know: make fin dec	0.37	(0.48)	0.00	1.00
Know: to invest	0.29	(0.45)	0.00	1.00
Know: to budget	0.60	(0.49)	0.00	1.00
Know: to save	0.57	(0.50)	0.00	1.00
White	0.64	(0.48)	0.00	1.00
Female	0.52	(0.50)	0.00	1.00
College grad	0.46	(0.50)	0.00	1.00
Parent college grad	0.29	(0.45)	0.00	1.00
Kids under 18	0.50	(0.93)	0.00	6.00
Married	0.55	(0.50)	0.00	1.00
Unemployed	0.05	(0.22)	0.00	1.00
Retired	0.21	(0.41)	0.00	1.00
Military or veteran	0.09	(0.29)	0.00	1.00
Census division	5.21	(2.52)	1.00	9.00
Observations	6389			

Note: CFPB National Financial Well-being Survey, 2016.

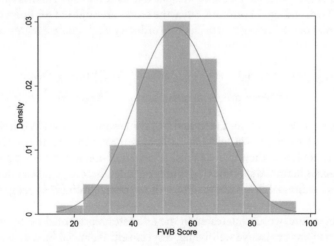

Figure 1. Financial well-being score distribution.
CFPB National Financial Well-being Survey, 2016.

We measure financial hardship as an indicator if the respondent has reported any of the following: not having enough food, not being able to afford housing, health care, or medications, and having had utilities (water, energy, telephone) shut off due to non-payment. About one-third of the respondents report some form of hardship in the last 12 months. We also have an indicator of the respondent having been a victim of financial fraud in the last 5 years (24 percent report they have been de-frauded). About 83 percent of the sample is banked – meaning they have a checking or savings account – and 14 percent have been contacted by a bill collector in the last year. About 12 percent of the respondents in the sample report receiving government food assistance, and 59 percent own their own home (including with a mortgage). Other measures are based on survey items that measure savings levels in 7 categories, ranging from $0 to over $75,000, with a mean of around $20,000. Income is measured in 9 categories, with a mean around $50,000.

Another set of questions in the survey measures respondents' perceptions of financial knowledge or 'know-how', including self reports (where 1 is yes and 0 is no) of knowing how to find financial advice (50 percent responding yes), how to make financial decisions (37 percent yes), how to invest (29 percent yes), how to budget (60 percent yes), and how to save (57 percent yes). The survey also includes a standard set of demographic characteristics. About two-thirds of the respondents report being white or Caucasian, with the remainder being people of color. About half of respondents are female, 46 percent are college graduates (including 2 and 4-year degrees), and 29 percent had a parent who attended college. About half of respondents have children under age 18, and 56 percent are currently married. Only 5 percent are unemployed, and 21 percent are retired from work. About 15 percent of respondents are in the military or are a military veteran.

These data provide a rich set of characteristics with useful variation to be able to estimate the factors that are associated with FWB scores, as well as how high or low FWB scores are associated with key financial outcomes. We next turn to our procedures to estimate FWB scores and relationships across measures.

5. Methods

One way to better understand financial well-being as a construct and the FWB scale as a particular measure of well-being is to rely on descriptive approaches used in population science, sociology, and demography. Prior studies have examined how measured financial attributes track with gender, age or other fixed factors, as well as preferences and behaviors (for example see Gerrans, Speelman, and Campitelli 2014, or Ruel and Hauser 2013 or the work of Halek and Eisenhauer 2001). Age cohorts are of particular interest since the FWB was in part constructed to account for age-based differences among people of working versus retirement ages. There are also very predictable patterns of financial behavior as people age, including accumulating savings and earning more income up until retirement, and de-cumulation after retirement.

To understand FWB scores over the lifecycle, we split our data into age cohorts of: 18–24, 25–34, 35–44, 45–54, 55–61, 62–69, 70–74, and age 75 or more. Since the scores are adjusted for those 62 and older, we intentionally split the data at that point. We begin with an OLS (ordinary least squares) regression of FWB scale scores in Equation (1).

$$Y_i = \alpha + \beta_1 \text{ Age Cats}_i + \beta_2 \text{ FinLit}_i + \beta_3 \text{ SWB}_i + \gamma \text{ Demo}_i$$
$$+ \sigma \text{ Resources}_i + \delta \text{ Perceptions}_i + \theta \text{ RegionFE}_i + \varepsilon_i \tag{1}$$

Y_i is the financial well-being (FWB) scale for individual i. β_1 is an estimate of the FWB scale for each age category (25–34, 35–44, 45–54, 55–61, 62–69, 70–74, and 75+), where age group 18–24 is the omitted category. We would generally predict that as people age, they have established consumption and earnings patterns that will lead to higher levels of FWB scores. Our initial specification simply includes these age category dummies as a baseline set of estimates. We then add additional covariates to observe how these β_1 estimates change with more explanatory variables.

Based on the prior literature, we are interested in the estimates represented by β_2 and β_3 in Equation (1), which are financial literacy and subjective well-being, respectively. Financial literacy is measured using objective quiz questions developed by Knoll and Houts (2012).[4] This scale is a percentage correct score represented by whole numbers (100 means all 9 questions were answered correctly, 0 means none). The subjective well-being scale is based on 3 commonly used survey items each with 7-point likert scales of levels of agreement or disagreement, drawn from scales used in prior studies, and scaled using an IRT method like the FWB scale.[5]

The estimates for γ are based on a vector of demographic characteristics, including gender, race, the highest education level in the household, the highest education level of the respondent's parents, the number of children under age 18, marital status, employment status (employed full or part time, unemployed, or retired from labor markets), and prior or current military service. These are included to account for most of the observed factors we predict might also influence the FWB scale score, although we have no specific priors on how these estimates should perform.

The estimates in σ are based on the household's reported economic or financial resources. This includes an indicator if the household has a bank account, if they own a home, if they have any investment accounts and if the household has any debt in collections (defined as having received a collector's notice in the last year). We measure financial inclusion by whether or not the individual has a formal checking or saving account, where we refer to this as banked. We also include participation in the stock, bond, or mutual fund markets. This vector also includes an indicator if the household was a victim of financial fraud in the last five years and separately if the household has received government assistance for obtaining food. Finally, this set of variables includes indicators of levels of savings ($0, $1–99, $100–999, $1k–5k, $5k–20k, $20k–75k, and $75k–), and levels of income (0–$20k, $20–30k, $30k–40k, $40k–50k, $50k–60k, $60k–75k, $75k–100k, $100k–150k, and $150k$^+$).

The final set of estimates include a vector of estimates in δ is based on a set of perceptions of financial knowledge or know-how, including self reports (where $1 =$ yes) of knowing how to find financial advice, how to make financial decisions, how to invest, how to budget, and how to save. We also include a vector of estimates represented by δ based on nine US regional fixed effects.[6] The error term ε_i is the standard error, adjusted for heteroskadsity (Freedman 2006). All estimates include national weights provided as part of the data distribution.

5.1. *Financial well being levels and financial conditions*

Studies of household financial decisions often use an array of financial outcomes, including financial status (savings), financial inclusion (whether or not an individual has access to financial products), financial hardship (experience of financial shocks), and financial knowledge (how financially 'literate' measured as individuals answer questions). We estimate coefficients for these types of outcomes using the following OLS specification:

$$Y_i = \alpha + \beta_1 \text{ Low FWB}_i + \beta_2 \text{ High FWB}_i + \gamma \text{ Demo}_i + \theta \text{ RegionFE}_i + \varepsilon_i \qquad (2)$$

where Y_i is the financial outcome for individual i. We estimate six outcomes: financial literacy (using the 0–100, 9-item quiz described above), subjective well-being (using the same three items described above), savings levels (seven levels), having financial investments (0–1, using a linear probability OLS specification), and the experience of material hardships.[7]

The Low FWB measure is an indicator variable for a respondent in the lowest quarter of the FWB scale distribution (below 48), and the High FWB measure is an indicator for being in the top quarter (63 and above). Thus β_1 and β_2 are the estimates conditional on having low or high FWB, with medium FWB as the constant. The same controls for demographics are included, as well as the age and income categories used in Equation (1). Savings levels are omitted, as are the other variables used in Equation (1). As in Equations (1), (2) also has δ regional fixed effects, and the adjusted error term ε_i, using survey provided weights.

6. Findings

We begin with a visual analysis of the FWB scale by age cohort, in order to compare these patterns to what we might predict based on standard life cycle explanations in household financial behaviors. Figure 2 shows that financial well-being increases with age, which is consistent with financial development as people's human capital improves and savings accrues. Each additional cohort sees an increase in financial well-being until age 75. Figure 3 shows a FWB summation score that uses the same measure for all age groups rather than the IRT score that uses different weighting after age 61; the patterns are similar. This is re-assuring that gains in FWB scores at older ages are not an artifact of the FWB scoring formula.

Figure 4 shows the FWB score by income levels, relative to the overall mean FWB score. There is a mostly normal distribution across all the income levels, with lower incomes generally showing lower levels of the FWB scale. This is not surprising, since those with greater incomes potentially have additional resources and a larger cushion with which to protect against financial shocks. Still, it is clear income does not precisely explain FWB scores.

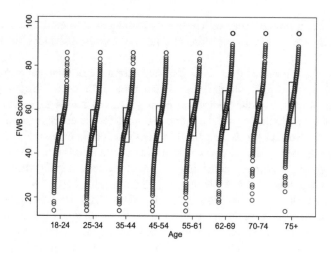

Figure 2. IRT financial well-being scale by age.
CFPB National Financial Well-being Survey, 2016.

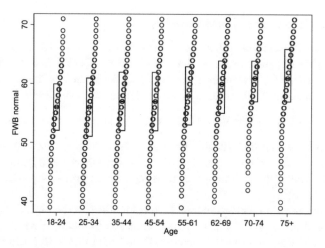

Figure 3. Summative financial well-being scale by age.
CFPB National Financial Well-being Survey, 2016.

Furthermore, Figure 5 shows a scatterplot of SWB and FWB. These two measures are positively correlated, as shown by the fitted line, but there is a great deal of variation in FWB scores at any given level of SWB score. Simple pairwise correlation statistics of FWB Score are 0.41 with subjective well-being. FWB is one of many factors influencing individuals' overall subjective well-being; financial security does not always generate happiness. It is this variation in FWB we explore next using the OLS regression estimates described in Equation (1).

Table 3 shows the stepwise estimates for the FWB scale adding additional covariates, beginning with only the age cohorts. In Column (1) the estimates for FWB score increase with each age cohort (relative to 18–24, the omitted category). Adding in financial literacy and SWB scores in Column (2) reduce these age group estimates only slightly. Both financial literacy and SWB score estimates for FWB scores are significantly different from 0. After controlling for demographics and regional fixed effects in Column (3), a 10 percentage point increase in financial literacy is related to a 1 point increase in FWB scores. A 10 point increase in SWB scores is associated with about a 3 point increase in FWB scores. Adding in economic resources and savings in Column (4) and self-reported knowledge in Column (5) greatly reduces the financial literacy estimates. The SWB score estimates are cut in half but remain still statistically different from 0.

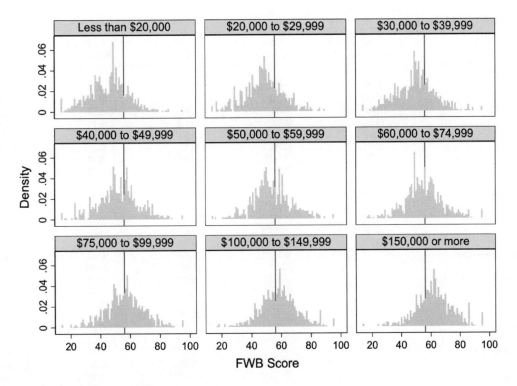

Figure 4. FWB distribution by income, FWBS 2016.
CFPB National Financial Well-being Survey, 2016.

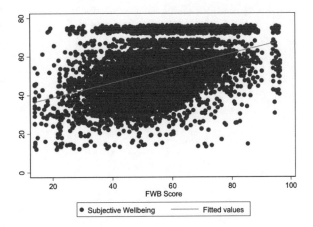

Figure 5. Financial well-being and subjective well-being.
CFPB National Financial Well-being Survey, 2016.

The other covariates generally show estimates that are consistent with higher or lower FWB in predictable ways. Being banked is associated with higher FWB scores, and having debt in collections is related to a lower score. Savings levels and income levels are strongly related to FWB scores, where more income and more savings are related to higher FWB scores. Self-reported financial know-how, especially related to savings, is also related to higher FWB scores. One exception is knowing how to make financial decisions, though this may not be a reliable measure as only 37 percent of respondents replied affirmatively. The lack of response may suggest a lack of confidence or a highly variable interpretation of the question.

Table 3. Financial well-being levels.

	(1) FWB score	(2) FWB score	(3) FWB score	(4) FWB score	(5) FWB score
Ref: Age 18–25					
25–34	0.10	0.01	−0.09	0.44	0.53
	(0.81)	(0.71)	(0.72)	(0.64)	(0.65)
35–44	1.49	0.80	0.85	0.58	0.94
	(0.82)	(0.72)	(0.77)	(0.71)	(0.72)
45–54	2.52**	2.35***	1.56*	0.74	1.09
	(0.80)	(0.70)	(0.73)	(0.67)	(0.68)
55–61	3.58***	3.14***	1.46	0.30	0.72
	(0.86)	(0.75)	(0.77)	(0.70)	(0.70)
62–69	8.28***	7.65***	4.55***	3.58***	3.85***
	(0.84)	(0.73)	(0.83)	(0.76)	(0.76)
70–74	10.02***	8.39***	4.49***	3.20***	3.81***
	(0.93)	(0.81)	(0.97)	(0.87)	(0.86)
75+	8.88***	7.99***	4.40***	3.07***	3.45***
	(0.91)	(0.82)	(0.98)	(0.89)	(0.89)
Financial literacy score		0.15***	0.09***	0.02	0.01
		(0.01)	(0.01)	(0.01)	(0.01)
Subjective wellbeing		0.42***	0.39***	0.30***	0.25***
		(0.01)	(0.01)	(0.01)	(0.01)
Female			0.06	−0.14	−0.18
			(0.35)	(0.30)	(0.30)
College grad			2.67***	−0.26	−0.39
			(0.41)	(0.38)	(0.37)
Parent college grad			2.03***	0.22	0.13
			(0.43)	(0.36)	(0.35)
Kids under 18			−1.41***	−0.42*	−0.36
			(0.22)	(0.19)	(0.19)
Married			2.81***	0.16	0.17
			(0.39)	(0.36)	(0.35)
Unemployed			−3.33***	−1.29	−1.22
			(0.82)	(0.71)	(0.72)
Retired			2.73***	2.23***	2.00***
			(0.60)	(0.51)	(0.50)
Military or veteran			1.24*	0.89	0.59
			(0.55)	(0.46)	(0.44)
Victim of fin fraud				−0.78*	−0.64*
				(0.32)	(0.31)
Banked				1.82***	1.63***
				(0.44)	(0.44)
Own financial investments				2.05***	1.57***
				(0.35)	(0.34)
Debt in collections				−5.06***	−4.69***
				(0.46)	(0.47)
Food assistance				−0.66	−0.81
				(0.55)	(0.55)
Ref: missing savings					
$0 saving				−9.13***	−8.04***
				(0.73)	(0.73)
$1 to 99				−9.41***	−8.45***
				(0.65)	(0.66)
$100 to 999				−6.92***	−6.15***
				(0.56)	(0.55)
$1k to 4999				−3.90***	−3.38***
				(0.50)	(0.49)
$5k to 19,999				0.54	0.37
				(0.48)	(0.47)
$20k to 74,999				3.60***	3.09***
				(0.52)	(0.51)

(continued)

Table 3. Continued

	(1) FWB score	(2) FWB score	(3) FWB score	(4) FWB score	(5) FWB score
$75k—				6.94***	6.13***
				(0.55)	(0.53)
Owns home				0.35	0.13
				(0.40)	(0.39)
Ref: 0–$20k income					
$20–30k				−0.55	−0.12
				(0.67)	(0.67)
$30k to 40k				0.64	1.17
				(0.65)	(0.64)
$40k to 50k				1.74*	2.20**
				(0.71)	(0.72)
$50k to 60k				2.27**	2.68***
				(0.72)	(0.72)
$60k to 75k				2.30***	2.78***
				(0.65)	(0.64)
$75k to 100k				2.84***	3.26***
				(0.65)	(0.65)
$100k to 150k				3.41***	3.82***
				(0.63)	(0.62)
$150k—				4.55***	4.75***
				(0.71)	(0.71)
Know: find advice					1.51***
					(0.33)
Know: make fin dec					−0.19
					(0.35)
Know: to invest					1.04**
					(0.38)
Know: to budget					0.83*
					(0.35)
Know: to save					3.19***
					(0.37)
Constant	50.99***	19.31***	21.73***	34.46***	34.05***
	(0.66)	(1.10)	(1.36)	(1.28)	(1.27)
Region FE	No	No	Yes	Yes	Yes
Controls	No	No	Yes	Yes	Yes
Observations	6389	6389	6389	6350	6345
Mean	54.25				
StDev	13.74				
r2	0.06	0.29	0.33	0.52	0.54

Note: CFPB National Financial Well-being Survey, 2016.
Standard errors in parentheses. Controls include race, gender, education, parent education, number of children, marital status, employment status, military service.
*p < 0.05, **p < 0.01, ***p < 0.001.

Generally, Table 3 shows age patterns where people age 62 and older have higher measured FWB scores and higher income and savings levels. Financial problems, such as debt in collections or not having savings at all, are related to lower FWB scores. Measured financial literacy has a relatively small association with FWB scores, especially controlling for self-assessed know-how. These results suggest that resources, financial skills, debt, and overall SWB are important correlates of FWB, whereas financial knowledge is likely only correlated with FWB through other factors (e.g. assets or skills).

Next we turn to FWB score levels. Summary Table 4 splits data by FWB levels. We can compare Column (1) for all respondents, to those in Column (2) with FWB scores in the lowest level, to those in the middle in Column (3), and to those in the highest level in Column (4).[8] Across all rows, the differences between Columns (2) and (4) are stark. Low-FWB score respondents have lower measured financial literacy scores, lower subjective well-being, lower savings levels, are less likely to have any investments, and have much higher rates of reporting material hardships.

We show estimates of financial outcomes using FWB score levels, as described in Equation (2), in Table 5. This table shows OLS estimates for indicators for people in the low-FWB and high-FWB groups. These estimates

Table 4. Well-being, savings, investing, and hardship by FWB levels.

	(1) All	(2) Lowest FWB group	(3) Middle FWB group	(4) Highest FWB group
FWB score	54.25	38.95	55.61	72.23
	(13.74)	(7.85)	(4.40)	(7.31)
Financial literacy score	67.09	60.44	67.16	75.94
	(21.11)	(20.31)	(20.71)	(19.65)
Subjective wellbeing	52.47	46.08	53.48	59.10
	(13.37)	(13.46)	(12.14)	(11.70)
Savings level	3.40	2.48	3.42	4.60
	(2.34)	(1.67)	(2.33)	(2.56)
Own financial investments	0.26	0.10	0.25	0.51
	(0.44)	(0.30)	(0.43)	(0.50)
Material hardship	0.34	0.70	0.24	0.05
	(0.47)	(0.46)	(0.42)	(0.21)
Observations	6389	1703	2918	1768

Note: CFPB National Financial Well-being Survey, 2016. Means. Robust standard errors in parentheses. Lowest FWB scores are under 48; Middle FWB scores are 48–62; Highest FWB scores are 63 and greater.

Table 5. Financial well-being level estimates for other outcomes.

	(1) Financial literacy score	(2) Subjective well-being	(3) Savings level	(4) Own financial investments	(5) Material hardship
Ref: Med FWB					
Low FWB	−1.02	−7.14***	−0.44***	−0.07***	0.39***
	(0.69)	(0.46)	(0.07)	(0.01)	(0.02)
High FWB	2.93***	6.18***	0.70***	0.16***	−0.12***
	(0.65)	(0.43)	(0.09)	(0.02)	(0.01)
Constant	42.59***	57.08***	1.40***	−0.15***	0.48***
	(1.80)	(1.16)	(0.19)	(0.03)	(0.04)
Region FE	Yes	Yes	Yes	Yes	Yes
Controls	Yes	Yes	Yes	Yes	Yes
Observations	6389	6389	6389	6389	6367
Mean	67.09	52.47	3.40	0.26	0.34

Note: CFPB National Financial Well-being Survey, 2016. Robust standard errors in parentheses
Controls include age, income, race, gender, education, parent education, number of children, marital status, employment status, military service.
Low FWB scores are under 48; High FWB scores are 63 and greater.
$^{*}p < 0.05, ^{**}p < 0.01, ^{***}p < 0.001.$

include covariates for age category, income level, race, gender, education level, parent's education, number of children, marital status, employment status, military service, and regional fixed effects. We exclude savings since it is a dependent variable in one estimate. All of these controls perform in a similar manner to the prior analysis.

Low-FWB is not statistically significant in terms of financial literacy in Column (1), but high FWB is – where people in the top group of FWB scores have financial literacy scores that are about 2.9 points higher than the middle group, controlling for other factors. This suggests that those with confidence in their financial futures potentially also seek out more financial knowledge. Column (2) shows low-FWB respondents have lower SWB, have higher-FWB, and have higher SWB, relative to the middle-FWB group. This correlation displays a clear link between financial struggle and overall utility.

Savings levels and having investments in Columns (3) and (4) show the same pattern – low-FWB have fewer financial assets and asset types, and high-FWB respondents have more. This suggest that a greater cushion to shield against financial shocks is reflected in the FWB measure. The estimates in Column (5) are especially stark, with low-FWB group respondents having almost 40 percentage points higher rates of material hardship, while high-FWB have 12 points lower material hardship rates, relative to the middle-FWB group. Recall that the FWB scale is a newer measure of financial well-being, which captures a subjective sense of someone's financial condition and consideration for the future. The patterns we see in this table are generally consistent with this construct – people who fare worse on these measures would also be likely to fare worse in terms of financial well-being.

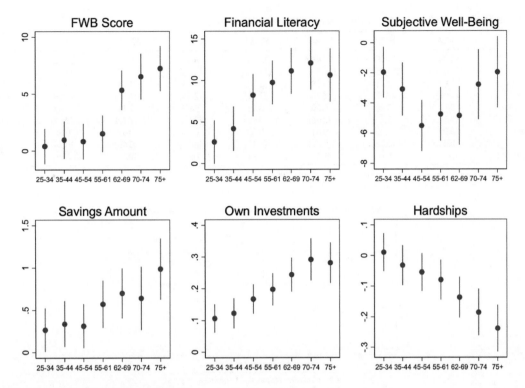

Figure 6. OLS estimates by age for financial outcomes.

CFPB National Financial Well-being Survey, 2016. Similar specification for each estimate as is used in Column (4) of Table 3, without savings levels. Controls include income level, race, gender, education and parent education levels, marital status, number of children, employment status, military status and regional fixed effects. Point estimate and 95% confidence intervals.

One problem with this exercise is we lack a clear benchmark for FWB scores. However, we can use the standard financial life cycle, widely used in economics and finance, to describe patterns of asset accumulation and decumulation through working and non-working years as a form of validation. We would expect these outcomes described in Table 5 would show predictable patterns by age group, including for FWB scores. We show the estimates for FWB score and these financial outcomes over the life course in Figure 6, using the same OLS estimation techniques as in Table 5. Each figure plots each outcome by age group, again controlling for other factors. The patterns are re-assuring that FWB follows the same age-group patterns as other measures. Notably, subjective well-being is more of a U shaped convex pattern across age cohorts, which may shine further light on differences between general subjective well-being and specific financial well-being measures over the life course. Younger people may feel initially higher general well-being despite their financial circumstances, then the reality of their finances settles in, lowering their sense of satisfaction. FWB scores follow a more positive path, increasing with age but not linearly. In general, financial well-being has a pattern of increasing over the life courses, and the life cycle patterns of financial well-being closely mimic what we observe in other measures.

Table 6 shows mean FWB score, savings levels, incomes and retirement rates by age group. The intent is to show the run up in FWB as retirement rates increase after age 50, even though income and savings levels are relatively flat.

7. Extension: exogenously predicting FWB scores

Since this is cross-sectional data without detailed respondent information, we have limited ability to predict FWB scores. However, we do have the respondent's current Census area (nine districts), and age range. We can use this information to estimate FWB scores based on the unemployment rate when the respondent was age 18 to 24, the ages when young adults enter into the labor force. Prior studies show entering the workforce during

Table 6. Mean financial well-being, savings, income and retirement status by age ranges.

	18–24	25–34	35–44	45–54	55–61	62–69	70–74	75–
FWB score	50.99	51.09	52.48	53.51	54.57	59.27	61.02	59.87
	(11.61)	(13.36)	(12.73)	(13.49)	(13.30)	(14.80)	(13.17)	(13.89)
Savings level	2.96	3.11	3.28	3.44	3.66	3.74	3.71	3.77
	(1.88)	(2.12)	(2.25)	(2.35)	(2.45)	(2.54)	(2.66)	(2.61)
Income level	5.71	5.26	5.59	5.91	5.62	5.11	4.83	3.95
	(2.78)	(2.75)	(2.68)	(2.76)	(2.82)	(2.77)	(2.71)	(2.49)
Retired	0.00	0.00	0.01	0.03	0.16	0.62	0.86	0.92
	(0.05)	(0.06)	(0.08)	(0.17)	(0.37)	(0.49)	(0.34)	(0.27)
Observations	414	1113	828	1074	707	1021	496	736

Note: CFPB National Financial Well-being Survey, 2016. Standard errors in parentheses
Seven savings levels from 0–75k; Nine income levels from 0–150k.

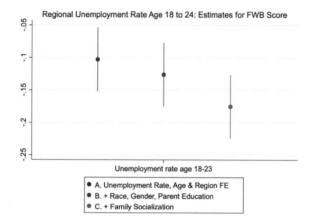

Figure 7. Unemployment rate in census division in early adulthood by age cohort.
FINRA National Financial Capability Survey, 2015.

more recessionary periods depresses later life economic status (Hershbein 2012; Oreopoulos, Von Wachter, and Heisz 2012). Here we use area unemployment rates by age cohort with age and division fixed effects, so the unemployment variable can identify differences in FWB scores based on variation across areas within an age cohort. We only can obtain regional unemployment rates from 1976 onward, meaning people age 62 and older are excluded from this analysis. This is a group all scored using the same formula and likely to still be in the workforce. Figure 7 plots the average unemployment rates in a region when an individual was between 18 and 24 by age, using from respondents from the 2015 NFCS.

We can additionally control for respondent fixed characteristics that are unlikely to be related to regional unemployment rates (gender, race, and parental education). Finally, we can control for respondents' family discussions of financial matters (saving, credit, smart shopping, provided an allowance or a savings account) as children. This is based on a series of questions in the survey we can include as controls. While FWB may influence response bias, generally these are activities that occurred before the respondent was 18 and would not be related to area unemployment rates. Figure 8 shows the estimates for each specification visually. All three estimates show lower FWB scores for age cohorts in regions with higher unemployment rates; these are statistically significant (relative to zero), although small in magnitude (as we would expect). This is consistent with FWB scores being influenced by economic contexts in formative early adulthood. While not an ideal identification strategy, given our limited data, this is re-assuring that FWB behaves generally as we would predict from prior studies.

8. Replicating financial well-being measures in existing survey data

Our last analysis is to try and replicate the FWB measure and the trends we see in these data with questions in another dataset. We use the National Financial Capability Study (NFCS) data (FINRA 2018) to show how the

FWB scale can be produced by proxy in other data. The United States Financial Industry Regulatory Authority (FINRA) Investor Education Foundation conducts the NFCS every three years. The survey was conducted online in 2018 among a representative sample of 27,091 adults. In 2018, NFCS did include the official FWB scale for the first time. The 2012, 2015, and 2018 NFCS data also include question items that approximate the types of topics that the FWB scale measures. We identified five questions that approximate items in the NFCS, capturing the abbreviated five-item scale the CFPB developed: (1) just getting by financially; (2) concern that money will not last; (3) never having the things you want in life; (4) financing controlling one's life; and (5) having money leftover at the end of the month. We then create a NFCS 'pseudo' FWB scale on the following survey items:

Mapping FWB Scale Items to NFCS Survey

FWB 5-Item Scale	NFCS Proxy Item
(1) I am just getting by financially	(1) How confident are you that you could come up with $2000 if an unexpected need arose within the next month?
(2) I am concerned the money I have or will save won't last	(2) Over the past year, would you say your household's spending was less than, more than, or equal to your household's income?
(3) Because of my money situation I feel like I will never have the things I want in life	(3) Overall, thinking of your assets, debts and savings, how satisfied are you with your current personal financial condition?
(4) My finances control my life	(4) I have too much debt right now
(5) I have money left over at the end of the month	(5) In a typical month, how difficult is it for you to cover your expenses?

We then estimate a FWB score using the same IRT graded response model with these proxy questions, where the estimated latent theta parameter is scaled the same way as the official FWB score.[9] Although this is not a summation score, if we estimate the classical scale reliability coefficient using the Cronbach's alpha measure of internal consistency, the 0.79 value is acceptable.

We run the same style of estimates for FWB scores as in Equation (1), although we lack some of the same controls. Our age groups are more condensed, and the measurement of assets is based on number of investments rather than amounts. Still, we are able to use many of the same variables as in the prior analysis. In Figure 9, we show visually that our coefficients of Pseudo-FWB score by age mimic the patterns for those of the FWB scale shown in the prior tables.

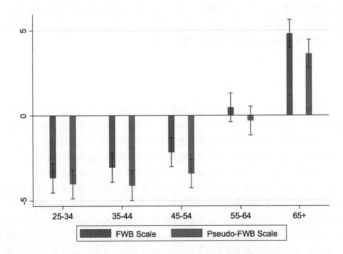

Figure 8. OLS estimates of FWB score based on unemployment rate by census division age 18–24.
CFPB National Financial Well-being Survey, 2016. Respondents age 61 and younger are included. A estimate only includes age cohort and Census division fixed effects. B estimate adds controls for race, gender, and parent education level. C estimate adds in family socialization controls based on respondent recalling that their family discussed saving, credit, smart shopping, or being provided an allowance or a savings account when they they were young. Point estimate and 95% confidence intervals.

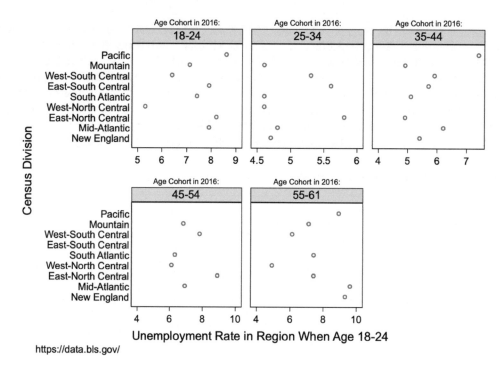

Figure 9. Financial well-being scale approximated using FINRA national financial capability survey.

FINRA National Financial Capability Survey, 2018. Pseudo FWB based on graded response model IRT: Can fund an emergency, poor credit, expenses less than income, confidence in financial future, financial satisfaction. IRT latent theta score using FWB scale methodology. Point estimate and 95% confidence intervals.

We also show estimates by age for the official FWB score that is included in the 2018 NFCS data side by side with the pseudo score – both have the same levels for each age cohort. Although not shown, we are able to produce similar patterns by age with prior year's of the NFCS before the FWB scale was added. The pseudo FWB scores perform well. Our intent is not to suggest a substitute for the official FWB scale items, but rather that the general concept of financial well-being can be replicated even in surveys that do not formally include the CFPB FWB survey items and scoring. This could present a strategy for researchers using other datasets, or even data collected from field studies, in cases where broader measures of financial well-being are useful in addition to traditional measures of financial status, inclusion, or hardships.[10]

9. Conclusions

Using the Financial Well-being Survey we show that financial well-being generally tracks the life cycle, rising with income and savings levels and increasing with age. However, there is significant variation in FWB score, even by income and age. The FWB score is not strongly associated with financial literacy and follows subjective well-being only to an extent, especially after middle age. Negative financial events tend to be associated with worse financial well-being, and positive behaviors are associated with higher scores.

The FWB scale is based on a definition of financial well-being that includes (1) having control of day-to-day and month-to-month finances; (2) having capacity to absorb a financial shock; (3) being on track to meet financial goals; and (4) having the freedom to make choices that allow enjoyment of life. Directly measuring financial well-being to capture these factors may be a useful strategy for evaluations of interventions and in future surveys. However, we also show that the FWB score may also be a measure that researchers can proxy for in existing surveys when proximate questions are available.

The concept of subjective financial well-being, and the FWB score as an applied measure using standardized items and scoring procedures, offers another construct to better understand household and consumer finances.

The FWB score is an alternative way to estimate financial status, mainly as a complement to asset or income measures. It may offer more insights into mechanisms for policy analysis, as well as to understand the longer term, more subjective impacts of programs.

Being a new concept and new measure, much more work is needed to understand how the FWB score operates. There are potential self-reporting biases or systematic biases by race or gender that may be problems with non-response in surveys relative to more objective measures. While all measures have issues with reliability and validity, the FWB score has yet to be compared to administrative data, such as credit reports or account balances, which would provide a way to externally validate the measure. The FWB score has also not been tested in a longitudinal panel format, so changes within respondents have not been documented. For example, there may be relative temporal effects of measures of financial well-being where some people experience differential rates of change in FWB score over time and in response to positive and negative shocks.

We are hopeful this descriptive exercise introduces researchers to a new concept and measure of financial well-being, ultimately expanding the toolbox of outcomes that are analyzed in household financial research. Financial well-being is a complementary way to capture how well people are doing financially, including their subjective perceptions of their financial health. We remain optimistic that measures like these will help the field to better understand the nuances of consumer financial behavior and uncover a way that people's financial well-being can ultimately be enhanced.

Notes

1. The scale has 5 questions with agree or disagree using a 1 to 7 scale, including: 'In most ways my life is close to my ideal', 'The conditions of my life are excellent', 'I am satisfied with my life', 'So far I have gotten the important things I want in life', 'If I could live my life over, I would change almost nothing'.
2. See the CFPB website: https://www.consumerfinance.gov/consumer-tools/financial-well-being/
3. The FWB score is estimated using software, flexMIRT 2.0 using a bifactor graded response model with one factor related to the latent financial well-being construct and one factor to account for whether each question was phrased negatively or positively.
4. The quiz items include: long-term returns; volatility; diversification; stock markets; life insurance; housing values; credit card payments; bonds and interest rates; and mortgage term length and interest costs.
5. SWB items include: I am satisfied with my life; I am optimistic about my future; If I work hard today, I will be more successful in the future.
6. The 9 divisions are: New England, Mid-Atlantic, East-North Central, West-North Central, South Atlantic, East-South Central, West-South Central, Mountain, and Pacific.
7. Hardships include any of these: worried whether food would run out; experienced food that did not last and did not have money to get more; could not afford a place to live or get health care, stopped taking needed medications due to costs, or, had utilities shut off due to non-payment.
8. The lowest quartile are under 48, the middle are between 48 and 62, and the highest are above 62.
9. We use the Stata command pfwb, developed by Austin Nichols. See: https://ideas.repec.org/c/boc/bocode/s458353.html.
10. See code at https://github.com/jmcollinswisc/fwb

Disclosure statement

No potential conflict of interest was reported by the authors.

ORCID

J. Michael Collins http://orcid.org/0000-0002-2280-2130
Carly Urban http://orcid.org/0000-0002-2187-3340

References

Atkinson, Adele, Stephen McKay, Sharon Collard, and Elaine Kempson. 2007. "Levels of Financial Capability in the UK." *Public Money and Management* 27 (1): 29–36.
Bergstresser, Daniel, and James Poterba. 2004. "Asset Allocation and Asset Location: Household Evidence From the Survey of Consumer Finances." *Journal of Public Economics* 88 (9–10): 1893–1915.
Beverly, Sondra G. 2001. "Measures of Material Hardship: Rationale and Recommendations." *Journal of Poverty* 5 (1): 23–41.
Bhattacharya, Jayanta, Janet Currie, and Steven Haider. 2004. "Poverty, Food Insecurity, and Nutritional Outcomes in Children and Adults." *Journal of Health Economics* 23 (4): 839–862.

Bricker, Jesse, Lisa J. Dettling, Alice Henriques, Joanne W. Hsu, Lindsay Jacobs, Kevin B. Moore, Sarah Pack, John Sabelhaus, Jeffrey Thompson, and Richard A. Windle. 2017. "Changes in US Family Finances From 2013 to 2016: Evidence From the Survey of Consumer Finances." *Federal Reserve Bulletin* 103: 1.

Browning, Martin, and Thomas F. Crossley. 2001. "The Life-cycle Model of Consumption and Saving." *Journal of Economic Perspectives* 15 (3): 3–22.

Deaton, Angus. 2008. "Income, Health, and Well-being Around the World: Evidence From the Gallup World Poll." *Journal of Economic Perspectives* 22 (2): 53–72.

Demirguc-Kunt, Asli, Leora Klapper, Dorothe Singer, Saniya Ansar, and Jake Hess. 2018. *The Global Findex Database 2017: Measuring Financial Inclusion and the Fintech Revolution.* New York: The World Bank. doi:10.1596/978-1-4648-1259-0.

Desmond, Matthew, and Carl Gershenson. 2016. "Housing and Employment Insecurity Among the Working Poor." *Social Problems* 63 (1): 46–67.

Diener, Ed. 1984. "Subjective Well-being." *Psychological Bulletin* 95 (3): 542–575.

Diener, Ed., and Robert Biswas-Diener. 2002. "Will Money Increase Subjective Well-being?" *Social Indicators Research* 57 (2): 119–169.

Diener, Ed., Eunkook M. Suh, Richard E. Lucas, and Heidi L. Smith. 1999. "Subjective Well-being: Three Decades of Progress." *Psychological Bulletin* 125 (2): 276.

Dolan, Paul, Tessa Peasgood, and Mathew White. 2008. "Do We Really Know what Makes Us Happy? A Review of the Economic Literature on the Factors Associated with Subjective Well-being." *Journal of Economic Psychology* 29 (1): 94–122.

Edelen, Maria Orlando, and Bryce B. Reeve. 2007. "Applying Item Response Theory (IRT) Modeling to Questionnaire Development, Evaluation, and Refinement." *Quality of Life Research* 16 (1): 5.

FINRA. 2018. "2018 National Financial Capability Study".

Freedman, David A. 2006. "On the so-called "Huber Sandwich Estimator" and "robust Standard Errors"." *The American Statistician* 60 (4): 299–302.

Gerrans, Paul, Craig Speelman, and Guillermo Campitelli. 2014. "The Relationship Between Personal Financial Wellness and Financial Wellbeing: A Structural Equation Modelling Approach." *Journal of Family and Economic Issues* 35 (2): 145–160.

Halek, Martin, and Joseph G. Eisenhauer. 2001. "Demography of Risk Aversion." *Journal of Risk and Insurance* 68: 1–24.

Hershbein, Brad J. 2012. "Graduating High School in a Recession: Work, Education, and Home Production." *The BE Journal of Economic Analysis & Policy* 12 (1). doi:10.1515/1935-1682.2599.

Hung, Angela, Andrew M. Parker, and Joanne Yoong. 2009. *Defining and Measuring Financial Literacy.* RAND Working Paper Series. Vol. WR-708, September 2, 1–28. doi:10.2139/ssrn.1498674

Johnson, Elizabeth, and Margaret S. Sherraden. 2007. "From Financial Literacy to Financial Capability Smong Youth." *The Journal of Sociology & Social Welfare* 34: 119.

Kahneman, Daniel, and Alan B. Krueger. 2006. "Developments in the Measurement of Subjective Well-being." *Journal of Economic Perspectives* 20 (1): 3–24.

Knoll, Melissa A. Z., and Carrie R. Houts. 2012. "The Financial Knowledge Scale: An Application of Item Response Theory to the Assessment of Financial Literacy." *Journal of Consumer Affairs* 46 (3): 381–410.

Kobau, Rosemarie, Joseph Sniezek, Matthew M. Zack, Richard E. Lucas, and Adam Burns. 2010. "Well-being Assessment: An Evaluation of Well-being Scales for Public Health and Population Estimates of Well-being Among US Adults." *Applied Psychology: Health and Well-Being* 2 (3): 272–297.

Lusardi, Annamaria, and Olivia S. Mitchell. 2007. "Baby Boomer Retirement Security: The Roles of Planning, Financial Literacy, and Housing Wealth." *Journal of Monetary Economics* 54 (1): 205–224.

Lusardi, Annamaria, and Olivia S. Mitchell. 2014. "The Economic Importance of Financial Literacy: Theory and Evidence." *Journal of Economic Literature* 52 (1): 5–44.

Lusardi, Annamaria, Maarten van Rooij, and Rob Alessie. 2011. "Financial Literacy and Stock Market Participation." *Journal of Financial Economics* 102 (2): 449–472.

Lyons, Angela C., and Tansel Yilmazer. 2005. "Health and Financial Strain: Evidence From the Survey of Consumer Finances." *Southern Economic Journal* 71: 873–890.

Mayer, Susan E., and Christopher Jencks. 1989. "Poverty and the Distribution of Material Hardship." *Journal of Human Resources* 24: 88–114.

Oreopoulos, Philip, Till Von Wachter, and Andrew Heisz. 2012. "The Short-and Long-term Career Effects of Graduating in a Recession." *American Economic Journal: Applied Economics* 4 (1): 1–29.

Poterba, James M., Steven F. Venti, and David A. Wise. 1994. "Targeted Retirement Saving and the Net Worth of Elderly Americans." *The American Economic Review* 84 (2): 180–185.

Rhine, Sherrie L. W., and William H. Greene. 2013. "Factors that Contribute to Becoming Unbanked." *Journal of Consumer Affairs* 47 (1): 27–45.

Rhine, Sherrie L. W., William H. Greene, and Maude Toussaint-Comeau. 2006. "The Importance of Check-cashing Businesses to the Unbanked: Racial/ethnic Differences." *Review of Economics and Statistics* 88 (1): 146–157.

Ruel, Erin, and Robert M. Hauser. 2013. "Explaining the Gender Wealth Gap." *Demography* 50 (4): 1155–1176.

Short, Kathleen S. 2005. "Material and Financial Hardship and Income-based Poverty Measures in the USA." *Journal of Social Policy* 34 (1): 21–38.

Taft, Marzieh Kalantarie, Zare Zardeini Hosein, and Seyyed Mohammad Tabatabaei Mehrizi. 2013. "The Relation Between Financial Literacy, Financial Wellbeing and Financial Concerns." *International Journal of Business and Management* 8 (11): 63.

Taylor, Mark. 2011. "Measuring Financial Capability and Its Determinants Using Survey Data." *Social Indicators Research* 102 (2): 297–314.

Xiao, Jing Jian, Cheng Chen, and Fuzhong Chen. 2014. "Consumer Financial Capability and Financial Satisfaction." *Social Indicators Research* 118 (1): 415–432.

Appendix. National financial well-being survey background

The National Financial Well-Being Survey was conducted in English and Spanish via web mode between October 27, 2016 and December 5, 2016. Overall, 6394 surveys were completed: 5395 from the general population sample and 999 from an oversample of adults aged 62 and older. The survey was designed to represent the adult population of the 50 U.S. states and the District of Columbia. The survey was fielded on the GfK KnowledgePanel using address-based sampling and dual-frame landline and cell phone random digit dialing methods. The survey sample was drawn from a recruited sample designed to be nationally representative of U.S. households. The GfK panel is the largest U.S. probability-based non-volunteer Internet panel, with a total of about 55,000 panel members. Recruitment is in both English and Spanish in order to ensure that different levels of language proficiency and acculturation are represented. GfK provides non-Internet households with a web-enabled computer and free Internet service so that they can participate as online panel members. The weighted GfK panel matches the U.S. adult (age 18 and older) Hispanic population on gender, age, marital status, housing ownership, education, region, Internet access, household size, language proficiency, and place of birth.

The sample for the National Financial Well-Being Survey from the KnowledgePanel called for 5000 completed surveys of adults in proportion to the U.S. population with respect to age, race/ethnicity, and household income below 200 percent of the federal poverty level, as well as an additional oversample of 1000 completed surveys of adults age 62 and older. The sample targets were specified with the percentages from the Current Population Survey (CPS) 2016 Annual Socioeconomic Supplement. Overall, 14,402 panelists were selected: 11,513 initially for the general population sample, 1647 for the age 62 and older oversample, and another 1242 focused on adults below 200 percent of the Federal poverty level, African American non-Hispanic, and Hispanic. From these 14,402 panelists, 6394 surveys were completed: 5395 from the general population sample (5000 from the general population sample originally drawn and 395 from the additional sample added focusing on panel members below 200 percent of the federal poverty level or who were African American non-Hispanic or Hispanic) and 999 from the age 62 and older oversample. The count of completed surveys excludes 72 panel members who completed the survey but were removed due to response quality concerns (70 from the original general population sample, 2 from the age 62 and older oversample, and 0 from the additional sample added later in the field period). For example, respondents who completed a survey in a substantially shorter than average amount of time were removed.

More detail on the National Financial Well-Being Survey is available at https://www.consumerfinance.gov/documents/5588/cfpb_nfwbs-puf-user-guide.pdf

Financial literacy and financial well-being among generation-Z university students: Evidence from Greece

Nikolaos D. Philippas and Christos Avdoulas

ABSTRACT

Financial knowledge has become an essential skill because of the instability of global markets, asymmetric information in those markets, increasing complexity of financial products, and the rapidly increasing growth in financial technology (Fintech). This study aims to be the first among its kind to evaluate the relation between financial literacy, financial fragility, and financial well-being in parallel with identifying their determinants. For this purpose, we design and distribute a questionnaire to a random sample of 456 university students in Greece. The university students represent Generation Z that experienced the effects of a unique in duration and consequences financial crisis. We analyze the data by using cross-tabulations, chi-square tests, logistic regressions, and a marginal effect analysis. The results show that male students, students who keep expense records, or their father is highly educated are more financially literate. We also examine the dimensions of financial fragility, and the results show that financially literate students are better able to cope with an unexpected financial shock. Thus, financial literacy can be a key driver of financial well-being among Greek university students. Furthermore, we discuss the likely policy prescriptions while accounting for related behavioral aspects and technological developments.

1. Introduction

Financial literacy has become an essential skill that is required for everyday life around the world. Because of the instability in the global economy, consumers face financial decisions that have become more complex due to the increased variety of financial products and challenges. For this reason, the significance of financial management skills in personal life has increased and more studies have explored this issue in the last decade. The global financial crisis has highlighted the significance of financial literacy and the need for financial knowledge and education. Furthermore, financial literacy contributes to a financial attitude that leads to financial well-being. Having financial knowledge is the key element for making sound financial decisions and is essential to financial well-being.

Financial literacy is the ability to understand and analyze financial options, plan for the future, and to respond appropriately to events. This ability can influence the conditions of life and work and can be very helpful in anticipating the future to increase income. Unfortunately, despite the importance of financial literacy, the research has shown that this ability in people around the world, especially in developing and underdeveloped countries, is not substantial. These populations face barriers such as the complexity of financial life, the existence of many options when making decisions, and not having enough time and money to learn about personal finance issues.

Therefore, these barriers cause low financial literacy in developing countries (Vitt et al. 2000). Financially literate people can make sound financial decisions and therefore are more able to achieve their financial goals and to hedge themselves against economic shocks and their associated risks that eventually lead to financial well-being. The lack of financial knowledge is the main driver that pulls people away from financial markets, as shown by Lusardi and Mitchell (2006). Moreover, the participation of individual investors in the financial market is increasing day by day due to the introduction of new financial services and products. The complexity in dealing with integrated financial products has increased in the last few decades that hinders the ability to understand financial concepts like inflation, interest, compound interest, risk management, and its application. Lusardi and Mitchell (2011b) and Atkinson and Messy (2012) argue that the financial knowledge that people need to deal with advanced financial products and services is at its lowest level.

The global financial crisis has left its mark on many countries, with Greece still experiencing its aftermath. Greece is still experiencing the financial cost from both the 2008 global financial crisis and domestic structural problems, and the negative consequences have affected the country's economy and society in a severe way. Unemployment rose to the extraordinary rate of 27% in 2013, whereas wages in both the public and, even more, in the private sector have sunk by 40–60%. Greeks' household budgets have dropped by around 30%, while they have lost some €587 billion throughout the global financial crisis. Since 2000 when Greece became a member of EMU, a geometrically rising credit expansion was entrusted to the credit industry in Greece – with no restrictions due to the low levels of interest rates and expansive monetary policies. Lending unscrupulously inevitably led to over-borrowing that equally led to over-indebtedness. According to official data, the Greek public and private debt has reached €532.18 billion, with a government debt to GDP that averaged 99.51% between 1980 and 2017. It reached an all-time high of 180.80 percent in 2016. Household loans accounted for around 46.2% of total bank credit to the private sector in September 2016; two-thirds of which were housing loans. The NPE's ratio (nonperforming exposure) of Greek banks rose during the first half of 2016 to 45.1% (the highest in the EU) and the total NPEs reached €107.6 billion in the third quarter of 2016. However, if private investors had been better informed on personal financial matters, they might have acquired more sophisticated financial products through risk diversification and might have had smaller exposures to debt through mortgages and consumer loans. Nevertheless, the gross gaming revenues in Greece have doubled the average of 27 countries in Europe and have reached about €11 billion. The stark contrast of the figures above is likely to generate inferences related to the importance of investing in people's financial literacy through awareness programs, initiatives, and national campaigns, especially for the young population, in order to mitigate erroneous financial behaviors.

The purpose of this study is to be the first of its kind to evaluate the relation among financial literacy, financial fragility, and financial well-being in parallel to identifying their determinants. Our sample comprises university students in Greece who represent a generation that grew up in a unique – in duration and consequences – financial crisis, which was comparable only to the Great Depression of 1929. Conceptually, this generation is more likely to have higher levels of financial awareness. On the other hand, the absence of a national strategy on financial literacy in Greece does not facilitate the process of experiential learning from good and bad past experiences.

Following Andreou and Philip (2018), we investigate the relation between financial literacy, financial fragility and financial well-being. For this purpose, we designed and distributed a survey that uses a random sampling of 456 university students in Greece. There are several important findings which stem from our estimation approach. First, we show that male students, students who keep expenses-record, or those whose father is high educated are more financially literate. Second, we measure the levels of the students' financial fragility and their 'absolute' financial knowledge with control variables for demographics and socioeconomics. We show that financially literate students are better able to cope with an unexpected financial shock. Third, we investigate whether financial literacy is a key determinant of financial well-being. The results show that financial literacy and low levels of financial fragility are key drivers of financial well-being among Greek university students. Finally, we discuss the likely policy prescriptions, taking into account related behavioral aspects and technological developments.

Our study is different from the empirical studies already conducted in three aspects. First, to the best of our knowledge, none of these studies has estimated the levels of financial literacy, financial fragility, and financial well-being in parallel with identifying the demographic and socioeconomic factors that affect these three financial components. Second, this study is the first of its kind in evaluating the relation between financial literacy, financial fragility and financial well-being. Third, we identify the lack of public policy actions to fight financial literacy in Greece and propose a holistic approach for financial education in Greece.

The study is organized as follows: in the next section, we discuss the related studies. In Section 3, we present the research method. Specifically, we present the survey instrument and the econometric method. In Section 4, we provide the statistics of our sample along with the empirical results from the econometric analysis. In Section 5, we discuss key policy actions in order to form a new generation of financially educated citizens along with a savings and effective culture to build financial awareness. The last section concludes the paper and suggests some unexplored avenues of research in the field.

2. Literature review

The complexity of financial decisions and the behavioral biases have threatened the quality of people's lives and have led to researchers investigating ways to deal with them. A focus on the young by examining financial literacy among students is an interesting starting point. Studies have shown that levels of financial literacy are low, especially among the young population and university students. Beal and Delpachitra (2003) survey 847 students of a regional Australian university with a substantial external student enrolment. They find that financial literacy is not high and this, no doubt, stems from the lack of financial-skill education in high schools. Xiao et al. (2007) survey 781 students at the University of Arizona and find that students who were in nonbusiness fields, those who were living in a campus dormitory, and those who received financial support had a low level of savings. Ergun (2018) analyzes the levels of financial literacy among university students in Estonia, Germany, Italy, Netherlands, Poland, Romania, Turkey, and the Russian Federation. Ergun examines 409 questionnaires, and the results show low levels of financial literacy among university students along with a strong relation between financial literacy and demographic characteristics. Andreou and Philip (2018) examine financial literacy and attitude as well as behavior among 881 university students in Cyprus. Their results show that 6.24% of the students answered all questions correctly with only 36.9% having good financial knowledge. By contrast, Chen and Volpe (1998) use data from 924 university students in 14 American universities and find that students who study business and economics had high levels of financial literacy. Furthermore, Oppong-Boakye and Kansanba (2013) use a sample of 203 undergraduate business students in Ghana. Their study finds that formal education is the major source of financial literacy for undergraduate students, followed by parents, the media, and peers. Sarigül (2014) survey 1,127 university students in Turkey. The results show that there is a strong relation between financial literacy and student characteristics. Albeerdy and Gharleghi (2015) investigate the factors that influence the financial literacy of university students in Malaysia and show that there is a significant relation between socioeconomic variables such as education and money attitude and the levels of financial literacy.

Shim et al. (2009) and Hogarth (2006) indicate that financial knowledge, financial fragility, and financial behavior affect financial well-being. Financial literacy develops a financial attitude that leads to financial well-being. They have found a strong positive relation between financial literacy and financial well-being. Joo and Grable (2004) show that an increase in financial literacy affects financial contentment which eventually turns into financial well-being. Klapper and Panos (2011) examine the relation between financial literacy and retirement planning in Russia. They find that only 36% of respondents in their sample understand interest compounding and only half can answer a simple question about inflation. In a country with widespread public pension provisions, they find that financial literacy is significantly and positively related to retirement planning that involves private pension funds.

Moreover, Gutter, Copur, and Garrison (2010) explore the relation between the financial behaviors and financial well-being of 15.797 college students in the US when controlling for demographic and financial characteristics and financial education and dispositions. The results show significant differences in the levels of financial well-being for various socioeconomic factors and financial behaviors. Chan, Chau, and Kim (2012) examine the relation between college students' money-related aptitudes, financial management practices, and financial well-being. Their findings confirm that students' tendency to engage in healthy financial management practices are related to attitudes toward debt, financial knowledge, and employment, while students who practice good financial management tend to incur less debt and show better financial well-being. Finally, Sabri et al. (2010) and Falahati and Paim (2011) examine the relations between personal and family backgrounds, academic ability, childhood consumer experience, financial socialization, financial literacy, and perceived financial well-being of Malaysian college students. They show that financial literacy is related to financial well-being, while there are important differences between the Malay and Chinese ethnic groups in Malaysia.

3. Research methodology

3.1. Data collection

According to statistics released by the Hellenic Statistical Authority for the academic year 2018–2019, there were 396,814 undergraduate students in all Greek universities. The survey used in this study covers 456 university students from Departments of Business Administration (55%) and Departments of Statistics and Insurance Science (45%). The data were collected through the use of a paper version that was self-administered. This research was conducted during the spring semester in 2016. Mostly senior students were targeted. Furthermore, the participation was optional and confidentiality measures were taken for personal data. Senior business school students were thought of as the primary group of interest due to more years of exposure to higher education and, specifically, business education.

3.2. Survey instrument

The survey instrument emphasized four pillars. The first pillar captures the demographic, parental, socioeconomic, and financial behavior characteristics of the participants. The second pillar emphasizes financial knowledge. The third pillar examines financial fragility, and the fourth pillar refers to financial well-being. Students were asked to answer 27 multiple-choice questions in total.

Specifically, the first pillar consists of 18 questions on participants' demographic characteristics, their parents' socioeconomic characteristics, their educational background, and some on their personal financial behavior as well as their perceptions of the effects of the financial crisis.

The second pillar includes five questions on numeracy (interest), compound interest, inflation, and risk diversification. The financial literacy pillar stems from five questions that define the levels of financial literacy of the students. These questions were based on the questions conducted by validated international financial literacy surveys in the literature, for example Lusardi and Mitchell (2014), Klapper, Lusardi, and Panos (2013) and Lusardi and Mitchell (2006). In order to define a 'Financially Literate' student we use three alternative scenarios. The first scenario indicates that a student is 'Financially Literate' when he or she correctly answers at least four questions. The second scenario indicates that a student is 'Financially Literate' if he or she correctly answers all these questions. The third scenario indicates that 'Financial Literacy' is an ordinal variable that denotes the number of respondent's correct answers.

The third pillar examines students' financial fragility in the sense of being exposed to an unexpected financial shock. Fragility was measured with a similar question those in Lusardi, Schneider, and Tufano (2011). Thus, we asked university students: 'How confident are you that you could come up with €300 if an unexpected need arose within the next month?' However, the amount of an unexpected shock was significantly reduced in order to be commensurate with students' allowance or income. This is in contrast with Lusardi, Schneider, and Tufano (2011) who asked for an amount of $2000. We define as 'Financially Fragile' a student who answered that 'I'm sure that I couldn't come up' or 'Maybe I couldn't come up' with €300 if an unexpected need arose in the next month.

The fourth pillar examines the perceived students' financial well-being in the sense of one's attitude toward financial status. It was measured using two questions adapted from Hira and Mugenda's (1999a, 1999b) measure of financial satisfaction: money saved and the current financial situation. These questions were thought of as relevant to the Greek economic environment and the Greek way of life. Therefore, we asked university students: 'Do you cover everyday expenses?' and 'If they are saving for long term'. We define a student as having a 'High level of Financial Well-being' if he or she responds that 'Most of the times' or 'Always I can cover everyday expenses' and 'Regularly' or 'Rarely' saves for the long term.

3.3. Empirical strategy

The main purpose of this study is to measure the levels of financial literacy, financial fragility, and financial well-being. First, we analyze the descriptive statistics of the variables included in the dataset. Second, we test the existence of dependencies between the financial literacy and sociodemographic variables along with the relation among financial literacy, financial fragility, and financial well-being by using the statistical Pearson X^2 test for independence (Pearson 1900). The chi-square test of independence determines whether there is an association between the categorical variables (i.e. whether the variables are independent or related).

Third, we use logistic regression models to determine the linkages between financial literacy, financial fragility, and financial well-being with a number of respondents' demographics, parental, and socioeconomic characteristics.[1] Logit(p) is the log of the odds ratio $p/(1-p)$ or likelihood ratio in which the dependent variable is one. In symbols, it is defined as:

$$\text{logit}(p) = \log\frac{p}{1-p} = \ln\frac{p}{1-p} \tag{1}$$

where p is the probability that a case is in a particular category. p can only range from zero to one where one denotes the probability of success. The logit(p) scale ranges from negative infinity to positive infinity and is symmetrical around the logit of 0.5 (which is zero). The formula below shows the relation between the usual regression equation ($a + bx$ ... etc.), which is a straight line formula, and the logistic regression.

The form of the logistic regression is:

$$\log(p(x)) = \log\left(\frac{p(x)}{1-p(x)}\right) = \beta_0 + \beta_1 x_1 + \beta_2 x_2 + \dots \tag{2}$$

in which p is the probability that a case is in a particular category, β_0 is the constant of the equation, and β_i are the coefficients of the predictor variables. Equation (2) looks just like a linear regression and although the logistic regression finds a 'best fitting' equation, just as a linear regression does, the principles on which it does so are rather different. Instead of using a least squared deviations for the best fit, it uses the maximum likelihood which maximizes the probability of getting the observed results given the fitted regression coefficients. A consequence of this method is that the goodness of fit and overall significance statistics used in the logistic regression are different from those used in a linear regression. p can be calculated with the following formula:

$$p = \frac{e^{\beta_0 + \beta_1 x_1 + \beta_2 x_2 + \dots}}{1 + e^{\beta_0 + \beta_1 x_1 + \beta_2 x_2 + \dots}} \tag{3}$$

in which p is the probability that a case is in a particular category, e is the base of natural logarithms, β_0 is the constant of the equation, and β_i are the coefficients of the predictor variables.

Finally, following Long (1997), we perform a marginal effect analysis in order to evaluate how the change in a response is related to the change in a covariate. Regarding binary independent variables, marginal effects are computed as the difference of the probability of success when the covariate equals one and zero otherwise, while holding all other variables constant at their means.

$$\text{Marginal Effect } X_k = \Pr(Y = 1|\bar{X}, X_k = 1) - \Pr(Y = 1|\bar{X}, X_k = 0) \tag{4}$$

in which X_k is the covariate variable; Y is the binary dependent variable; $\Pr(Y = 1|\bar{X}, X_k = 1)$ is the probability of success when the covariate equals one; and $\Pr(Y = 1|\bar{X}, X_k = 0)$ is the probability of success when the covariate equals zero. In other words, with binary independent variables, the marginal effects measure discrete change, that is, how do the predicted probabilities change as the binary independent variable changes from zero to one?

4. Empirical results

4.1. Preliminary analysis

This unique dataset provides rich demographic and socioeconomic information and invaluable insights for Greek university students' financial penetration, vulnerability, literacy, fragility and financial wellbeing. Table 1 (Panels A and B) provide summary statistics regarding the frequency and proportion of the respondents' demographic, parental information, socioeconomic and financial behavior characteristics that are tabulated across female and male students and for the entire sample. Our dataset consisted of 51% male respondents. The age distribution was about 75.4% of individuals between 18 and 22 years of age, 23% between 23 and 28, and about 1.5% was over 29 years old. The vast majority of the respondents (97.1%) were Greeks while only 2.9% had a different nationality. Of the participants, 69.5% had no or less than two years of working experience, 18.9% had two to four years of working experience, while only a 11.6% of total respondents had more than four years working experience. Their father's education level was almost smoothly distributed. Only 27% of the sample had a father with at least a BS degree, while the majority of them had a father with a lower or upper high school degree. As for their mother's education level, 35.8% answered that their mother had a BS, MS, or a PhD degree, while 46.6% answered that their mother had an upper or lower high school degree or a primary school degree. Of the respondents, 91% had a father with a job while 20.8% answered that their mother was unemployed.

The survey asked university students to report their parents' gross monthly income. In our sample, the monthly gross income categories are: €1,000–€1999 with a proportion of 40.2%, while 21.7% have a parental monthly income between €2000 and €2999, 20.7% have a parental monthly income under €1000, and only 17.4% have a parental monthly gross income over €3000. We also include a variable labeled 'Income change' if the individual responded 'Yes' to the question, 'Did you (your family) experience an unexpected significant reduction of your gross income during the Global Financial Crisis (%)'. The summary statistics show that a huge 98.5% of the participants reported they suffered a negative income shock during the global financial crisis. Specifically, about a 55.9% answered that they had lost about 20–50% of their monthly gross income, 31.1% answered that they had lost over a 50% of their monthly gross income while 61.4% answered that they had reduced their standard of living.

Next, we asked participants to report their concerns about their future and their future income in parallel with questions about their daily financial behavior (Table 1 Panel B). Specifically, 92.5% were concerned about their future while 48% were concerned about their future family income. When respondents were asked about their daily financial behavior, the majority reported that they held a bank account (80.4%) and that they manage their bank account on their own (80.7%). Furthermore, about 55.3% of the participants reported that they kept a record of their expenses and only 6.6% of the respondents had investment experience, while almost 5% of the respondents saved the same amount of euros each month.

Moreover, the survey asked university students to report on their confidence that they could come up with €300 if an unexpected need arose within the next month as well as their perceived financial well-being in the sense of one's attitude toward financial status. The summary statistics show that the majority of the participants (82%) responded that 'I'm sure that I could come up' or 'Maybe I could come up' with €300 if an unexpected need arose in the next month. Respondents reported that they 'Always' or 'Most of the times' could cover everyday expenses (54.8%), while they were 'Regularly' or 'Rarely' saving for the long term (75%).

Table 2 reports the descriptive statistics tabulated across financially literate students, financially illiterate students, and for the entire sample. We denote as 'Financially Literate' a student who answered five questions correctly. In Table 2 we use two alternative scenarios for the financial literacy variable. The first scenario indicates that 'Financial Literacy' is a binary variable that equals one if the student correctly answers four or more questions and zero otherwise. The second scenario denotes that 'Financial Literacy' is an ordinal variable equaling 0,1,2,3,4, or 5 to capture the proficiency of the respondent. The results show that Greek university students have average financial knowledge scores which are below the baseline of 50% in all scenarios. Table 2 also reports the summary statistics of the variables used in the regression analysis over the entire dataset. The results show that the number of males is higher in the sample of financially literate students than in the sample of financially illiterate students. The number of students with highly educated parents is greater in the sample of financially literate students, while the number of university students who keep records of expenses is higher in the sample of financially literate students than in the sample of financially illiterate students. The difference in the means of the two samples is statistically significant for the variables mentioned above. This significance provides evidence that the demographics, parental, or financial behavior characteristics are associated with high levels of financial knowledge.

The Spearman (1904) non-parametric measures of rank correlations between the alternative scenarios of financial literacy and demographic and socioeconomic variables are reported in Table 3. The results show that Financial Literacy is correlated with Financial Fragility and Financial Well-being at the 5% statistical significance

Table 1. Respondents' characteristics.

Variables		Female Students		Male Students		Entire sample	
		Frequencies	%	Frequencies	%	Frequencies	%
Panel A							
Demographics							
Gender		222	48.7	234	51.3	456	100
Age	18–22	183	40.1	161	35.3	344	75.5
	23–28	34	7.5	71	15.6	105	23
	29+	5	1.1	2	0.4	7	1.5
Nationality	Greek	212	46.5	231	50.7	443	97.1
	Other	10	2.2	3	0.7	13	2.9
Work Experience in years	None	68	14.9	60	13.2	128	28.1
	< 2	85	18.6	104	22.8	189	41.4
	2–4	41	9	45	9.9	86	18.9
	4–6	11	2.4	15	3.3	26	5.7
	> 6	17	3.7	10	2.2	27	5.9
Parents' Information							
Father's Education	No education	0	0	2	0.4	2	0.4
	Primary School	19	4.2	14	3.1	33	7.3
	Lower High School	16	3.5	15	3.3	31	6.9
	Upper High School	54	11.9	71	15.7	125	27.7
	Post-secondary education	45	10	51	11.3	96	21.2
	BSc	69	15.3	54	11.9	123	27.2
	MSc/PhD	17	3.8	25	5.5	42	9.3
Mother's Education	No education	0	0	0	0	0	0
	Primary School	14	3.1	10	2.2	24	5.3
	Lower High School	20	4.4	12	2.6	32	7.1
	Upper High School	72	15.9	83	18.3	155	34.2
	Post-secondary education	37	8.2	43	9.5	80	17.7
	BSc	73	16.1	67	14.8	140	30.9
	MSc/PhD	6	1.3	16	3.5	22	4.9
Father's Unemployment	No	201	44.1	213	46.7	414	90.8
	Yes	21	4.6	21	4.6	42	9.2
Mother's Unemployment	No	175	38.4	186	40.8	361	79.2
	Yes	47	10.3	48	10.5	95	20.8
Monthly Income	< €1.000	54	13	32	7.7	86	20.7
	€1.001–€1.999	76	18.3	91	21.9	167	40.2
	€2.000–€2.999	35	8.4	55	13.3	90	21.7
	€3.000–€4.500	21	5.1	20	4.8	41	9.9
	> €4.500	17	4.1	14	3.4	31	7.5
Income Change	No change	2	0.4	5	1.1	7	1.5
	Under 20%	25	5.5	27	5.9	52	11.4
	20–50%	128	28.1	127	27.9	255	55.9
	Over 50%	67	14.7	75	16.4	142	31.1
Reduction of Standard of Living	No	90	19.7	86	18.9	176	38.6
	Yes	132	28.9	148	32.5	280	61.4

(*continued*).

Table 1. Continued.

Variables		Female Students		Male Students		Entire sample	
		Frequencies	%	Frequencies	%	Frequencies	%
Panel B							
Financial Behavior							
Keep expenses' record	No	96	21.1	108	23.7	204	44.7
	Yes	126	27.6	126	27.6	252	55.3
Hold of a Bank account	No	45	9.9	44	9.7	89	19.6
	Yes	177	38.9	189	41.5	366	80.4
Manage my account	No	40	8.8	48	10.5	88	19.3
	Yes	182	39.9	186	40.8	368	80.7
Saving	Each month same amount	13	2.9	9	2.0	22	4.8
	When I have enough money	14	3.1	22	4.8	36	7.9
	When I want to buy sth	26	5.7	29	6.4	55	12.1
	I don't save	130	28.5	129	28.3	259	56.8
	I don't have money to save	39	8.6	45	9.9	84	18.4
Investment Experience	No	210	46.1	216	47.4	426	93.4
	Yes	12	2.6	18	3.9	30	6.6
Financial Fragility							
How confident are you that you could come up with €300 if an unexpected need arose within the next month?	I'm sure that I couldn't come up	20	4.5	20	4.5	40	9.0
	Maybe I couldn't come up	18	4.0	22	4.9	40	9.0
	Maybe I could come up	96	21.6	82	18.4	178	40
	I'm sure that I could come up	84	18.9	103	23.1	187	42
Financial Well-being							
Cover everyday expenses	Never	62	13.6	58	12.7	120	26.3
	Almost never	41	9.0	45	9.9	86	18.9
	Most of the times	58	12.7	78	17.1	136	29.8
	Always	61	13.4	53	11.6	114	25
Long –Term Saving	No money to save	55	12.1	46	10.1	101	22.1
	Never	10	2.2	3	0.7	13	2.9
	Rarely	101	22.1	113	24.8	214	46.9
	Regularly	56	12.3	72	15.8	128	28.1
Future Concerns							
Concern about your future	No	9	2.0	25	5.5	34	7.5
	Yes	213	46.7	209	45.8	422	92.5
Concern about your future income	No	124	27.2	113	24.8	237	52
	Yes	98	21.5	121	26.5	219	48

Note: This table reports the summary statistics regarding the frequency and proportion of the respondent characteristics that are tabulated across female students, male students, and for the entire sample.

level. Also, the scenario in which a student is Financially Literate is correlated with the aforementioned variables at higher levels than the alternative scenarios of financial literacy. The correlations among financial literacy, financial fragility, and financial well-being variables with demographics, parental and financial behavior variables provide evidence that students' demographic characteristics and financial behaviors could influence their levels of financial literacy.

4.2. Determinants of financial literacy

Our 'Financial Literacy' variable stems from five questions in the survey which are similar to those originally developed by Klapper, Lusardi, and van Oudheusden (2015). In order to define their levels of financial literacy, participants were asked to answer the following questions:

Q_1: Suppose you need to borrow €100. Which is the lower amount to pay back: €105 or €100 plus three percent?
[€105; **€100 plus three percent**; don't know; refused to answer]

Table 2. Descriptive statistics – financially literate vs financially illiterate.

	Entire Sample		Financial Literate		Financial Illiterate		
Variables	Mean	St. Dev	Mean	St. Dev	Mean	St. Dev	Diff
Financial Literacy							
Scenario 1 (at least 4 correct answers)	0.49	0.501	1.00	0.000	0.38	0.486	−0.62**
Scenario 2 (continuous approach)	2.37	1.217	5.00	0.000	2.98	1.024	−2.01**
Demographics							
Gender	0.49	0.500	0.51	0.487	0.48	0.500	0.139**
Age	0.26	0.473	0.22	0.414	0.27	0.486	0.056
Nationality	0.03	0.167	0.01	0.107	0.03	0.178	0.021
Work Experience	1.2	1.092	1.07	0.980	1.23	1.116	0.163
Parents' Information							
Father's Education	3.81	1.375	3.91	1.271	3.78	1.399	−0.123*
Mother's Education	3.76	1.246	3.73	1.296	3.77	1.236	0.039
Father's Unemployment	0.09	0.289	0.07	0.254	0.10	0.297	0.030
Mother's Unemployment	0.208	0.409	0.216	0.413	0.207	0.405	−0.009
Monthly Income	1.8	1.606	1.70	1.151	1.82	1.629	0.116
Income Change	2.17	0.678	2.14	0.730	2.17	0.666	0.038
Reduction of Standard of Living	0.61	0.487	0.60	0.492	0.62	0.487	0.015
Financial Behavior							
Keep expenses' record	0.55	0.498	0.65	0.480	0.53	0.500	−0.11**
Hold of a Bank account	0.80	0.397	0.81	0.397	0.80	0.398	−0.003
Manage my account	0.81	0.395	0.77	0.421	0.82	0.389	0.042
Saving	2.76	1.000	2.82	0.941	2.75	1.014	−0.071
Investment Experience	0.07	0.248	0.06	0.233	0.07	0.252	0.011
Future Concerns							
Concern about your future	0.93	0.263	0.92	0.272	0.93	0.261	0.006
Concern about your future income	0.48	0.500	0.51	0.503	0.47	0.500	−0.039

Note: This table presents the statistics of the variables used in the regression analysis. The first two columns give the means and standard deviations (St.Dev.) of the variables for the entire sample. Next, it gives the means and standard deviations of the variables for the subsamples of financially literate (5 correct answers) and financially illiterate students. The first scenario indicates that 'Financial Literacy' is a binary variable that equals one if the student correctly answers four or more questions and zero otherwise. The second scenario denotes that 'Financial Literacy' is an ordinal variable that equals 0,1,2,3,4, or 5 to capture the proficiency of the respondent. Diff denotes the t-statistics for testing the difference of means between financially literate and financially illiterate students. The *denotes a p-value < 0.1; **denotes a p-value < 0.05; and ***denotes a $p < 0.01$.

Table 3. Correlation matrix for financial literacy variables.

	Gender	Age	Father's Education	Monthly Income	Keep record	Manage my account	Financial Literacy (5 correct)	Financial Literacy (> 4 correct)	Financial Literacy (continuous)	Financial Fragility
Age	−0.15**									
Father's Education	0.018	−0.003								
Monthly Income	−0.08*	−0.038	0.288**							
Keep record	0.029	0.054	0.018	−0.076*						
Manage my account	0.032	0.08*	−0.036	−0.099**	−0.108**					
Financial Literacy (5 correct)	−0.10**	−0.037	0.037	−0.018	0.094**	−0.042				
Financial Literacy (> 4 correct)	−0.13**	0.006	0.010	0.008	−0.009	−0.033	0.489**			
Financial Literacy (continuous)	−0.11**	−0.06	0.032	0.012	0.015	−0.050	0.705**	0.593**		
Financial Fragility	−0.057	0.045	0.073	0.091*	0.156**	0.074*	0.088*	0.057	0.071	
Financial Well-being	−0.014	0.049	−0.057	0.027	0.237**	0.198**	0.15**	0.13	0.014	0.524**

Note: This table presents the Spearman (1904) non-parametric measures of rank correlation for the most important variables. The *indicates a p-value < 10% and **indicates a p-value < 5%. Correlations for the rest of the database are available on request.

Q2: Suppose you put money in the bank for two years and the bank agrees to add 15 percent per year to your account. Will the bank add more money to your account the second year than it did the first year, or will it add the same amount of money both years?
[**More**; the same; don't know; refused to answer]

Q_3: Suppose you had €100 in a savings account and the bank adds 10 percent per year to the account. How much money would you have in the account after five years if you did not remove any money from the account?

[**More than €150**; exactly €150; less than €150; don't know; refused to answer]

Q_4: Suppose over the next 10 years the prices of the things you buy double. If your income also doubles, will you be able to buy less than you can buy today, the same as you can buy today, or more than you can buy today?

[Less; **the same**; more; don't know; refused to answer]

Q_5: Suppose you have some money. Is it safer to put your money into one business or investment, or to put your money into multiple businesses or investments?

[One business or investment; **multiple businesses or investments**; don't know; refused to answer]

Table 4 presents the results of these questions. Results show that the level of financial literacy for Greek university students in absolute terms (students answered correctly all five financial knowledge questions) is 19.3%. For comparison reasons, if we apply the measurement level of financial literacy when participants have to answer at least four questions correctly, the level of financial literacy is 50%. Thus, the levels of financial literacy support the conjecture that university students in Greece have greater knowledge than the general population in Greece (45%), which is consistent with Klapper, Lusardi, and van Oudheusden (2015). Specifically, 81% and 77.4% of the respondents correctly answered the inflation question and the diversification question respectively, while the majority of the respondents correctly answered the questions on numeracy (interest) and the compound interest rate. Also, a higher percentage of male students had at least four correct responses as compared to female students. This result indicates that male students may be more financially knowledgeable. Overall, the results are in accordance with the studies in the literature review and are consistent with a similar study of Cypriot undergraduate students (Andreou and Philip 2018).

Proceeding with the cross-tabulation analysis, we use the 16 demographic, socioeconomic, and financial variables reported in Table 1 (Panels A and B) to investigate their effect on financial literacy. The results show that financial literacy is strongly dependent only on 'Gender', 'Father's Education', and 'Keep records of income/expenses' at the 5% significance level. The results show that in males, financial literacy is related to 'Gender', 'Father's Education', 'Father's Unemployment', 'Saving', and 'Keep records of income/expenses' at the 10% significance level, while for females, none of the examined variables are significantly related with financial literacy.[2]

Next, we perform a regression analysis to estimate models of the determinants of financial literacy. Table 5 (Panels A and B) present the results of the logistic regression and the ordinary least squares represent the determinants that influence students' levels of financial literacy. In general, the results show that among independent variables, 'Gender', 'Father's Education Level' and 'Keep record of expenses' are three determinants that are statistically significant. Furthermore, in terms of model criteria, the test results in Cox and Snell (1989), Nagelkerke (1991) and Hosmer and Lemeshow (1989) also show that the logistic regression model explains the variation in the dependent variable in a better way.

Further, the results in Table 5 (Panels A and B) show that students whose father has an upper high school degree, a BS degree, or a MS/PhD degree has 3.5 times, 3.1 times, or 2.2 times, respectively, higher possibility of being financially literate than those whose father has no education. The odds ratio for 'Gender' shows that male students are 2.02 times more likely to show acceptable levels of financial literacy than female students. Also, students who keep a record of expenses have a higher possibility of being financially literate than those who do not.

Next, we perform a marginal effects analysis in order to investigate how the probability of a student being financially literate changes as a determinant variable changes from zero to one while holding all other variables at their means. Figure 1 presents the marginal effects for the statistically significant factors from the logistic regressions and Table 7 presents their predicted probabilities. The results show that male students have a 0.115 greater predicted probability of being financially literate than female students, while students whose father has a BS degree or a MS/PhD degree have 0.162 and 0.106 greater predicted probabilities, respectively, of being financially literate than those whose father has no education. Also, students who keep a record of expenses have a 0.015 greater predicted probability of being financially literate than those who do not. Overall, the results of

Table 4. Responses to financial literacy questions.

	Female Students		Male Students		Entire sample	
	Frequencies	%	Frequencies	%	Frequencies	%
Distribution of answers						
Q_1. Suppose you need to borrow €100. Which is the lower amount to pay back: €105 or €100 plus three percent?						
€105	60	13.2	52	11.4	112	24.6
€100 plus three percent	**11**	**24.3**	**147**	**32.2**	**258**	**56.6**
Don't know	51	11.2	35	7.7	86	18.9
Q_2. Suppose you put money in the bank for 2 years and the bank agrees to add 15% per year to your account. Will the bank add more money to your account the second year than it did the first year, or will it add the same amount of money both years?						
More	**143**	**31.4**	**160**	**35.1**	**303**	**66.4**
The same	73	16.0	69	15.1	142	31.1
Don't know	6	1.3	5	1.1	11	2.4
Q_3. Suppose you had €100 in a savings account and the bank adds 10% per year to the account. How much money would you have in the account after 5 years if you did not remove any money from the account?						
More than €150	**102**	**22.4**	**151**	**33.1**	**253**	**55.5**
Exactly €150 or Less than €150	112	24.6	80	17.5	192	42.1
Don't know	8	1.8	3	0.7	11	2.4
Q_4. Suppose over the next 10 years the prices of the things you buy double. If your income also doubles, will you be able to buy less than you can buy today, the same as you can buy today, or more than you can buy today?						
Less or More	20	4.4	54	11.8	74	16.2
The same	**196**	**43**	**174**	**38.2**	**370**	**81.1**
Don't know	6	1.3	6	1.3	12	2.6
Q_5. Suppose you have some money. Is it safer to put your money into one business or investment, or to put your money into multiple businesses or investments?						
One business or investment	38	8.3	34	7.5	72	15.8
Multiple businesses or investments	**170**	**37.3**	**183**	**40.1**	**353**	**77.4**
Don't know	14	3.1	17	3.7	31	6.8
Distribution of correct answers						
No correct answers	2	0.4	4	0.9	6	1.3
1 correct answer	15	3.3	16	3.5	31	6.8
2 correct answers	37	8.1	30	6.6	67	14.7
3 correct answers	72	15.8	52	11.4	124	27.2
4 correct answers	63	13.8	77	16.9	140	30.7
5 correct answers	33	7.2	55	12.1	88	19.3
Pearson Chi-Square			11.248**			
Spearman correlation			−0.115**			

Note: This table presents the patterns of responses to the five financial literacy questions that are tabulated across female students, male students, and the entire sample. The Pearson Chi-Squares indicate the values for Pearson (1900) statistic for a pairwise comparison between the number of correct answers and gender. The Spearman (1904) correlation denotes a nonparametric measure of rank correlation between the number of correct answers and gender. The *indicates a p-value $< 10\%$; **indicates a p-value $< 5\%$; and the ***indicates a p-value $< 1\%$.

the marginal effects strengthen the results of the odds ratio by showing that those factors influence students' financial literacy levels at the 5% statistical significance level.

4.3. Financial fragility

We measure students' financial fragility with a similar question to that in Lusardi, Schneider, and Tufano (2011). However, we significantly reduced the amount of the unexpected shock w to be commensurate with students' allowance or income. Therefore, the students were asked whether they could cover an unexpected shock of €300 if it arose in the next month, Lusardi, Schneider, and Tufano (2011) uses $2000. The cross-tabulation analysis shows that 42% claimed that they were sure that they could cover the amount, while 40% claimed that maybe they could cover the amount. Almost 60% of the participants were not that sure or they could not cover the amount of €300.[3]

Furthermore, we examine the relation between students' financial fragility and their 'absolute'/excellent financial literacy (e.g. answered correctly all five questions) along with a number of the other financial behavior variables. The Pearson's chi-square values show significant dependency between financial fragility and 'Work Experience', 'Keep record of expenses', and 'Hold a bank account' in the 1% statistical significance level while the dependency between Financial Fragility and Financial Literacy was barely below the acceptable level of 10%. However, from the characteristics of the sample, 52.9% of the students with excellent financial literacy were certain that they could cover an unexpected economic shock. By contrast, only 35% of the students' with lower financial literacy answered that they could cover the unexpected amount. Recognizing this difference, we could assume that students with financial knowledge learned to manage their finances for rainy days.[4]

Next, we perform a logistic regression analysis to estimate the determinants of financial fragility. The regression uses explanatory variables which capture students' demographic characteristics and their financial behavior as well as their parents' background. Table 6 (Panels A and B) present the coefficients and odds ratios. In general, the results show that among the independent variables, 'Work Experience', 'Father's Education Level', 'Keep record of expenses', 'Saving', and 'Financial Literacy' are five factors that influence students' financial fragility at the 5% statistical significance level. Furthermore, in term of information criteria, the results for Cox and Snell (1989), Nagelkerke (1991) and Hosmer and Lemeshow (1989) show that the logistic regression model has a good fit with the data and explains 33% of the variation in the dependent variable.

Moreover, the results in Table 6 (Panels A and B) show that students whose father has a BS degree or a MS/PhD degree have a 1.2 times and a 2.01 times higher possibility, respectively, of not being financial fragile than those whose father has no education. The odds ratio for 'Work Experience' shows that students who have two to four years of work experience are 0.36 times more likely to show low levels of financial fragility than students with no proper work experience. Also, students who do not keep a record of expenses have a higher possibility of being financial fragile than those who do, while students who do not save money have a 1 times higher possibility of

Table 5. Determinants of financial literacy.

Variables		OLS Model	Logit Model 1		Logit Model 2	
		Coef	Coef	Odds Ratios	Coef	Odds Ratios
Panel A[a]						
Demographics						
Gender		2.367***	0.751***	2.472***	−0.832***	2.235***
Age	23–28	−0.328**	−0.232	0.793	−0.465	0.628
	29+	−1.815***	−0.950	0.142	−0.335	0.421
Nationality	Greek	0.236	0.664	1.942	−0.639	0.528
Work Experience in years	< 2	0.150	0.369	1.446	−0.138	0.871
	2–4	0.032	0.018	1.018	−0.144	0.728
	4–6	0.573**	0.010	1.747	−0.318	1.343
	> 6	0.447	0.914	2.495	0.295	0.469
Parents' Information					−0.757	
Father's Education	Primary School	−1.394	0.558	1.345	0.011	0.965
	Lower High School	0.282	0.663	1.940	0.021	1.021
	Upper High School	0.737**	1.181*	3.257*	1.253*	3.502*
	Post-secondary education	0.299	0.830*	2.294*	−0.105	0.900
	BSc	0.486*	0.747*	2.111*	1.133*	3.106*
	MSc/PhD	0.484**	0.875**	2.398**	0.820**	2.271**
Mother's Education	Primary School	0.386	0.146	0.989	0.644	1.205
	Lower High School	0.023	−0.638	1.157	0.492	1.904
	Upper High School	−0.187	−0.766	0.529	−0.087	1.636
	Post-secondary education	−0.091	−0.343	0.465	−0.254	0.917
	BSc	−0.030	−0.400	0.710	−0.291	0.775
	MSc/PhD	−0.099	0.111	0.670	0.566	0.748
Father's Unemployment	Yes	−0.144	−0.389	0.678	−0.602	0.547
Mother's Unemployment	Yes	0.208	0.537	1.711	0.168	1.183
Monthly Income	€1.001 – €1.999	0.151	−0.075	0.928	−0.134	0.875
	€2.000 – €2.999	0.263	0.178	1.195	0.091	1.096
	€3.000 – €4.500	0.176	−0.371	0.690	−0.192	0.825
	> €4.500	0.608*	0.713	2.040	0.531	1.701
Income Change	Under 20%	−0.250	−0.156	0.855	−0.526	0.591
	20–50%	−0.221	−0.416	0.660	−0.628	0.533
	Over 50%	−0.241	−0.369	0.691	−0.610	0.543

(continued)

Table 5. Continued.

Variables		OLS Model	Logit Model 1		Logit Model 2	
		Coef	Coef	Odds Ratios	Coef	Odds Ratios
Panel B[b]						
Financial Behavior						
Keep expenses' record	Yes	−0.212	−0.402	0.669	1.107**	0.899**
Hold of a Bank account	Yes	−0.135		0.599	0.102	0.735
Manage my account	Yes	−0.255	−0.386	0.680	−0.469	0.626
Saving	When I have enough money	−0.167	−0.643	0.526	−0.156	0.855
	When I want to buy sth	−0.488	−0.468	0.230	−0.784	0.457
	I don't save	0.055	−0.345	0.708	0.342	1.408
	I don't have money to save	−0.173	−0.524	0.592	−0.146	0.864
Investment Experience	Yes	−0.175	−0.407	0.666	−0.063	0.939
Future Concerns						
Concern about your future income	Yes	0.011	−0.081	0.922	0.180	1.197
Constant		3.708***	1.542	4.673	−0.343	0.710
Models' Information						
−2Log Likelihood		650.21	555.01		360.9	
Cox and Snell (1989)		0.104	0.122		0.159	
Nagelkerke (1991)		0.109	0.163		0.24	
Hosmer and Lemeshow (1989)		2.875	3.847		14.00**	

[a]This table presents the results of the logistic regression and the ordinary least squares on the factors that influence students' financial literacy. The coefficients for the OLS model and the coefficients and odds ratios for the logit models are presented with their statistical validity. The dependent variable (Financial Literacy) in the OLS model denotes the respondents' correct answers in a continuous way. The dependent variable (Financial Literacy) in the logit model 1 equal one if the student correctly answers four or more questions and zero otherwise. The dependent variable (Financial Literacy) in logit model 2 equals one if the student correctly answers all questions and zero otherwise. The *denotes a p-value < 0.1; **denotes a p-value < 0.05; and the ***denotes a p-value < 0.01.

[b]This table presents the results for the logistic regression and the ordinary least squares on the factors that influence students' financial literacy. The coefficients for the OLS model and the coefficients and odds ratios for the logit models are presented with their statistical validity. The dependent variable in the OLS model denotes the respondents' correct answers in a continuous way. The dependent variable (Financial Literacy) in logit model 1 equals one if the student correctly answers four or more questions and zero otherwise. The dependent variable (Financial Literacy) in logit model 2 equals one if the student correctly answers all questions and zero otherwise. Cox and Snell (1989) and Nagelkerke (1991) measure the proportion of the variance that the model is able to explain. The Hosmer and Lemeshow (1989) test estimates the goodness of fit with the data. The *denotes a p-value < 0.1; **denotes a p-value < 0.05; and the ***denotes a p-value < 0.01.

being financially fragile than those who save. The results also show that financially illiterate students have a 1.6 times higher possibility of being financially fragile than financially literate students.

Next, we perform a marginal effects analysis in order to investigate how the probability of a student being financially fragile changes as a determinant variable changes from zero to one, holding all other variables at their means. Figure 2 presents the marginal effects for the statistically significant factors from the logistic regressions that influence students' financial fragility while Table 7 presents the predicted probabilities. The results show that students whose father has a BS degree or a MS/PhD degree have 0.033 and 0.024, respectively, greater predicted probabilities of not being financially fragile than those whose father has no education. The predicted probabilities for 'Work Experience' show that students who have more than two years of work experience have over a 0.056 greater predicted probability of showing low levels of financial fragility than students with no proper work experience. Also, students who do not keep a record of expenses have a 0.118 greater predicted probability of being financial fragile than those who do. Furthermore, students who do not have money to save have a greater predicted probability of being financial fragile, while students' with high levels of financial literacy have a 0.152 greater predicted probability of not being financially fragile. Overall, the results of the marginal effects strengthen the results of the odds ratio by showing that the determinants influence students' financial fragility levels at the 5% statistical significance level.

4.4. Financial well-being

Financial well-being is the ultimate outcome of financial literacy. The financial attitude of an individual also determines the level of financial well-being of the respondents. A positive and healthy financial attitude leads to

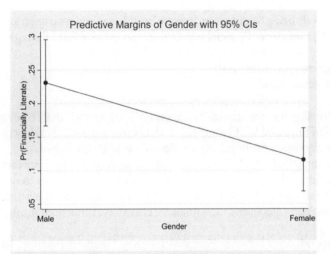

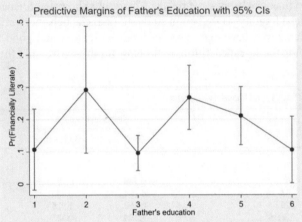

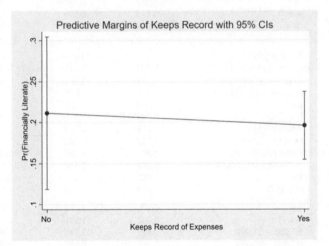

Figure 1. Financial literacy determinants' marginal effects.

Note: Figures present the plots of the predicted probabilities of someone being financially literate for the statistically significant factors in the logistic regressions that influence students' financial literacy, while holding all the other covariates at their mean. They also show the 95% confidence intervals for each predicted probability.

a higher level of financial well-being. We measure financial well-being with two questions adapted from Hira and Mugenda's (1999a, 1999b) measure of financial satisfaction: money saved and the current financial situation.

Q_1: Could you cover everyday expenses?
Q_2: Do you save for your future?

Therefore, we asked university students can you 'Cover everyday expenses?' and 'If they are saving for long term'. We define as 'High level of Financial Well-being' the students who respond that they can 'Most of the times' or 'Always' cover everyday expenses and 'Regularly' or 'Rarely' saves for the future.

The cross-tabulation analysis shows that over a half of the students could cover everyday expenses or could cover them most of the time, while only 26% answer that they could not cover these expenses. Furthermore, over a vast majority of the students, 71%, do not save or rarely save money for their future. These are interesting signs which show that the recent global and local financial crises have influenced the financial behavior of Greek university students.[5]

Next, we test the dependencies between Financial Literacy, Financial Fragility, Financial Well-being and demographic, parental, and financial behavior variables. The results show that financial well-being depends on 'Financial Literacy', 'Financial fragility' as well as on students' financial behavior variables. This finding means that Greek university students who have high levels of financial literacy and good financial behavior have a higher possibility of achieving the so-called 'future well-being' for themselves and their families.[6]

Table 6. Determinants of financial fragility and financial well-being.

Variables		Financial Fragility		Financial Well-being	
		Coeff	Odds Ratios	Coeff	Odds Ratios
Panel A[a]					
Demographics					
Gender		−0.248	0.781	−0.004	0.996
Age	23–28	−0.164	0.849	−0.251	0.778
	29+	0.650	1.916	0.927	2.528
Nationality	Greek	−1.134	0.322	1.160	3.189
Work Experience in years	< 2	−0.012	0.988	1.204***	3.334***
	2–4	−1.002*	0.367**	1.260***	3.527***
	4–6	−0.513	0.599	1.338*	3.811*
	> 6	0.040	1.041	2.296***	9.938***
Parents' Information					
Father's Education	Primary School		3.012		1.220
	Lower High School	1.103	3.314	1.105	4.626
	Upper High School	1.198	1.891	0.532	1.173
	Post-secondary education	0.637	0.649	0.160	0.839
	BSc	0.432*	1.265*	−0.175**	0.988**
	MSc/PhD	0.235*	2.010*	−0.012**	3.019**
Mother's Education	Primary School	0.102	0.128	−0.711	0.181
	Lower High School	−0.052	0.199	−0.621	0.537
	Upper High School	0.617	0.287	−0.782	0.458
	Post-secondary education	0.247	0.339	−0.726	0.484
	BSc	−0.082	0.277	−0.164	0.312
	MSc/PhD	−0.284	0.128	−0.626	0.995
Father's Unemployment	Yes	0.108	1.114	0.167	1.182
Mother's Unemployment	Yes	0.087	1.091	0.024	1.024
Monthly Income	€1.001 – €1.999	0.435	1.545	0.302	1.352
	€2.000 – €2.999	−0.565	0.569	0.447	1.564
	€3.000 – €4.500	0.042	1.043	0.340	1.404
	> €4.500	−2.183	0.113	0.151	1.163
Income Change	Under 20%	−0.836	0.434	−0.871	0.419
	20–50%	−0.234	0.792	−0.232	0.793
	Over 50%	−0.584	0.458	−0.358	0.699

(continued).

Table 6. Continued.

Variables		Financial Fragility		Financial Well-being	
		Coeff	Odds Ratios	Coeff	Odds Ratios
Panel B[b]					
Financial Behavior					
Keep expenses' record	Yes	−0.833**	0.435**	0.305	1.356
Hold of a Bank account	Yes	0.267	0.733	0.099	0.599
Manage my account	Yes	−0.052	0.949	1.499***	4.478***
Saving	When I have enough money	2.896***	1.038***	4.856***	19.464***
	When I want to buy sth	1.224**	0.976**	2.928**	17.749**
	I don't save	−0.185	0.338	0.983	12.110
	I don't have money to save	−0.096	0.055	−0.179	0.895
Investment Experience	Yes	0.034	0.166	−0.120	0.887
Future Concerns					
Concern about your future income	Yes	−0.434	0.648	0.131	1.141
Financial Literacy	Literate	0.545	1.641**	0.798*	1.878*
Financial Fragility	Fragile			−4.483***	0.011***
Constant			6.860		0.009**
Models' Information					
−2Log Likelihood		1001.8***		1553.7***	
Cox and Snell (1989)		0.296		0.652	
Nagelkerke (1991)		0.328		0.658	
Hosmer and Lemeshow (1989)		9.878**		13.110***	

[a]Panel A presents the results of the logistic regression on the factors that influence students' financial fragility and financial well-being. The coefficients and odds ratios for the logit models are presented with their statistical validity. The dependent variable 'Financial Fragility' equals one if the student responds that 'I'm sure that I couldn't come up' or 'Maybe I couldn't come up' with €300 if an unexpected need arose in the next month and zero otherwise. The dependent variable 'Financial Well-being' equals one if the student responds that he or she can 'Most of the times' or 'Always' cover everyday expenses and 'Regularly' or 'Rarely' saves for the future and zero otherwise. The Financial Literacy variable equals one if the student correctly answers all questions and zero otherwise. The *denotes a p-value < 0.1; **denotes a p-value < 0.05; and the ***a denotes p-value < 0.01.

[b]Panel B presents the results of the logistic regression on the factors that influence students' financial fragility and financial well-being. The coefficients and odds ratios for the logit models are presented with their statistical validity. The dependent variable 'Financial Fragility' equals one if the student responds that 'I'm sure that I couldn't come up' or 'Maybe I couldn't come up' with €300 if an unexpected need arose in the next month and zero otherwise. The depended variable 'Financial Well-being' equals one if the student responds that 'Most of the times' or 'Always' covers everyday expenses and 'Regularly' or 'Rarely' saves for the future and zero otherwise. Financial Literacy variable equals one if the student correctly answers all questions and zero otherwise. Cox and Snell (1989) and Nagelkerke (1991) measure the proportion of the variance that the model is able to explain. the Hosmer and Lemeshow (1989) test estimates the goodness of fit with the data. The *denotes a p-value < 0.1; **denotes a p-value < 0.05; and the ***denotes a p-value < 0.01.

To identify the factors that influence students' financial well-being, we perform a logistic regression analysis. Important variables that explain financial well-being are included in the regression as explanatory variables to capture students' demographic characteristics and financial behavior as well as their parents' background. Table 6 (Panels A and B) present the logistic regression's coefficients and odds ratios. In general, the results show that among the independent variables, 'Work Experience', 'Father's Education Level', 'Manage my bank account', 'Saving', 'Financial Literacy', and 'Financial Fragility' are the six factors that influence students' financial well-being at the 5% statistical significance level. Furthermore, in term of information criteria, the results for Cox and Snell (1989), Nagelkerke (1991) and Hosmer and Lemeshow (1989) show that the logistic regression model has a good fit with the data and explains 65% of the variation in the dependent variable.

Furthermore, the results in Table 6 (Panels A and B) show that students whose father has a BS degree or a MS/PhD degree have 1 and 3 times, respectively, higher possibilities of having higher levels of financial well-being than those whose father has no education. The odds ratio for 'Work Experience' shows that students who have two years of work experience are 3–9 times more likely to have high levels of financial well-being than students with no proper work experience. Also, students who manage their bank account on their own have a four times higher possibility of having higher levels of financial well-being than those who do not, while students who save money have a 17–19 times higher possibility of having higher levels of financial well-being than those who do not save. The results show that financially literate students have a 1.8 times higher possibility of having

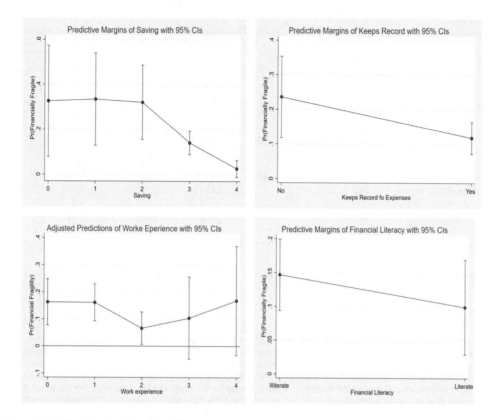

Figure 2. Financial fragility determinants' marginal effects.

Note: Figures present the plots of the predicted probabilities of someone being financially fragile for the statistically significant factors in the logistic regressions that influence students' financial fragility, while holding all the other covariates at their mean. They also show the 95% confidence intervals for each predicted probability.

higher levels of financial well-being than financially illiterate students, while no financially fragile students have a better possibility of showing higher levels of financial well-being.

Next, we perform a marginal effects analysis to investigate how the probability of a student with a higher level of financial well-being changes as a determinant variable changes from zero to one, holding all other variables at their means. Figure 3 presents the marginal effects for the statistically significant factors from the logistic regressions. Table 7 presents the predicted probabilities for the statistically significant factors. The results show that students whose father has a MS/PhD degree have greater predicted probability of having higher levels of financial well-being than those whose father has no education. The predicted probabilities for 'Work Experience' show that students who have more than two years of work experience have over a 0.2 greater predicted probability of showing high levels of financial well-being than students with no proper work experience. Also, students who save money have a greater predicted probability of having higher levels of financial well-being while students' who manage their own account have 0.237 greater predicted probability of having higher levels of financial well-being. Finally, financially literate students have a 0.126 greater predicted probability of having higher levels of financial well-being than financially illiterate students while financial fragile students have a low predicted probability of having higher levels of financial well-being. Overall, the results of the marginal effects strengthen the results of the odds ratio by showing that the factors influence students' levels of financial well-being at the 5% statistical significance level.

5. Policy recommendations

Financial education in schools should be part of a coordinated holistic national strategy. The education system should be involved in the development of the strategy. As a young pupil can understand the importance of saving

Table 7. Marginal effects for the determinants of financial literacy, fragility and well-being.

Variables		Financial Literacy	Financial Fragility	Financial Well-being
Demographics				
Gender		0.115***		
Work Experience in years	< 2		−0.002	0.201***
	2–4		0.096*	0.214**
	4–6		0.059*	0.232
	> 6		0.006**	0.466**
Parents' Information				
Father's Education	Primary School	0.050	0.210	0.115
	Lower High School	0.002	0.153	0.250
	Upper High School	0.187	0.172	0.355
	Post-secondary education	−0.010	0.075	0.031
	BSc	0.162**	0.033*	−0.031
	MSc/PhD	0.106**	0.024*	−0.002*
Financial Behavior				
Keep expenses' record	Yes	0.015*	0.118*	
Saving	When I have enough money		0.008**	0.003**
	When I want to buy sth		0.005	0.255***
	I don't save		0.185	0.267
	I don't have money to save		0.300	0.703
Manage my account	Yes			0.237***
Financial Literacy	Literate		0.152**	0.126*
Financial Fragility	Fragile			−0.908***

Note: Table 7 presents the marginal effects (dy/dx) for the statistically significant factors from the logistic regressions that influence students' financial literacy, financial fragility, and financial well-being at the 5% statistical significance level. The Financial Literacy variable equals one if the student correctly answers all questions and zero otherwise. The dependent variable 'Financial Fragility' equals one if the student respond that 'I'm sure that I couldn't come up' or 'Maybe I couldn't come up' with €300 if an unexpected need arose in the next month and zero otherwise. The dependent variable 'Financial Well-being' equals one if the student responds that he or she can 'Most of the times' or 'Always' cover everyday expenses and 'Regularly' or 'Rarely' saves for the future and zero otherwise. The *denotes a p-value < 0.1; **denotes a p-value < 0.05; and the ***denotes a p-value < 0.01. The marginal effects for the rest of the database are available on request.

money from the age of four, financial education should start as early as possible, ideally from the beginning of formal schooling and carry on until the end of the students' time at school. Financial education should ideally be a core part of the school curriculum. Unfortunately, the Greek public education system is based on a strict institutional framework, so financial education can be taught as an elective subject in the curriculum or integrated into other subjects like mathematics, economics, social science, citizenship, or history.

Greek authorities have not carried out any systematic and harmonized activities in schools or universities at the national level that focus solely on financial education unlike other European countries such as the Netherlands, Spain, Belgium, Croatia, and France. Further, the authorities scarcely imposed sanctions on creditors for inappropriate behavior and violations of the law. Basic financial principals were not covered while new technology trends in the financial sector such as Fintech, Insurtech, Digital Currencies, and Behavioral Finance are also excluded from the deliverable education in schools and universities. Knowledge of these subjects are crucial for individuals to meet the challenges in a currently dynamic global economic environment.

Therefore, we propose a holistic approach to financial education should consist of three pillars. The first pillar must deal with the lack of evidence about the levels of financial literacy and financial behavior in Greece. The collection of data can use national or international instruments such as the OECD/INFE survey for adults and the PISA financial literacy assessment for 15-year-old students. Both took place in 2015, and the PISA financial literacy assessment will be done again in 2018. We emphasize that for Greece, the OECD/INFE survey instrument does not clearly represent real financial and behavioral attitudes while the Greek results for the PISA assessment represent only general useful insights about mathematics and reading. Continuously measuring levels of financial literacy in Greece especially for specific groups such as immigrants, new parents, and elderly citizens as well as the construction of a national financial literacy index could be the first step in identifying the real financial behavior.

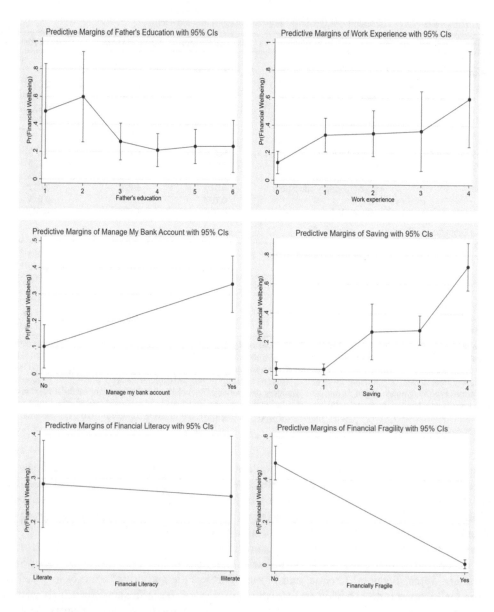

Figure 3. Financial well-being determinants' marginal effects.

Note: Figures present the plots of the predicted probabilities of someone achieving financial well-being for the statistically significant factors in the logistic regressions that influence students' financial fragility while holding all the other covariates at their mean. They also show the 95% confidence intervals for each predicted probability.

The second pillar refers to the adoption of a new financial education program that would mainly be implemented in primary and secondary schools. Financial education should start in primary school. Young students should be educated about financial matters as early as possible in their lives in order to form a new generation of financially educated citizens and a savings and effective investment culture as well as to build financial awareness.

The third pillar refers to actions which should be promoted to provide relevant, user-friendly financial information to the public, especially to the elderly, while free information services should be developed by formal policymakers in coordination with specialist organizations. Taking into account these principles we strongly recommend the creation of a financial education website under the responsibility of the Ministry of Education or a university which would provide useful financial content.

These proposed actions would offer the basic financial knowledge necessary for every individual. They would contribute to the formulation of a new generation of financially educated citizens. Fighting financial ignorance and populism would help society to avoid incorrect consumer decisions and to easily understand the importance of the structural reforms needed. These poor decisions affect not only the people making them but also those who will undergo the consequences of these decisions as a side effect. Financially educated citizens benefit the economy as a whole by increasing competitiveness, innovation, and the quality of the financial products and services offered. Therefore, apart from the personal benefits, the financial education of all citizens is necessary for the smooth operation of the financial system and its stability. Under these conditions, the financial markets can operate effectively, and the economy can grow at sustainable rates.

6. Conclusions

The purpose of this study is to be the first among its kind, To do so, we measure the levels of financial literacy, financial fragility, and financial well-being to evaluate their influence among university students in Greece. These students reflect a generation that grew up in a unique financial crisis that rivaled the Great Depression of 1929. We also investigate the roles of demographic, socioeconomic and financial behavior characteristics on the change in financial literacy, financial fragility and financial well-being. Our study was inspired by previous works on measuring the levels of these variables; for example, Chen and Volpe (1998), Ergun (2018), Andreou and Philip (2018), and Gutter, Copur, and Garrison (2010) as well as on evaluating the relations among them; for example, Shim et al. (2009), Hogarth (2006) and Gutter, Copur, and Garrison (2010). Our findings are in accordance with very few studies in the literature, although Andreou and Philip (2018) and Sabri et al. (2010) are similar.

Our analysis produced the following results. First, the levels of financial literacy in Greek university students in absolute terms were 19.3%. Second, we analyze data using cross-tabulations, chi-square tests, logistic regressions, and marginal effect analyses. The results show that male students and students who keep a record of expenses or their father is highly educated are more financially literate. Third, we measure the levels of financial fragility, and we examine the relation between it and students' 'absolute' financial knowledge after adding control variables for demographics and socioeconomics. We show that financially literate students are better able to cope with an unexpected financial shock. Fourth, we investigate whether financial literacy is a key determinant of financial well-being. Hence, we perform a logit model and a marginal effect analysis to evaluate the relation between financial well-being, financial literacy, and financial fragility along with demographics and socioeconomic variables. The results show that financial literacy and low levels of financial fragility are key drivers of financial well-being among Greek university students. Further, we discuss the likely policy prescriptions that account for the related behavioral aspects and technological developments.

Our study is different from the empirical studies already conducted in three respects. First, to the best of our knowledge, none of these studies has estimated the levels of financial literacy, financial fragility and financial well-being in parallel with the identification of the demographic and socioeconomic factors that affect these three financial components. Second, this study is the first of its kind to evaluate the relation between financial literacy, financial fragility, and financial well-being among university students in Greece who are members of Generation Z. Third, we identify the lack of public policy actions on fighting financial literacy in Greece and propose a holistic approach for financial education.

A state should create the conditions for the well-being of its citizens. That well-being is strongly dependent on financial well-being. Therefore, the financial education of the entire population is necessary to address future challenges such as longevity, over-indebtedness, reduced quality of life, and future reductions in pensions. The proposed actions would contribute to the formulation of a new generation of financially educated citizens by offering the basic financial knowledge necessary for every individual. Apart from the personal benefits, financial education would improve the smooth operation of the financial system and its stability.

Similar to other research, the present study has some limitations. The small sample size is the primarily limitation. The sample size can be increased by including students from different field of studies. While the results from the survey act as a pilot study in understanding the financial literacy levels in Greece, they are limited to drawing broader conclusions for the entire population. Therefore, a nationally representative household survey that is carried out as a policy step would allow a comprehensive assessment of the level of financial knowledge in Greece. The outcome of such a survey would enable policymakers and social planners to identify the priority areas and population segments in which to initiate programs for enhancing the financial capability of the country. Its results would also enable the country to benchmark its policy initiatives against other countries and coordinate its initiatives on the global front. An investigation of insurance and pension income literacy in Greece are also left for future research.

Notes

1. According to Chen and Tsurumi (2010), logit and probit models differ in the assumption of the underlying distribution. Logit assumes the distribution is logistic (i.e., the outcome either happens or it does not). Probit models assume the underlying distribution is normal which means, essentially, that the observed outcome either happens or does not but this reflects a certain threshold being met for the underlying latent variable which is normally distributed. In practice the end result of these different distributional assumptions is that coefficients differ, usually by a factor of about 1.6. However, if we look at marginal effects (meaning the effects on the predicted mean of the outcome holding other covariates at the mean or averaging over observed values) the logit and probit models will make essentially the same predictions. So, if we are looking at marginal effects, the choice probably does not matter. On the other hand, if we are not going to go about calculating the margins, then the logit has the obvious advantage of generating coefficients that can be transformed into the familiar odds ratio by exponentiating the coefficient. Probit coefficients are essentially uninterpretable – given a probit model we would report average marginal effects for this very reason. The odds of an outcome occurring is a ratio of successes to failures (an odds of 1 would correspond to a probability of 0.5). Odds ratios, then, reflect the predicted change in the odds given a one unit change in the predictor. Thus, the odds ratio reflects change relative to the base odds of the outcome occurring. Given an outcome that either rarely occurs or almost always occurs, a small change in probability can correspond to a large odds ratio.
2. The cross-tabulation analysis and the Pearson (1900) Chi-Square's statistic for each pairwise comparison between financial literacy and demographic, parental, and socioeconomic variables are available on request.
3. Cross-tabulation analysis results are available on request.
4. Pearson (1900) Chi-Square's statistic for each pairwise comparison between financial literacy and demographics, parental, and socioeconomic variables are available on request.
5. Cross-tabulation analysis results are available on request.
6. Pearson (1900) Chi-Square's statistic for each pairwise comparison between financial literacy and demographics, parental, and socioeconomic variables are available on request.

Disclosure statement

No potential conflict of interest was reported by the authors.

References

Albeerdy, M. I., and B. Gharleghi. 2015. "Determinants of the Financial Literacy among College Students in Malaysia." *International Journal of Business Administration* 6 (3): 15–24.

Andreou, P. C., and D. Philip. 2018. "Financial Knowledge among University Students and Implications for Personal Debt and Fraudulent Investments." *Cyprus Economic Policy Review* 12 (2): 3–23.

Atkinson, A., and F. A. Messy. 2012. *Measuring Financial Literacy: Results of the OECD/International Network on Financial Education (INFE) Pilot Study*. OECD Working Papers on Finance, Insurance and Private Pensions 15, OECD.

Beal, D. J., and S. B. Delpachitra. 2003. "Financial Literacy among Australian University Students." *Economic Papers: A Journal of Applied Economics and Policy* 22 (1): 65–78.

Chan, S. F., A. W. Chau, and Y. K. Kim. 2012. "Financial Knowledge and Aptitudes: Impacts on College Students' Financial Well-Being." *College Student Journal* 46: 1.

Chen, G., and H. Tsurumi. 2010. "Probit and Logit Model Selection." *Communications in Statistics—Theory and Methods* 40: 159–175.

Chen, H., and R. P. Volpe. 1998. "An Analysis of Personal Financial Literacy among College Students." *Financial Services Review* 7 (2): 107–128.

Cox, D. R., and E. J. Snell. 1989. *Analysis of Binary Data*. 2nd ed. London: Chapman and Hall/CRC.

Ergun, K. 2018. "Financial Literacy among University Students: A Study in Eight European Countries." *International Journal of Consumer Studies* 42: 2–15.

Falahati, L., and L. Paim. 2011. "Gender Differences in Financial Well-being among College Students." *Australian Journal of Basic and Applied Sciences* 5 (9): 1765–1776.

Gutter, M. S., Z. Copur, and S. Garrison. 2010. *M.S. Financial Capabilities of College Students From States with Varying Financial Education Policies*. Denver, CO: National Endowment for Financial Education.

Hira, T. K., and O. Mugenda. 1999a. "Do Men and Women Differ in Their Financial Beliefs and Behaviors?" In *Proceedings of Eastern Family Economics Resource Management Association, Eastern Family Economics Resource Management Association*, edited by K. Kitt, 1–8. Austin, TX.

Hira, T. K., and O. Mugenda. 1999b. "The Relationships Between Self-worth and Financial Beliefs, Behavior, and Satisfaction." *Journal of Family and Consumer Sciences* 91 (4): 76–82.

Hogarth, M. 2006. "Financial Education and Economic Development." International Conference hosted by the Russian G8 Presidency in Cooperation with the OECD.

Hosmer, D., and S. Lemeshow. 1989. *Applied Logistic Regression*. New York: John Wiley & Sons.

Joo, S., and J. E. Grable. 2004. "An Exploratory Framework of the Determinants of Financial Satisfaction." *Journal of Family and Economic Issues* 25 (1): 162–171.

Klapper, L., A. Lusardi, and G. A. Panos. 2013. "Financial Literacy and Its Consequences: Evidence from Russia During the Financial Crisis." *Journal of Banking & Finance* 37: 3904–3923.

Klapper, L., A. Lusardi, and P. van Oudheusden. 2015. *Financial Literacy Around the World: Insights from the Standard & Poor's Rating Services Global Financial Literacy Survey*.

Klapper, L., and G. A. Panos. 2011. "Financial Literacy and Retirement Planning: The Russian Case." *Journal of Pension Economics and Finance* 10 (04): 599–618.

Long, J. S. 1997. "Regression Models for Categorical and Limited Dependent Variables." *Advanced Quantitative Techniques in the Social Sciences Series*, Vol. 7.

Lusardi, A., and O. S. Mitchell. 2006. *Financial Literacy and Planning: Implications for Retirement Well-being*. Working Paper, Pension Research Council, Wharton School, University of Pennsylvania.

Lusardi, A., and O. S. Mitchell. 2011b. "Financial Literacy and Planning: Implications for Retirement Wellbeing." In *Financial Literacy: Implications for Retirement Security and the Financial Marketplace*, edited by A. Lusardi, and O. S. Mitchell, 17–39. Oxford: Oxford University Press.

Lusardi, A., and O. S. Mitchell. 2014. "The Economic Importance of Financial Literacy: Theory and Evidence." *Journal of Economic Literature, American Economic Association* 52 (1): 5–44.

Lusardi, A., D. J. Schneider, and P. Tufano. 2011. "Financially Fragile Households: Evidence and Implications." *Brookings Papers on Economic Activity*, pp. 83–150.

Nagelkerke, N. D. 1991. "A Note on a General Definition of the Coefficient of Determination." *Biometrika* 78: 691–692.

Oppong-Boakye, P. K., and R. Kansanba. 2013. "An Assessment of Financial Literacy Levels among Undergraduate Business Students in Ghana." *Research Journal of Finance and Accounting* 4 (8): 36–49.

Pearson, K. 1900. "On the Criterion That a Given System of Deviations From the Probable in the Case of a Correlated System of Variables is Such That it Can Be Reasonably Supposed to Have Arisen from Random Sampling." *The London, Edinburgh, and Dublin Philosophical Magazine and Journal of Science* 50 (302): 157–175.

Sabri, F. M., M. MacDonald, T. K. Hira, and J. Masud. 2010. "Childhood Consumer Experience and the Financial Literacy of College Students in Malaysia." *Family and Consumer Sciences Research Journal* 38 (4): 455–467.

Sarigül, H. 2014. "A Survey of Financial Literacy Among University Students." *Journal of Accounting & Finance* 64: 207–224.

Shim, S., J. J. Xiao, B. L. Barber, and A. C. Lyons. 2009. "Pathways to Life Success: A Conceptual Model of Financial Well-being for Young Adults." *Journal of Applied Developmental Psychology* 30: 708–723.

Spearman, C. 1904. "The Proof and Measurement of Association Between Two Things." *The American Journal of Psychology* 15: 72–101.

Vitt, L. A., C. A. Anderson, J. Kent, and D. Lyter. 2000. *Personal Finance*. Washington, DC: fannies mea foundation.

Xiao, J. J., S. Shim, B. Barber, and A. Lyons. 2007. *Academic Success and Well-being of College Students: Financial Behaviours Matter*. Tucson, AZ: Take Charge American Institute for Consumer Financial Education and Research.

Financial literacy and student debt

Nikolaos Artavanis and Soumya Karra

ABSTRACT

Using a large sample of over 1000 students from a major, land-grant, public university in Massachusetts, we examine the financial literacy level of college students, and its implications on the repayment of student debt. We find low levels of financial literacy (39.5%), particularly among female (26%), minority (24%) and first-generation (33%) students. Based on survey responses, we show that students with a deficit in financial literacy are more likely to underestimate future student loan payments; 38.2% of low-literacy students underestimate future payments by more than $1000 annually, while high financial literacy reduces the probability of significant payment underestimation by 17–18 percentage points. Furthermore, we find evidence of a financial literacy wage gap as students with low financial literacy expect significantly lower starting salaries than their high-literacy peers. As a result, low-literacy students are more vulnerable to unexpected, adverse shocks on their payment-to-income ratios that can impair their future creditworthiness and undermine their ability to service debt post-graduation.

1. Introduction

In recent years, the increase in outstanding student debt and student loan default rates have raised concerns regarding the net value of higher education outcomes and the consequences of over-indebtedness for young borrowers (Mueller and Yannelis. 2018). These facts highlight the importance of financial literacy for young adults, who are more susceptible to financial mistakes (Agarwal et al. 2009). The topic is increasing in relevance, as nowadays students are expected to make long-term, life-changing decisions on education and debt accumulation despite evidence that they exhibit low levels of financial literacy (Lusardi, Mitchell, and Curto 2010).

In this study, we explore the links between financial literacy and student debt using a large sample of 1040 students from a land-grant, public university in Massachusetts. Our survey includes three questions on financial literacy that have been extensively used in the past literature (Lusardi and Mitchell 2008; Lusardi, Mitchell, and Curto 2010; Hastings, Madrian, and Skimmyhorn 2013), and provides information on demographics and student loan characteristics (debt amount, interest rate, maturity), which we use to estimate future loan payments. We compare these estimates to students' responses regarding the amounts they expect to pay upon graduation, examine whether realized differences are systematically associated with financial literacy, and assess the impact of possible biases on their payment-to-income ratios.

Our results indicate alarmingly low levels of financial literacy among undergraduate students. We find a literacy rate of just 39.5% and an even lower college-weighted rate (36%). We document a significant financial literacy gender gap as female students exhibit considerably lower literacy rates (26%) than their male peers (56%), consistent with findings of previous studies (Ford and Kent 2010; Lusardi, Mitchell, and Curto 2010; Bucher-Koenen et al. 2017). We also find a significant deficit in literacy among minority (24%) and first-generation students (33%), and higher literacy rates for Honors students (44%). In addition, there is significant variation in financial literacy rates among disciplines; students majoring in Business, Engineering and Computer Science exhibit high rates of financial literacy, which may underscore the role of financial knowledge (Mahdavi and Horton 2014) and numeracy (Christelis, Jappelli, and Padula 2010; Gerardi, Goette, and Meier 2013).

We use information on self-reported student loan characteristics to show that students with low literacy levels significantly underestimate future debt payments both in the intensive and the extensive margin.[1] We find that 38% (19.5%) of respondents with low (high) literacy underestimate student loan payments by at least $1000 annually. Furthermore, the average low-literacy student underestimates payments by $575 annually, in contrast to literate students whose average bias is close to zero. Our regression results indicate that financial literacy reduces the probability of significant payment underestimations by 17–18 percentage points after controlling for student characteristics. This negative relationship between financial literacy and payment underestimation remains strongly robust in a wide array of tests that examine alternative explanations (e.g. debt forgiveness, IDRs, passive responses, high numeracy/SAT scores).

Next, we document for the first time, to our best knowledge, a substantial 'financial literacy wage gap' in expected starting salaries. We focus on business majors and show that low-literacy students expect significantly lower starting salaries ($48,596) than their literate peers ($57,410), a gap that persists when we consider only senior, better-informed students with close proximity to the job market. This finding along with the fact that our survey responses are very close to average realized starting salaries support the view that these expectations are on average correct and that differences between literacy groups reflect actual labor market outcomes rather than over(under)-estimation of future wages. Differences in expected starting salaries remain significant across genders and are double as large as the well-documented gender wage gap (Becker 1957). The financial literacy wage gap also persists within majors, which alleviates concerns that the results are driven by high-literacy students self-selecting into high-earning professions.

We combine our previous findings to assess the impact of payments miscalculations on the ability to repay debt for students of different literacy levels. Low-literacy students have higher expected payment-to-income (PTI) ratios (8.23%) than their literate peers (6.79%), due to higher debt burdens and lower expected salaries post-graduation. More importantly, borrowers with a deficit in financial literacy are more exposed to unexpectedly higher PTI ratios post-graduation (9.72%), once we correct for the underestimation of future payments. The effect is more pronounced at the right tail of the distribution; for instance, even though only 14.5% of low-literacy students expect to graduate with a PTI above 10%, the actual percentage is 39.5%. These unexpected shocks on the debt-to-income ratios for low-literacy students can impair their future creditworthiness and undermine their ability to service student loans post-graduation.

The contribution of our study to the literature is threefold. First, we contribute to the growing body of literature on the incidence of financial literacy (see Hastings, Madrian, and Skimmyhorn 2013; Lusardi and Mitchell 2014), particularly among young adults (Lusardi, Mitchell, and Curto 2010; Bucher-Koenen et al. 2017; Anderson, Conzelmann, and Austin Lacy 2018). In this context, our work provides additional evidence on the level of financial literacy of college students, using one of the largest sample from a single institution, and documents significant deficits in financial literacy for female, minority and first-generation students.

Second, our results provide a causal link between financial literacy and financial outcomes, which is hard to establish without relying on an exogenous source of variation in financial literacy (Fernandes, Lynch Jr, and Netemeyer 2014). Here instead, we focus on the relationship between literacy levels and financial mistakes for which the direction of causality is very hard to challenge (Klapper, Lusardi, and Panos 2013) and show that low-literacy students are more likely to underestimate the future payments of the student loans they describe.

Finally, our finding that low-literacy students are more likely to experience an unexpected, adverse shock on their debt-to-income ratios post-graduation provides a plausible explanation for the higher student loan default rates in recent years. Looney and Yannelis (2015) attribute this trend to non-traditional borrowers, who exhibit higher propensity to default despite having lower debt-to-income ratios, on average. Our results suggest that the ability of low-literacy students to repay their student loans can be undermined by unexpected shocks in their debt-to-income ratios that are realized upon graduation. Such shocks, which are shown to be of prime importance for household default (see Sullivan, Warren, and Lawrence Westbrook 2001[2], in our case originate from the numerator (underestimation of payments) rather than the denominator (income shock).

The remainder of the study is organized as follows. The next section describes our data and methodology. Section 3 presents our results on financial literacy, the underestimation of future student loan payments and the effect of this bias on payment-to-income ratios. Lastly, Section 4 discusses our findings and concludes the study.

2. Data

Our survey was completed in the spring semester of 2017 in a major, land-grant, public university in Massachusetts. Following approval from the Institutional Review Board, a 'paper-and-pencil' questionnaire was circulated mainly through personal interviews on campus and in classrooms. The survey was designed to be compact, with questions in a multiple-choice format and a short completion time frame (less than 10 min). Our total sample is 1040 undergraduate students, which represents approximately 5% of total enrollment.

In the first part of the survey, we assess students' financial literacy from three questions that test basic knowledge in the areas of interest compounding, inflation and diversification. This set of questions, also known as the 'Big Three' (Hastings, Madrian, and Skimmyhorn 2013), has been extensively used in the literature, and enables comparisons with findings of previous studies. The questions used to assess financial literacy (correct answers noted in bold) are presented below:

1. Suppose you had $100 in a savings account and the interest rate was 2% per year. After 5 years, how much do you think you would have in the account if you left the money to grow?
   (a) **More than $102**   (b) Exactly $102   (c) Less than $102   (d) I don't know

2. Imagine that the interest rate on your savings account was 1% per year and inflation was 2% per year. After 1 year, how much would you be able to buy with the money in this account?
   (a) More than today   (b) Exactly the same   (c) **Less than today**   (d) I don't know

3. Please tell me whether this statement is true or false. *'Buying a single company's stock usually provides a safer return than a stock mutual fund.'*
   (a) True   (b) **False**   (c) I don't know

Additionally, we collect students' demographics, such as age, gender, and ethnicity, and characteristics, such as class rank and major to group respondents by their home college. Respondents also note whether they are first-generation or Honors students.

The third part of the survey pertains to information on student debt and expected starting salaries. We gather information on funding sources of tuition (personal funds, student loans, scholarships) and the type of student debt (federal, private, both) held, if any. Respondents also self-report amounts of current and total student debt by graduation (in $10,000 brackets), as well as the average interest rate (in 3% brackets) and the average maturity (5-year brackets) of these loans. Another novel item in our study is that we ask students to provide the expected monthly loan payment for their student debt (in $100 brackets) and their expected starting salary post-graduation (in $10,000 brackets). Finally, we use a separate dataset that includes information on actual starting salaries from the business school to compare expectations to actual labor market outcomes on remuneration for business majors.

3. Empirical results

3.1. Financial literacy

A robust finding of the past literature is that individuals exhibit low levels of financial literacy across different demographic groups and countries (Lusardi and Mitchell 2011; Klapper and Panos 2011).[3] The problem is more pronounced for young adults who are more prone to financial mistakes (Agarwal et al. 2009). There is mounting evidence that young adults (Lusardi, Mitchell, and Curto 2010; Bucher-Koenen et al. 2017; Anderson,

Table 1. Financial literacy across groups of interest.

	Fin.Literate (All 3)	Dif.	Int.Rate (Q1)	Inflation (Q2)	Diversify (Q3)	N
Total	39.52		87.6	67.88	53.27	1,040
Gender						
Male	56.22	–	92.92	79.61	66.31	466
Female	25.96	−30.26***	83.28	58.36	42.68	574
Ethnicity						
White	40.49	–	86.85	69.01	53.78	768
Asian	41.29	0.80	93.53	68.66	52.74	201
Hispanic	27.27	−13.22*	77.27	59.09	56.82	44
Afr. American	18.52	−21.98**	81.48	44.44	37.04	27
Year						
Freshman	41.84	6.09	85.82	72.34	55.32	141
Sophomore	44.82	9.07**	86.55	71.43	57.70	357
Junior	35.24	−0.51	88.83	65.33	49.00	349
Senior	35.75	–	88.60	62.69	51.30	193
College						
Business School	49.12	–	91.98	70.43	64.16	399
Comp. Sciences	63.64	14.51*	95.45	84.09	70.45	44
Engineering	50.00	0.88	91.43	82.86	58.57	70
Humanities	26.42	−22.71***	88.68	50.94	41.51	53
Natural Sc	29.79	−19.34***	81.70	68.09	42.13	235
Public Health	15.12	−34.01***	82.56	47.67	26.74	86
Social Sciences	43.52	−5.60	85.19	68.52	61.11	108
Other	17.78	−31.35***	80.00	62.22	35.56	45
Parents Education						
NonFirstGen	41.03	–	87.36	68.59	54.87	831
FirstGen	33.49	−7.54**	88.52	65.07	46.89	209
Honors						
NonHonors	36.67	–	86.27	67.69	51.21	619
Honors	43.71	7.03**	89.55	68.17	56.29	421

Notes: The table presents the percentage of students who responded correctly to all three questions (High Financial Literacy) and to each question (Interest rate, Inflation, Diversification) separately within each group of interest. Column 'Diff' shows differences in means with respect to the reference group (in italics) with significance at the 1%, 5%, and 10% levels indicated by ***, **, and *, respectively. The last column reports the sample size for each group.

Conzelmann, and Austin Lacy 2018) have a deficit in financial literacy because they lack experience in handling financial matters on their own.

Our study uses one of the largest samples collected from a single college in the literature (1040 students). Confining our survey to a rather homogeneous group of young, well-educated individuals attending the same institution limits the effect of unobservables, such as intelligence and education, that can proxy for financial knowledge, but are hard to control for (see Behrman et al. 2010).

We assess financial literacy from the three questions on interest compounding, inflation and risk diversification, as described previously. Following the literature, we define as financially literate a respondent who answers all three questions correctly. Table 1 presents our results. Overall, we find an alarmingly low level of financial literacy; only 39.5% of students answered all three questions correctly. This finding is concerning given the educational background of our respondents. Since our sample is heavily skewed on business majors, we also weight our results by college enrollment to provide university-representative estimates, which yields an even lower literacy rate of 35.97%.

Consistent with Lusardi and Mitchell (2014), we find that respondents were more likely to answer the interest rate question correctly (88%) compared to the inflation (68%) and the diversification (53%) questions. According to our criterion, for scoring purposes, an 'I don't know answer' and incorrect answers are equivalent. Lusardi, Mitchell, and Curto (2010) argue that 'textitI do not know' responses may reflect even lower levels of financial literacy than wrong ones, however we find mixed evidence regarding this claim; specifically, 'I don't know' responses appear to be more associated with the type of the question rather than performance in the remaining survey (see Figure A1).[4]

Our results document a substantial gender gap in financial literacy. In our sample, female students exhibit significantly lower literacy rates (26%) than their male peers (56%), consistent with past findings in the literature, both for young individuals (Chen and Volpe 2002; Ford and Kent 2010; Lusardi, Mitchell, and Curto 2010) and other groups of interest (Lusardi and Mitchell 2008; Bucher-Koenen et al. 2017). The sources of this persistent difference remain a subject of open debate. Ford and Kent (2010) argue that female college students are more intimidated by and less interested in financial markets; however, we find that the gender gap persists not only across disciplines (Figure 1) but also within business majors (Figure A2). It is plausible that, as suggested by Fonseca et al. (2012), the gap in financial literacy between males and females is better explained by differences on how literacy is produced for the two groups (differences in coefficients) rather than differences in characteristics.

We also find evidence of a significant financial literacy deficit in minorities, which has been also documented in previous studies (Lusardi and Mitchell 2007; Lusardi, Mitchell, and Curto 2010; Lusardi and Tufano 2015); only 27% of Hispanics and 18.5% of African-American students responded to all three questions correctly.[5] In contrast, Asian students exhibit literacy levels close to the sample average.[6] Our results indicate that first-generation students constitute another vulnerable group in terms of financial literacy. Consistent with the empirical findings of Lusardi, Mitchell, and Curto (2010) and Mahdavi and Horton (2014), students whose parents have not attended college exhibit significantly lower levels of literacy (33.5%). Shim et al. (2010) also highlight the importance of parents' influence on current financial learning and behaviors, specifically on financial decisions associated with college. Finally, we find that Honors students exhibit significantly higher literacy levels (43.7%) compared to their non-Honors peers (36.7%).

Our survey results indicate that there is significant variation in financial literacy among disciplines. Not surprisingly, business majors exhibit higher literacy levels (49%) than their peers in other schools, consistent with the findings of Mahdavi and Horton (2014) that business education has a significant impact on financial literacy. However, the fact that almost half of business majors still fail to respond to all three questions correctly suggests that financial knowledge is a necessary but not a sufficient condition for financial literacy (Mahdavi and Horton 2014). Interestingly, students in engineering and computer science - who follow a curriculum that is hardly focused on financial knowledge - also exhibit high levels of financial literacy comparable to business majors. The fact that these colleges have high SAT scores, which may proxy for cognitive ability (Lusardi, Mitchell, and Curto 2010), and require high level of numeracy (Christelis, Jappelli, and Padula 2010; Gerardi, Goette, and Meier 2013), suggests that these factors are also closely related to financial literacy.

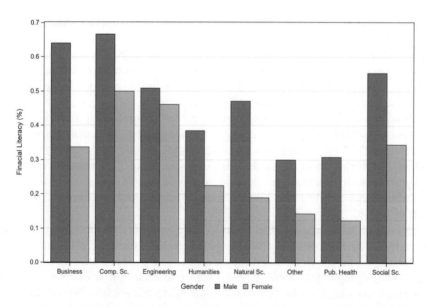

Figure 1. Financial literacy by college and gender. The figure presents the percentage of financially literate male and female students within each college ($N = 1040$). Survey participants are defined as financially literate if they have responded correctly to all three financial literacy questions.

Table 2. Marginal effects on financial literacy.

	Literacy = 1 if fin. literate, 0 otherwise			
Dep. Variable:	(1)	(2)	(3)	(4)
Female	−0.2823***	−0.2801***	−0.2858***	−0.2557***
	[0.0233]	[0.0233]	[0.0232]	[0.0254]
Minority		−0.1642***	−0.1532**	−0.1333**
		[0.0631]	[0.0626]	[0.0622]
First Gen.			−0.0535	−0.0525
			[0.0367]	[0.0362]
Honors			0.0878***	0.0914***
			[0.0290]	[0.0291]
Business				omitted
				–
Engineering				−0.0526
				[0.0504]
Other Colleges				−0.1547**
				[0.0316]

Notes: The table presents average marginal effects from a logistic regression, where the dependent variable (*Literacy*) takes the value 1 if the participant has answered correctly all three questions on financial literacy and zero otherwise (*N = 1040*). Independent variables include indicator variables of student characteristics (gender, minority, first-generation and honors status) and a partition to College groups with Business school majors being the reference group. Engineering includes students in the Colleges of Engineering and Computer Science. Corresponding standard errors using the Delta method are shown in brackets and significance at the 1%, 5%, and 10% levels is indicated by ***, **, and *, respectively.

In Table 2, we examine these patterns more formally in a regression setting. In univariate regressions (not reported), all independent variables are significantly associated with the level of financial literacy. Gender and minority are shown to have the highest marginal effects; female students are 26–28 percentage points less likely to exhibit high financial literacy, while being a minority student reduces the respective probability by 13–16 percentage points. By contrast, Honors students are 9 percentage points more likely to be financially literate. Interestingly, the effect of first-generation status, even though significant on its own, is subsumed once we include gender and honors status. Finally, students who attend colleges other than business, engineering, and computer science are 15 percentage points less likely to be financially literate, after controlling for all the aforementioned characteristics.

3.2. Student debt

The literature suggests that lack of financial skills, particularly on understanding interest compounding and the concept of time value of money, are related to inefficient decisions regarding debt. Bernheim (1998) shows that most households lack adequate decision-making skills, especially when it comes to interest compounding. Individuals with low financial literacy are more likely to hold costly mortgages (Moore 2003) and accumulate higher amounts of debt (Stango and Zinman 2009). Gerardi, Goette, and Meier (2013) find that a deficit in literacy increases the probability of default, while Lusardi and Tufano (2015) show that individuals with low debt literacy tend to incur higher fees and costs on their debt obligations.

Despite the plethora of documented relationships between literacy and financial behaviors or outcomes, causality claims are hard to establish (Klapper, Lusardi, and Panos 2013). Due to the potential effect of latent variables, researchers have to rely on exogenous sources of variation in financial literacy to establish causality. However, the efficiency of this approach is always subject on validity of the instrument used (see Fernandes, Lynch Jr, and Netemeyer 2014). Here, instead, we provide a causal link between literacy and outcomes by focusing on financial mistakes, for which the causal direction is difficult to challenge (Klapper, Lusardi, and Panos 2013); specifically, we show that low-literacy students are more likely to underestimate payments of the loans they describe.

Furthermore, two features of the survey support the view that the documented relationship is not an artifact of latent variables. First, we use a rather homogeneous sample of young, well-educated adults that alleviates

Table 3. Summary statistics on student debt and expected salaries.

	Total	Female	Minority	First Gen.	Honors	Fin.Literate
Panel A						
Funding Source(s)						
Private Funds	83.74	83.54	68.57	71.98	90.45	86.03
Student Loans	64.38	63.92	77.14	83.09	56.80	59.80
Scholarships	62.63	64.80	81.43	64.25	75.66	62.99
Loan Type						
Federal Loans	39.59	41.33	45.71	52.66	37.47	36.03
Private Loans	6.39	6.13	2.86	3.86	5.73	6.86
Both	18.01	16.29	25.71	27.05	11.69	15.69
None	36.01	36.25	25.71	16.43	45.11	41.42
Exp. Starting Salary						
< $30,000	11.81	15.24	14.29	10.63	11.93	6.13
$30–40,000	16.84	22.59	25.71	20.29	14.80	11.76
$40–50,000	22.56	24.52	14.29	23.19	19.33	17.65
$50–60,000	23.04	19.09	22.86	22.22	21.24	28.43
$60–70,000	15.39	11.73	11.43	13.04	18.62	20.83
> $70,000	10.36	6.83	11.43	10.63	14.08	15.20
N	1,033	571	70	207	419	408
Panel B						
Total Student Debt						
< $10,000	17.60	19.17	24.07	9.47	22.46	18.03
$10–20,000	25.64	25.56	22.22	26.04	25.42	29.51
$20–30,000	24.73	25.00	18.52	26.04	27.12	22.54
$30–40,000	11.53	10.00	12.96	19.53	8.47	9.84
$40–50,000	10.02	10.83	18.52	8.88	6.36	7.79
> $50,000	10.47	9.44	3.70	10.06	10.17	12.30
Interest Rate						
0-3%	15.17	16.67	14.81	15.38	18.22	16.39
3–6%	32.17	28.61	31.48	34.91	24.58	36.07
6–9%	8.95	9.17	14.81	12.43	8.47	7.79
9–12%	1.67	1.67	7.41	2.96	2.12	1.64
I don't know	42.03	43.89	31.48	34.32	46.61	38.11
Maturity						
< 5 years	28.68	30.56	27.78	27.81	34.75	28.69
5–10 years	48.25	47.50	48.15	48.52	44.92	45.90
11–15 years	15.93	15.56	16.67	17.16	16.10	16.80
16–20 years	4.55	3.61	3.70	5.92	2.12	5.33
> 20 years	2.58	2.78	3.70	0.59	2.12	3.28
Exp. Mon. Payment						
< $200	27.16	27.78	29.63	20.71	31.78	30.74
$200–300	39.15	40.00	31.48	35.50	40.68	34.02
$300–400	21.40	20.56	24.07	25.44	17.80	20.49
$400–500	6.83	7.22	5.56	10.65	5.51	9.43
> $500	5.46	4.44	9.26	7.69	4.24	5.33
N	659	360	54	169	236	244

Notes: The table summarizes student responses on characteristics of student debt and expected salaries as percentages of the respective sample. In Panel B, the sample includes only respondents that reported a non-zero total student debt (upon graduation). The sample size is reported in the last row of each panel.

concerns of an unobservable, such as intelligence and education, driving our results (Behrman et al. 2010). Second, we focus on student loans for which eligibility is less of a consideration compared to other credit products (e.g. credit cards, personal loans), due to affluent federal funding.

In Table 3 (Panel A), we present information on funding sources, loan types and expected salaries for our total sample and selected subgroups. The majority of students rely on a mix of funding sources to pay for college. Over 80% use personal and family funds to pay at least partially for college education, while two-thirds hold some amount of student debt. Consistent with the findings of Lee and Mueller (2014), first-generation students rely more on student loans (83%) and are more likely to believe that they can afford college education only through external funding (28%). By contrast, Honors students rely relatively less on debt and more on scholarships and private funds. Most of the students with debt are holding federal loans, while a noteworthy portion of our sample is holding both federal and private loans.

Panel A (Table 3) also summarizes survey responses regarding expected starting salaries. The median expected salary is close to $50,000, which is in accordance with the official statistics of our institution, and over one half of our sample expects annual earnings between $40,000 and $60,000 post-graduation. Female students expect on average lower starting salaries than their male peers and are less likely to appear in the higher income brackets consistent with the well-documented gender wage gap (Becker 1957). Minority students also expect relatively lower starting salaries on average, while Honors students expect higher remuneration than their non-Honors peers post-graduation.

In Panel B (Table 3), we provide information on loan characteristics for students who hold debt (debt amount, maturity and interest rate), along with the amounts they expect to pay monthly to service these student loans.[7] The median student borrows between $20,000 and $30,000, while 20% of students holding debt carry a significant burden in excess of $40,000, post-graduation. First-generation students are less likely to carry low balances (9.4%), while the respective percentage is more than double for Honors students (22.5%), consistent with results on the use of private funds, presented earlier.

The majority of student loans has maturity less than 10 years. Almost half of the loans have a mid-term repayment horizon (5–10 years) and only a small fraction (7%) involves maturities longer than 15 years. Reflecting the current low interest rate environment, the majority of students borrows at interest rates below 6%. We find evidence that first-generation and particularly minority students are exposed to high-cost borrowing.[8]

However, the most striking finding is that a large percentage of students cannot provide even a rough estimate of their borrowing cost (42%). This inability to determine the cost of borrowing is very concerning and appears to span across literacy levels (44% for low and and 38% for high-literacy students) but is significantly smaller for minority (31%) and first-generation students (34%), which may reflect the importance of paying attention to loan terms, when borrowing at a higher cost.

Students, in general, expect relatively low monthly payments on their loans. Over 80% of the sample believes that the monthly payment will not exceed $400, while 27% expects to pay less than $200 per month to service student debt. These expectations are largely inconsistent with the high debt amounts and the relatively short maturities reported earlier in our survey. The dominant expected payment bracket (39%) is between $200 and $300 per month, which includes the average monthly payment reported in the College Scorecard of our institution.

In the last column of Table 3, we report summary statistics for high-literacy students, but we refrain from making causal claims because differences with the total sample may be due to unobservables (e.g. wealth). In general, high-literacy students appear to rely more on private funds, are less likely to borrow to finance their education and expect, on average, higher starting salaries.[9]

3.3. Financial literacy and loan payment underestimation

In this section, we compare amounts that students expect to pay for their loans – as per their responses – and payments that correspond to the self-reported characteristics of their loans and relate differences to financial literacy. We define *expected payment* (*Exp_Pay*) as the bracket midpoint of the survey response for each student, and we estimate *actual payment* (*Actual_Pay*) using the midpoints of the self-reported loan characteristics and applying a normal amortization schedule with monthly compounding. The difference between expected (*Exp_Pay*) and actual payment (*Actual_Pay*) is our first measure of *payment underestimation* (*Under*). Because our responses come in the form of brackets (see Table 3) that can affect the accuracy of our estimates, we focus on 'inside' brackets, where the potential bias is limited. Thus, we exclude observations with debt amount and maturity greater than $50,000 and 20 years, respectively, and students who expect to pay more than $500 per month.[10] We also exclude loans with very short maturity (less than 5 years) and students who hold no debt or cannot provide their cost of borrowing. We examine all variables on an annual basis.

Figure 2 presents the distribution of differences between expected and actual payments (*Under*) by literacy group. For the entire sample, the bias on estimating future loan payments appears to be limited; the average and median underestimation are just $351 and $89, respectively, on an annual basis, suggesting that students are able

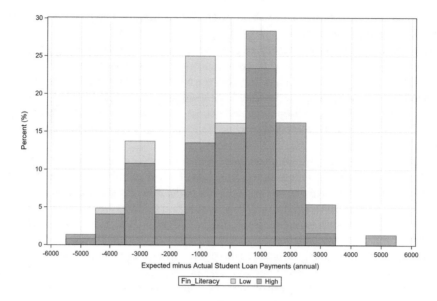

Figure 2. Underestimation of student loan payments. The figure presents a histogram of the annual underestimation of student loan payments for students of low (dark gray) and high (light gray) financial literacy (*N* = 213). Underestimation is defined as the difference between the midpoint of the expected payment bracket as per survey responses minus the actual payment calculated using self-reported loan characteristics as described in Section 3.3.

to estimate their future payments correctly on average. But, once we condition on the level of financial literacy, the story changes dramatically. Low-literacy students are more likely to underestimate their payments both in the extensive and the intensive margin, as shown in Figure 2; the median student with low financial literacy underestimates future loan payments by $560 (mean:$-575$) annually. By contrast, high-literacy students tend to overestimate future loan payments, with a median overestimation of $587 (mean: $25).

It is important to note the sign of 'bias' cannot be treated symmetrically for several reasons. First, overestimation may reflect intentions for early repayment of the loan. This appears to be more plausible in the case of high-literacy students that have both lower debt balances and higher expected starting salaries (see Table 3). Second, our survey takes place in a low interest rate environment, which means that it is highly unlikely that the underestimation reflects expectations of refinancing at lower interest rate in the future. More importantly, the sign of miscalculation has entirely contrasting impact on the borrower's future creditworthiness. Specifically, a student who underestimates (overestimates) payments is exposed to a negative (positive) shock with respect to debt obligations she has to service in the future. For these reasons, we mainly focus on the underestimation of student loan payments that poses a threat to future debt paths.

In our tests, we prioritize our focus on large underestimations of future payments for two reasons. First, we want to examine economically meaningful biases that can have a substantial effect on the ability to repay debt in the future. Second, due to the bracket format of our survey, a small bias may arise even if the answer is correct. [11] Therefore, to further examine economically meaningful biases, we define *Under1K* as an indicator variable that takes the value of one, if the underestimation is greater than $1000 annually, and zero otherwise.

We find that 38.2% of low-literacy students exhibit considerable underestimation of future payments exceeding $1000 per year, while the respective percentage for high-literacy students is just 18%. In Table 4, we examine this pattern more formally in a regression framework, where the variable *Under1K* serves as our dependent variable. We find that large underestimations of debt payments are significantly and negatively related to the level of financial literacy, even after controlling for a host of student characteristics. The results indicate that financially literate students are 17 percentage points less likely to underestimate student loan payments by more than $1000 annually than their low-literacy peers. Furthermore, all other student characteristics are not significantly related to large underestimations, once we control for the level of financial literacy.

Our main results remain qualitatively unchanged in a series of robustness tests, which we present in Table 5. First, we examine whether the underestimation of loan payments reflects expectations for writing off part of

Table 4. Marginal effects on payment underestimation.

Dep. Variable:	$Under1K = 1$ if $Under < -1000$, 0 otherwise			
	(1)	(2)	(3)	(4)
Literacy	−0.1820***	−0.1787***	−0.1693**	−0.1682**
	[0.0675]	[0.0690]	[0.0697]	[0.0700]
Female		0.0405	0.0455	0.0471
		[0.0659]	[0.0658]	[0.0694]
Minority		−0.0313	−0.0224	−0.0251
		[0.1113]	[0.1114]	[0.1128]
First Gen.			0.0091	0.0082
			[0.0705]	[0.0709]
Honors			−0.0989	−0.0994
			[0.0773]	[0.0781]
Business				−
				−
Engineering				0.0153
				[0.1230]
Other Colleges				0.0134
				[0.0705]

Notes: The table presents average marginal effects from a logistic regression, where the dependent variable (*Under1K*) takes the value one if actual loan payments exceed expected payments by more than $1000 annually ($N = 213$). Expected loan payments are the midpoints of the respective brackets from survey responses. Actual payments are estimated from self-reported loan characteristics as described in Section 3.3. Independent variables include indicator variables of financial literacy, student characteristics (gender, minority, first generation and honors status) and a partition to College groups with Business school majors being the reference group. Engineering includes students in the Colleges of Engineering and Computer Science. Engineering includes students in the Colleges of Engineering and Computer Science. Corresponding standard errors using the Delta method are shown in brackets and significance at the 1%, 5%, and 10% levels is indicated by ***, **, and *, respectively.

the debt in the future. For example, student borrowers that get employed in the public sector are eligible for federal debt forgiveness under the Public Service Loan Forgiveness (PSLF) program. To alleviate this concern, we repeat our analysis by excluding majors, who are more likely to work in the public sector upon graduation; specifically, we exclude students majoring in Education, Public Health, Agriculture and the Humanities. Our results in Table 5 (Panel A) indicate that financially literate students in majors that are mainly employed in the private sector are 15 percentage points less likely to significantly underestimate their loan payments.

Second, we investigate whether the documented underestimation is due to ignoring possible participation in Income Driven Repayment programs (IDRs). Abraham et al. (2018) show that IDRs can be particularly beneficial for low income graduates as they limit loan payments to a certain fraction of income (e.g. 15%), even though participation rates remain relatively low due to poor framing of available programs. To address this concern, we recalculate our dependent variable, limiting actual payments to 15% of the expected starting salary, as per each student's response. In Panel B, the coefficient of financial literacy remains negative and statistically significant, suggesting that our results remain robust even if we assume universal participation in IDRs.

Next, we examine whether the reported bias reflects responses that are based on public information and average statistics rather than the loan characteristics of debt that students report. The U.S. Department of Education publishes annually a College Scorecard that includes summary statistics on enrollment, graduation rates, student debt, and labor outcomes for each institution. For our University, the College Scorecard reports an average for monthly student loan payments that falls in the bracket between $200 and $300 per month. To examine whether students blindly adopt this statistic as a biased signal of their future debt burden, we exclude responses that fall in this particular bracket. Even though our sample reduces considerably, the effect of financial literacy on loan payment underestimation, becomes even larger (−21 perc. points), suggesting that the role of literacy remains significant across expected payment brackets.

Finally, we consider a subsample that includes only students in Business, Engineering and Computer Science. These colleges exhibit the highest financial literacy rates in our sample (Table 2) but also have students with strong numeracy skills and high SAT scores that can proxy for cognitive ability (Lusardi, Mitchell, and Curto 2010). Interestingly, even in these subgroups (e.g. Business majors), we observe significant variation in

3
3

3** 5. Marginal effects on payment underestimation - robustness tests.

	Panel A: Exclude Public Sector			Panel B: IDR Programs		
	(1)	(2)	(3)	(1)	(2)	(3)
Literacy	−0.1610** [0.0724]	−0.1577** [0.0733]	−0.1480** [0.0736]	−0.1554** [0.0670]	−0.1555** [0.0683]	−0.1505** [0.0687]
Female		0.0583 [0.0696]	0.0702 [0.0695]		0.0300 [0.0644]	0.0377 [0.0641]
Minority		−0.0389 [0.1234]	−0.0137 [0.1236]		−0.0504 [0.1107]	−0.0335 [0.1106]
First Gen.			−0.0126 [0.0769]			−0.0398 [0.0698]
Honors			−0.1182 [0.0827]			−0.1150 [0.0769]
N	163			198		

	Panel C: Exclude Scorecard Replies			Panel D: High SAT/Numeracy		
	(1)	(2)	(3)	(1)	(2)	(3)
Literacy	−0.2188** [0.0888]	−0.2219** [0.0895]	−0.2088** [0.0909]	−0.2096** [0.0960]	−0.2103** [0.9961]	−0.1903* [0.0997]
Female		0.0325 [0.0853]	0.0374 [0.0850]		0.0158 [0.0930]	0.0193 [0.0918]
Minority		−0.0392 [0.1300]	−0.0409 [0.1325]		−0.0270 [0.1304]	−0.0193 [0.1288]
First Gen.			0.0040 [0.0903]			0.0676 [0.0936]
Honors			−0.1028 [0.1025]			−0.1771 [0.1112]
N	114			107		

Notes: The table presents average marginal effects from a logistic regression, where the dependent variable (*Under*1K) takes the value 1 if actual loan payments exceed expected payments by more than $1000 annually, for alternative samples and definitions of actual payments. Panel A excludes students in the colleges of Public Health, Education, Agriculture and Humanities. Panel B calculates payment underestimation by limiting actual payments to 15% of expected starting salary. Panel C excludes observations with expected loan payments in the bracket that corresponds to the average monthly payment published at the College Scorecard of the U.S. Department of education for our institution ($200–$300). Panel D includes only students in high SAT/numeracy colleges (Business, Engineering and Computer Science). Corresponding standard errors using the Delta method are shown in brackets and significance at the 1%, 5%, and 10% levels is indicated by ***, **, and *, respectively.

financial literacy (see Figure A2). Since we do not have measures of numeracy or cognitive ability at the individual level, we focus on a sub-group of high numeracy-high SAT score students in an attempt to control for these factors. Our results in Panel D indicate that financial literacy is significantly and negatively related to the probability of underestimating future loan payments, even within a group that admittedly has higher than average numeracy skills and has achieved particularly high SAT scores.

We conclude this section with a discussion on issues that may threaten the validity of our inferences on the relationship between financial literacy and loan payment underestimation. The first is measurement errors. Since we do not observe the actual loan terms, we cannot rule out the possibility that the self-reported loan characteristics are not entirely accurate. In an attempt to address this issue, our survey uses wide-range brackets for loan amounts, maturity and expected payments,[12] and includes an 'I do not know' option for the interest rate question. The large size of the sample and the close correspondence of survey results to average university statistics (e.g. debt amounts, expected payments) and well-established findings in the literature (e.g. more aggressive borrowing by first-generation students, higher interest rates for minorities) increase our confidence that our responses convey reliable information to a large degree. It is important to note that our main inferences remain largely valid, even if the inputs are not entirely accurate, because both loan characteristics and expected payments are self-reported. In other words, here we examine whether the disclosed future payments correspond to the loans described by the respondents, and we find that for low-literacy students this is significantly less likely to be the case.

The second concern is related to selection issues. Our survey design – a paper-and-pencil questionnaire that was circulated through interviews and in classrooms – limits concerns regarding participation, drop-out rates, or response time and methods that are more pronounced in internet surveys. However, we exclude a large portion of students who hold debt but fail to specify their borrowing cost (42%). Selection issues arise from this group to the extent that the low-literacy borrowers underestimate their future payments relatively less than their high-literacy peers. For these omitted observations, we use reported debt amounts, maturities and expected payments to estimate the 'implied' interest rate from these characteristics. We find that among students who do not provide their borrowing cost, low-literacy borrowers have significantly lower 'implied' interest rates, which are more likely to be negative (22%) – a clear indication of payment underestimation – than their high-literacy peers (15%). These results suggest that, under reasonable assumptions, the negative relationship between financial literacy and payment underestimation is also present in the excluded group.

3.4. Financial literacy and expected starting salaries

Our survey also provides information on the expected starting salaries. This data item is particularly important, not only because it reflects borrowers' expectations on future income that can be used to service student loans, but also due to the fact that it contributes as a factor to current debt decisions. That is, regardless of whether these expectations are correct or not, they are relevant, because students are using them to decide how much they can afford to borrow today.

We initially focus on business majors, for whom we have additional information on realized starting salaries. We use the midpoints of the expected starting salary brackets[13] and examine how expectations compare to realized outcomes in the labor market. As shown in Table 6 (Panel A), despite the use of rather broad brackets in our survey, the average expected and actual salaries are very close. Differences in means are very small and insignificant for the business school sample, across genders and within most departments.

This close correspondence between expected and actual salaries is very important for our analysis for a number of reasons. First, it suggests that students are well-informed about job market conditions and that their expectations for future remuneration are correct on average (Betts 1996). Second, it supports the view that our sample is representative of the population and that the variation in responses reflects primarily individual-specific factors other than major and gender. Third, it justifies to some extent the use of survey responses as a proxy for actual outcomes with respect to starting salaries.

Table 6. Expected and actual starting salaries.

	Panel A			Panel B			Panel C (only juniors/seniors)		
	Act. Salary (1)	Exp. Salary (2)	Dif. (3):(1)-(2)	Exp. Salary (Lit = 1) (4)	Exp. Salary (Lit = 0) (5)	Dif. (6):(4)-(5)	Exp. Salary (Lit = 1) (7)	Exp. Salary (Lit = 0) (8)	Dif. (9):(6)-(7)
Total	52,971	52,915	56	57,410	48,596	8,814***	55,556	48,150	7,406**
Gender									
Female	51,014	49,949	1065	54,697	47,538	7,159***	52,857	46,519	6,338***
Male	55,092	55,792	−700	58,798	50,479	8,319***	56,774	50,833	5,941
Department									
Accounting	58,886	54,508	4,377***	57,222	50,600	6,622**	56,667	50,000	6,667*
Finance	57,114	55,231	1,883	59,250	48,800	10,450***	55,357	46,500	8,857**
HTM	42,998	45,455	−2,457	53,333	42,500	10,833***	56,429	42,778	13,651***
Management	55,815	52,222	3,593**	54,333	50,714	3,619	56,111	50,000	6,111*
Marketing	48,164	47,619	545	49,706	46,200	3,506	45,909	47,272	−1,315
OIM	57,897	58,333	−436	61,296	54,524	6,772***	61,607	56,111	5,556*
Sports Mgt	44,427	50,676	−6,249**	55,000	49,483	5,517	57,000	48,636	8,364

Notes: The table presents average starting salaries for business majors (class of 2017) by department and gender (1). Column (2) reports the average expected starting salaries by department and gender from the survey that are further refined to high (4) and low financial literacy (5) students (N = 399). Panel C includes only junior and senior students (N = 207). Differences in means are reported using a simple t-test (column (3)) and a two-sample t-test (columns (6) & (9)) with significance at the 1%, 5%, and 10% levels indicated by ***, **, and *, respectively.

In Panel A (Table 6), we also find evidence of the well-documented gender wage gap (Becker 1957; Loury 1997; Bobbitt-Zeher 2007) not only in realized outcomes but also in expectations. Female business majors expect lower remuneration (−5843$) on average, and indeed receive significantly lower mean starting salaries (−4078$) upon graduation compared to their male peers. The fact that the gender wage gap from our survey responses is comparable to realized outcomes suggests that female students are aware of it and adjust their expectations accordingly.

Next, we examine expected salaries by financial literacy level. In Panel B (Table 6), we find that financially literate students expect significantly higher starting salaries ($57,410) than their low-literacy peers ($48,596). To our best knowledge, this is the first documentation of a 'financial literacy wage gap' in the form of expectations, which is not only large ($8814), but also highly significant.

Table 6 shows that the financial literacy wage gap persists across genders; $7159 for female and $8319 male students. Interestingly, it appears to dominate the gender wage gap in magnitude. As a result, the average literate female student expects a starting salary that is more than $4000 higher than the remuneration of the average low-literacy male. Naturally the question arises whether the well-know gender wage gap can be at least partially explained by financial literacy, as women exhibit a significant deficit in this dimension both in our study and the prior literature.

An alternative explanation for the documented financial literacy wage gap could be that high (low) financial literacy students systematically overestimate (underestimate) their actual future wages for some reason (e.g. confidence). To alleviate this concern, we focus on a subsample that includes only juniors and seniors in Panel C. These students are admittedly better-informed about labor conditions, as they typically have had internships in the past and are about to enter or are currently in the job market. Since our survey took place during the spring semester, seniors are likely to have completed the recruitment process and therefore know their starting salary with certainty.[14] Even though our sample reduces by half, differences across financial literacy groups remain large and significant, suggesting that they reflect differential performance in the job market rather than systematic biases in exceptions.

Another possible explanation for the financial literacy wage gap could be that financially literate students self-select in high-earning majors. However, even within majors, there are significant differences in financial literacy rates (Figure A2) and expected starting salaries between high and low-literacy groups (Table 6). These differences are particularly pronounced in majors with high starting salaries and high level of financial literacy, like accounting, finance and operations information management.

Finally, we find that the financial literacy wage gap is not unique to business majors. In Table A1, we show that there are significant differences in expected started salaries among students with high and low financial literacy at the university level ($7807), for both female ($4336) and male ($7476) students, and within disciplines with a sizable sample.

Collectively our findings support the view that our survey replies are not systematically biased and that they provide information on actual future outcomes. Nevertheless, in the next section, we will take these expectations on starting salaries at face value because they are part of the information set that our respondents use to make financial decisions. That is, reported expectations regarding future income remain important, even if they are not entirely accurate, because they determine the amount of debt borrowers expect to be able to repay post-graduation.

3.5. Financial literacy and ability to pay

Our previous results indicate that low-literacy students are more likely to underestimate student loan payments, while they also expect significantly lower starting salaries. Both of these features affect their payment-to-income ratio (PTI) – also known as debt-to-income or debt service ratio – which is defined as the ratio of required debt payments to disposable income. The PTI ratio affects access to future credit (Johnson and Li 2010), as it serves as an indicator for the ability to service debt in the future, and is used by lenders to access borrowing capacity.[15] In practice, a PTI ratio greater than 10% from non-mortgage debt may result to significant borrowing constraints and future exclusions from the credit market.

To examine the effect of payment underestimation on future creditworthiness, we first estimate the *expected PTI* for each student by scaling expected loan payments with the midpoint of the expected starting salary bracket.[16] Similarly, we calculate the *actual PTI* as the ratio of annual payments, estimated from self-reported loan characteristics, to the expected annual remuneration. It is important to note that we use the term 'actual' to describe the correction in annual payments through the provided loan terms. The 'true' PTI may differ from our 'actual' PTI to the extend that loan terms are not reported accurately or salary expectations do not reflect realized outcomes.[17]

In Figure 3, we plot the histograms of the two variables. Once we correct annual loan payments, the PTIs (Figure 3(b)) of high-literacy students, who are more prone to overestimation, tend to be lower than the expected

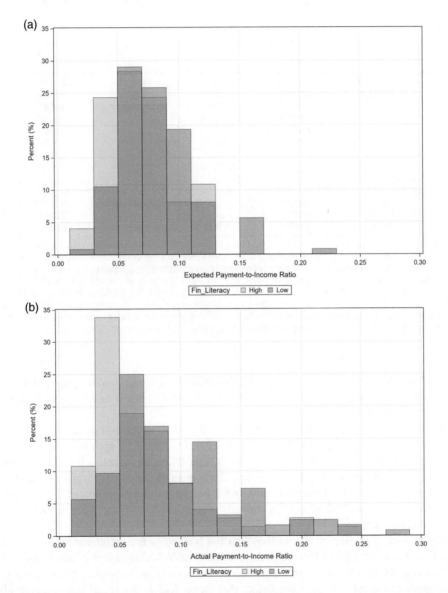

Figure 3. Expected and actual payment-to-income ratios. The figures present the distribution of annual expected (a) and actual (b) payment-to-income (PTI) ratios for students with low (dark gray) and high (light gray) financial literacy ($N = 198$). Expected (actual) PTI is defined as the ratio of expected (actual) annual loan payments to expected salary from survey responses. Expected payments are the bracket midpoints of the survey responses and actual payments are calculated using self-reported loan characteristics as described in Section 3.3. (a) Expected PTI and (b) Actual PTI.

Table 7. Expected & actual payment-to-income ratios.

	Panel A					
	Mean	25th Perc.	Median	75th Perc.	Above 10%	Above 15%
Expected PTI						
Total sample	7.69%	5.45%	7.64%	9.33%	13.13%	4.04%
High Fin.Literacy	6.79%	4.62%	6.67%	8.31%	10.81%	0.00%
Low Fin.Literacy	8.23%	6.46%	7.64%	9.33%	14.52%	6.45%
Actual PTI						
Total sample	8.62%	4.76%	7.15%	11.24%	30.30%	12.63%
High Fin.Literacy	6.78%	4.07%	5.24%	8.47%	14.86%	5.41%
Low Fin.Literacy	9.72%	5.76%	8.52%	12.24%	39.52%	16.95%

	Panel B					
	Expected PTI			Actual PTI		
Dep. Variable:	(1)	(2)	(3)	(4)	(5)	(6)
Literacy	−0.014***	−0.012**	−0.010*	−0.029***	−0.027***	−0.025***
	[0.0042]	[0.0042]	[0.0042]	[0.0073]	[0.0074]	[0.0075]
Female		0.005	0.005		0.004	0.004
		[0.0042]	[0.0042]		[0.0074]	[0.0075]
Minority		0.016	0.016		0.016	0.016
		[0.0089]	[0.0092]		[0.0179]	[0.0173]
Honors			−0.007			−0.014
			[0.0047]			[0.0083]
First Gen.			0.008			0.007
			[0.0048]			[0.0085]
Constant	0.082***	0.077***	0.076***	0.097***	0.093***	0.093***
	[0.0029]	[0.0034]	[0.0039]	[0.0051]	[0.0067]	[0.0078]
R^2	0.050	0.078	0.104	0.068	0.077	0.092

Notes: Panel A presents summary statistics (mean, median and the 25th & 75th percentile) of expected and actual payment-to-income (PTI) ratios. Expected PTI is defined as ratio of expected annual payments to expected salary from survey responses (midpoints). Actual PTI is defined as the ratio of annual student loan payments, estimated from self-reported loan characteristics as described in Section 3.3 to expected starting salary. The last two columns report the percentage of population with PTIs above the 10% and 15% threshold, respectively. Panel B presents results from OLS regressions, where the dependent variable is the expected PTI (columns (1)–(3)), defined as the ratio of expected payments over expected salary and actual PTI (columns (4)–(6)), defined as the estimated payments from loan characteristics over expected salary ($N = 198$). Independent variables include indicators for gender, minority, honors and first generation status. Corresponding robust standard errors are shown in brackets and significance at the 1%, 5%, and 10% levels is indicated by ***, **, and *, respectively.

(Figure 3(a)), and largely concentrated around the 5% threshold. By contrast, low-literacy students, who tend to underestimate future payments, are exposed to significantly higher PTI ratios than the ones expected, which in some cases exceed 25% of their future income.

Table 7 presents summary statistics for the PTI ratios of the total sample and of subgroups by literacy level. The difference between average expected (7.69%) and actual (8.62%) PTIs appears to be entirely driven by low-literacy students, who underestimate their actual PTIs by 18.2%, on average. By contrast, financially literate respondents appear to remain largely unaffected. The impact of the payment underestimation on PTIs is significant for the majority of low-literacy students, but it becomes more pronounced in the right side of the distribution; for instance, at the 75th percentile, students with a deficit in financial literacy are exposed to PTIs over 12% (instead of the expected 9.33%).

Another way to assess the effect of the underestimation bias on future creditworthiness is by focusing on the sample that exceeds a certain PTI threshold. According to Table 7, almost 40% of low-literacy students will graduate with a PTI greater than 10%, when just 15% expects to cross this threshold. Similarly, while only 6.45% of low-literacy students expect to exceed the higher threshold of 15%, the actual percentage is almost triple (17%).

In Panel B, we examine the relationship between financial literacy and PTIs more formally in a regression framework. High-literacy students have lower expected PTIs, however the relationship weakens once we include socio-economic characteristics (columns (1) –(3)). By contrast, once we correct for the miscalculation of future payments the effect of financial literacy on PTI burdens becomes larger, highly significant and persists even when we control for student characteristics (columns (4) –(6)). Collectively, our findings indicate that, due to the failure to accurately estimate future debt burdens, low-literacy students are exposed to significant, adverse, and – more importantly – unexpected shocks on their PTI ratios.

Such unexpected shocks have long been recognized by the the household finance literature as a crucial factor of household default. Typically, these shocks originate from the denominator, due to adverse life-events (e.g. unemployment, illness/death, divorce) that cause a sharp decline on disposable income, which in turn impairs borrowers' ability to continue servicing debt (Sullivan, Warren, and Lawrence Westbrook 2001; Elul et al. 2010; Morrison et al. 2013). In our case, however, we have a similar adverse, unexpected change in the PTI that originates from the numerator, due to the underestimation of future loan payments.

Our finding that low-literacy students significantly underestimate their future loan burden provides a plausible explanation for the increased student default rates in recent years. Looney and Yannelis (2015) attribute this trend to non-traditional borrowers - students who typically come from disadvantaged backgrounds and attend for-profit institutions. The fact that these borrowers exhibit higher default rates, despite having lower PTIs than traditional student borrowers, seems puzzling. However, if non-traditional borrowers also exhibit low financial literacy levels and systematically underestimate their future loan payments, then the adverse, unexpected shocks in post-graduation debt burdens could play an important role in explaining the high delinquency rates we observe.

4. Conclusion

Our study provides compelling, new evidence on the alarmingly low level of financial literacy for undergraduates, particularly among female, minority, and first-generation students. More importantly, we show that students with a deficit in financial literacy are more likely to significantly underestimate future loan payments, which can impair their ability to repay student debt through exposure to unexpectedly higher PTI upon graduation.

Furthermore, we document for the first time a 'financial literacy wage gap', as low-literacy students systematically expect lower starting salaries that their high-literacy peers. Given the importance of early labor market decisions on career paths and lifetime income, the effect of financial literacy on starting salaries can shed light on other documented relationships of literacy with long-term outcomes, including wealth accumulation (Lusardi, Michaud, and Mitchell 2017) and retirement planning (Lusardi and Mitchell 2007).

Finally, our results pose new, intriguing questions for future research. We show that the 'financial literacy wage gap' dominates the gender wage gap in magnitude, and we document a significant deficit in financial literacy for female students. Collectively, these findings suggest that financial literacy can play an important role in explaining gender differences in remuneration, at least in early career stages. Also, the fact that low-literacy students are exposed to unexpected, adverse shocks in the payment-to-income ratios post-graduation provides an alternative explanation for the rising default rates in student loans, which Looney and Yannelis (2015) attribute to non-traditional borrowers. It is for future research to determine whether the higher default rate of these borrowers, despite their lower debt burden, is due to lack of financial literacy, poor labor outcomes, or both.

Notes

1. It is important to note that if students also underestimate the amount of debt they hold, as suggested by Akers and Chingos (2014), then our estimates are by definition conservative and they constitute lower bounds of the actual underestimation.
2. This is the essence of the 'double-trigger' default models, where negative equity is a necessary condition, and a 'life event' ((e.g. job loss, death/illness, divorce) which results in inability to continue servicing debt is a sufficient condition for mortgage default (see Riddiough and Elliott Thompson 1991; Vandell 1995; Elul et al. 2010).
3. A deficit in financial literacy has been associated with a number of inefficient financial outcomes, including debt problems (Lusardi and Tufano 2015) and increased propensity to default (Gerardi, Goette, and Meier 2013; Urban et al. 2014), suboptimal investment strategies (Van Rooij, Lusardi, and Alessie 2011; Hastings and Tejeda-Ashton 2008) and use of credit instruments (Lusardi and Tufano 2015), lower rates of wealth accumulation (Lusardi, Michaud, and Mitchell 2017) and less efficient wealth management (Hilgert, Hogarth, and Beverly 2003) and retirement planning (Lusardi and Mitchell 2007, 2008).

4. We find that students that respond 'I do not know' in questions 1 and 2 are less likely to answer the remaining two questions correctly and more likely to answer them both incorrectly. However, this pattern is reversed in question 3. Interestingly, the first two questions involve computations, while the third relies purely on financial knowledge. It is plausible that students with strong numerical skills but no financial knowledge, prefer to abstain from answering the last question.
5. It is important to note that our minority student sample size is limited (71), but it is representative of the university's enrollment.
6. The financial literacy level of Asian students is not due to the influx of international students; in fact, these students exhibit similar literacy rates (38.9%) to Asian in-state students.
7. We note that these figures are self-reported. Akers and Chingos (2014) find that undergraduates underestimate the amount of student debt they hold, in which case, our estimates can be seen as a lower bound of the actual underestimation of student loan payments.
8. Among students who report their interest rate, about 30% of minority and 23% of first-generation students borrow at the high-cost brackets (6–12%), when the respective percentage for the entire sample is just 17%.
9. In a recent study, Anderson, Conzelmann, and Austin Lacy (2018) find that student borrowers exhibit higher student debt literacy than non-borrowers. We do not find any corroborating evidence here, however we should point out that we are looking at financial literacy from the standard 'Big-Three' questions, while Anderson, Conzelmann, and Austin Lacy (2018) define debt literacy as the level of awareness on government provisions related to student debt repayment.
10. Our results on the relative underestimation of actual payments of high and low-literacy students remain robust, if we include these observations.
11. For instance, due to the 'in-bracket' range of the expected payment question and the use of midpoints, a bias of up to $600 may appear, even if the student responds correctly. This is the case, for example, if the actual monthly payment is $200 and the respondent marks $200–300 per month as the expected amount to pay. Due to the use of the midpoint $250, the student will appear to underestimate her payments by $600 annually.
12. This creates a different type of measurement error that we attempt to address by focusing on large payment underestimations (see endnote 11).
13. For the extreme brackets 'less than $30,000' and 'more than $70,000', we use $25,000 and $75,000, respectively.
14. Differences in expected remuneration between low and high financial literacy seniors remain large, but the power of the sample is low, due to the reduced sample size.
15. Widely used cutoff points are 36% for total debt (Quercia, McCarthy, and Wachter 2003) and 28% for just housing expenses (front-end ratio). Federal Housing Administration limits for qualifying mortgages are 31% and 43%, for front-end and back-end ratios, respectively.
16. It should be noted that our estimates are conservative as expected salaries refer to before-taxes income.
17. See Sections 3.3 and 3.4 for a discussion on these concerns.

Acknowledgements

The authors are thankful to Stefanos Kechagias, Georgios Panos, Carly Urban, George Tziros, two anonymous referees, and seminar participants at the IFIN 2018 (University of Glasgow), the FMA 2019 Annual meeting, the HEFW 2019 Summit, and Virginia Tech for helpful comments and suggestions. The authors also wish to thank student respondents who participated in our survey. All errors are our own.

Disclosure statement

No potential conflict of interest was reported by the authors.

References

Abraham, Katharine G., Emel Filiz-Ozbay, Erkut Y. Ozbay, and Lesley J. Turner. 2018. "Framing Effects, Earnings Expectations, and the Design of Student Loan Repayment Schemes." Technical Report. National Bureau of Economic Research.

Agarwal, Sumit, John C. Driscoll, Xavier Gabaix, and David Laibson. 2009. "The Age of Reason: Financial Decisions Over the Life Cycle and Implications for Regulation." *Brookings Papers on Economic Activity* 2009 (2): 51–117.

Akers, Elizabeth J., and Matthew M. Chingos. 2014. *Are College Students Borrowing Blindly*. Brookings: Brown Center on Education Policy.

Anderson, Drew M., Johnathan G. Conzelmann, and T. Austin Lacy. 2018, July. The State of Financial Knowledge in College: New Evidence from a National Survey. Working Paper.

Becker, Gary S. 1957. *The Economics of Discrimination*. Chicago: University of Chicago press.

Behrman, Jere R., Olivia S. Mitchell, Cindy Soo, and David Bravo. 2010. "Financial Literacy, Schooling, and Wealth Accumulation." Working Paper. National Bureau of Economic Research.

Bernheim, Douglas D. 1998. "Financial Illiteracy, Education, and Retirement Saving." Working Paper. Wharton School Pension Research Council, University of Pennsylvania.

Betts, Julian R. 1996. "What Do Students Know About Wages? Evidence From a Survey of Undergraduates." *Journal of Human Resources* 31 (1): 27–56.

Bobbitt-Zeher, Donna. 2007. "The Gender Income Gap and the Role of Education." *Sociology of Education* 80 (1): 1–22.

Bucher-Koenen, Tabea, Annamaria Lusardi, Rob Alessie, and Maarten Van Rooij. 2017. "How Financially Literate are Women? An Overview and New Insights." *Journal of Consumer Affairs* 51 (2): 255–283.

Chen, Haiyang, and Ronald P. Volpe. 2002. "Gender Differences in Personal Financial Literacy among College Students." *Financial Services Review* 11 (3): 289–307.

Christelis, Dimitris, Tullio Jappelli, and Mario Padula. 2010. "Cognitive Abilities and Portfolio Choice." *European Economic Review* 54 (1): 18–38.

Elul, Ronel, Nicholas S. Souleles, Souphala Chomsisengphet, Dennis Glennon, and Robert Hunt. 2010. "What 'Triggers' Mortgage Default?" *The American Economic Review* 100 (2): 490–494.

Fernandes, Daniel, John G. Lynch, Jr., and Richard G. Netemeyer. 2014. "Financial Literacy, Financial Education, and Downstream Financial Behaviors." *Management Science* 60 (8): 1861–1883.

Fonseca, Raquel, Kathleen J. Mullen, Gema Zamarro, and Julie Zissimopoulos. 2012. "What Explains the Gender Gap in Financial Literacy? The Role of Household Decision Making." *Journal of Consumer Affairs* 46 (1): 90–106.

Ford, Matthew W., and Daniel W. Kent. 2010. "Gender Differences in Student Financial Market Attitudes and Awareness: An Exploratory Study." *Journal of Education for Business* 85 (1): 7–12.

Gerardi, Kristopher, Lorenz Goette, and Stephan Meier. 2013. "Numerical Ability Predicts Mortgage Default." *Proceedings of the National Academy of Sciences* 110 (28): 11267–11271.

Hastings, Justine S., Brigitte C. Madrian, and William L. Skimmyhorn. 2013. "Financial Literacy, Financial Education, and Economic Outcomes." *Annual Review of Economics* 5 (1): 347–373.

Hastings, Justine S., and Lydia Tejeda-Ashton. 2008. "Financial Literacy, Information, and Demand Elasticity: Survey and Experimental Evidence from Mexico." Working Paper. National Bureau of Economic Research.

Hilgert, Marianne A., Jeanne M. Hogarth, and Sondra G. Beverly. 2003. "Household Financial Management: The Connection Between Knowledge and Behavior." *Federal Reserve Bulletin* 89: 309.

Johnson, Kathleen W., and Geng Li. 2010. "The Debt-Payment-to-Income Ratio As An Indicator of Borrowing Constraints: Evidence From Two Household Surveys." *Journal of Money, Credit and Banking* 42 (7): 1373–1390.

Klapper, Leora, Annamaria Lusardi, and Georgios A. Panos. 2013. "Financial Literacy and Its Consequences: Evidence from Russia During the Financial Crisis." *Journal of Banking & Finance* 37 (10): 3904–3923.

Klapper, Leora, and Georgios A. Panos. 2011. "Financial Literacy and Retirement Planning: The Russian Case." *Journal of Pension Economics & Finance* 10 (4): 599–618.

Lee, Jason, and John A. Mueller. 2014. "Student Loan Debt Literacy: A Comparison of First-Generation and Continuing-Generation College Students." *Journal of College Student Development* 55 (7): 714–719.

Looney, Adam, and Constantine Yannelis. 2015. "A Crisis in Student Loans?: How Changes in the Characteristics of Borrowers and in the Institutions they Attended Contributed to Rising Loan Defaults." *Brookings Papers on Economic Activity* 2015 (2): 1–89.

Loury, Linda Datcher. 1997. "The Gender Earnings Gap Among College-Educated Workers." *ILR Review* 50 (4): 580–593.

Lusardi, Annamaria, Pierre-Carl Michaud, and Olivia S. Mitchell. 2017. "Optimal Financial Knowledge and Wealth Inequality." *Journal of Political Economy* 125 (2): 431–477.

Lusardi, Annamaria, and Olivia S. Mitchell. 2007. "Baby Boomer Retirement Security: The Roles of Planning, Financial Literacy, and Housing Wealth." *Journal of Monetary Economics* 54 (1): 205–224.

Lusardi, Annamaria, and Olivia S. Mitchell. 2008. "Planning and Financial Literacy: How Do Women Fare?" *American Economic Review* 98 (2): 413–17.

Lusardi, Annamaria, and Olivia S. Mitchell. 2011. "Financial Literacy Around the World: An Overview." *Journal of Pension Economics and Finance* 10 (4): 497–508.

Lusardi, Annamaria, and Olivia S. Mitchell. 2014. "The Economic Importance of Financial Literacy: Theory and Evidence." *Journal of Economic Literature* 52 (1): 5–44.

Lusardi, Annamaria, Olivia S. Mitchell, and Vilsa Curto. 2010. "Financial Literacy among the Young." *Journal of Consumer Affairs* 44 (2): 358–380.

Lusardi, Annamaria, and Peter Tufano. 2015. "Debt Literacy, Financial Experiences, and Overindebtedness." *Journal of Pension Economics & Finance* 14 (4): 332–368.

Mahdavi, Mahnaz, and Nicholas J. Horton. 2014. "Financial Knowledge Among Educated Women: Room for Improvement." *Journal of Consumer Affairs* 48 (2): 403–417.

Moore, Danna L. 2003. *Survey of Financial Literacy in Washington State: Knowledge, Behavior, Attitudes, and Experiences.* Olympia, WA: Washington State Department of Financial Institutions.

Morrison, Edward, Arpit Gupta, Lenora Olson, Lawrence Cook, and Heather Keenan. 2013. "Health and Financial Fragility: Evidence from Car Crashes and Consumer Bankruptcy." *University of Chicago Coase-Sandor Institute for Law & Economics Research Paper* 655: 13–81.

Mueller, Holger M., and Constantine Yannelis.. 2018. "The Rise in Student Loan Defaults." *Journal of Financial Economics* 131 (1): 1–19.

Quercia, Roberto G., George W. McCarthy, and Susan M. Wachter. 2003. "The Impacts of Affordable Lending Efforts on Homeownership Rates." *Journal of Housing Economics* 12 (1): 29–59.

Riddiough, Timothy J., and Howard Elliott Thompson. 1991. "Equilibrium Mortgage Default Pricing with Non-Optimal Borrower Behavior." PhD Thesis. Madison: University of Wisconsin.

Shim, Soyeon, Bonnie L. Barber, Noel A. Card, Jing Jian Xiao, and Joyce Serido. 2010. "Financial Socialization of First-year College Students: The Roles of Parents, Work, and Education." *Journal of Youth and Adolescence* 39 (12): 1457–1470.

Stango, Victor, and Jonathan Zinman. 2009. "Exponential Growth Bias and Household Finance." *The Journal of Finance* 64 (6): 2807–2849.

Sullivan, Teresa A., Elizabeth Warren, and Jay Lawrence Westbrook. 2001. *The Fragile Middle Class: Americans in Debt*. Yale University Press.

Urban, Carly, Maximilian Schmeiser, J. Michael Collins, and Alexandra Brown. 2014. State Financial Education Mandates: It's all in the Implementation. *Financial Industry Regulatory Authority*

Vandell, Kerry D. 1995. "How Ruthless is Mortgage Default? A Review and Synthesis of the Evidence." *Journal of Housing Research* 6 (2): 245–264.

Van Rooij, Maarten, Annamaria Lusardi, and Rob Alessie. 2011. "Financial Literacy and Stock Market Participation." *Journal of Financial Economics* 101 (2): 449–472.

Appendix

Table A1. Expected starting salaries across colleges.

	Exp. Salary (Lit= 1)	Exp. Salary (Lit= 0)	Dif.	N
Total	54,167	46,360	7,807***	1,033
Gender				
Female	49,218	44,882	4,336***	571
Male	56,954	49,478	7,476***	462
College				
Business School	57,410	48,596	8,814***	398
Comp. Sciences	66,786	61,875	4,911*	44
Engineering	60,143	60,714	−571	70
Humanities	37,308	38,684	−1,377	51
Natural Sciences	48,478	43,528	4,951***	232
Public Health	45,000	43,611	1,389	85
Social Sciences	46,702	41,557	5,145**	108
Other	40,000	47,432	−7,432	45

Notes: The table reports average expected starting salaries for students of high (*Lit* = 1) and low (*Lit* = 0) financial literacy. The last two columns report differences in means with a two-sample t-test (6), where significance at the 1%, 5%, and 10% levels indicated by ***, **, and *, respectively, and the sample size of each group.

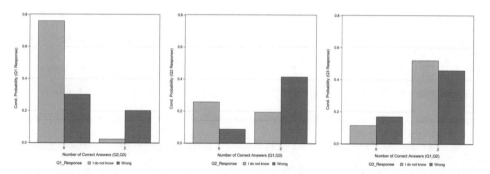

Figure A1. Performance of wrong respondents by question. The figure presents the conditional probability of responding incorrectly (0) or correctly (2) on both remaining questions, given that the response on the first (a), second (b) or third question (c) is 'I don't know' (light gray) or wrong (dark gray). (a) Q1: Wrong/I don't know, (b) Q2: Wrong/I don't know and (c) Q3: Wrong/I don't know.

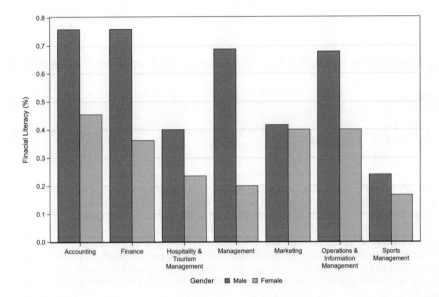

Figure A2. Financial literacy of business school students by major and gender. The figure presents the percentage of financially literate male and female students in each business major ($N = 399$). Survey participants are defined as financially literate if they have responded correctly to all three financial literacy questions.

Keep your customer knowledgeable: financial advisors as educators

Milena Migliavacca

ABSTRACT

Educational programmes aimed at increasing financial literacy are typically scarcely effective or have relatively quick 'decay' periods. In this paper, I provide evidence that financial advisors are an effective way to increase investors' financial awareness. I check this relationship using three measures of financial literacy: basic, advanced and overall; and also test different typologies of advisors. Results indicate that financial advisors have a significant educational role; in particular, the presence of independent financial advisors tends to increase the 'advanced' financial literacy of their clients. The study has potentially important policy implications, as it provides robust evidence that investors' financial literacy can be increased in a gradual and stable way that does not directly affect public funds.

1. Introduction

Financial literacy is widely recognised among scholars, practitioners and policy-makers as an essential determinant of individual financial awareness and the overall stability of the financial system (OECD 2016). The relevant literature (among others, Lusardi and Mitchell 2008a, 2011b; Gathergood and Weber 2014) provides extensive evidence of widespread financial illiteracy thus suggesting the need for more effective educational programmes (Bucher-Koenen and Ziegelmeyer 2013; Stolper and Walter 2017). The lack of convergence on financial literacy's determinants, though, might undermine these initiatives at their root. A rich body of literature provides heterogeneous insights on the possible determinants of financial literacy (Lusardi 2008; Lusardi and Mitchell 2008b; Monticone 2010; Van Rooij, Lusardi, and Alessie 2011, 2012). Moreover, even the literature focused on the effectiveness of financial education programmes on financial literacy provides conflicting evidence.[1] A stream of contributions provides evidence that *ad hoc* educational programmes are scarcely effective or have a quick decay period (e.g. Lusardi 2003; Mandell 2008; Willis 2008; Fernandes, Lynch, and Netemeyer 2014; Brown et al. 2016; Carpena et al. 2017), in contrast with other studies (e.g. Bruhn et al. 2016; Skimmyhorn 2016; Berg and Zia 2017), which document a positive influence of financial education interventions, not always necessarily on financial literacy *per se*, but on virtuous behaviours (e.g. delinquency rate, debt balances, probability of facing adverse legal actions).

The consistently mixed findings on the impact of financial education programmes determined a recent shift in the literature towards studies designed to assess which approaches make such interventions more effective. This stream of literature (e.g. Locke and Latham 2002; Drexler, Fischer, and Schoar 2014; Berg and Zia 2017; Cai and Song 2017) points out alternatives to standard training (e.g. multi-random games, *ad hoc* soap operas, etc.) that proved to be more effective in terms of outcome on both theoretical knowledge and financial behaviours. Some of these approaches also entailed setting precise goals and dates, individualised counselling, teaching financial management rules of thumb, which are financial management tools frequently used by financial advisors.

To the best of our knowledge, though, fewer empirical studies and with mixed results (e.g. Hackethal, Haliassos, and Jappelli 2012; Hung and Yoong 2013; Calcagno and Monticone 2015; Kramer 2016) consider that, at least in principle, the presence of a financial advisor may directly improve his/her clients' financial literacy. The role of advisors within the global financial industry is gaining importance, particularly in the light of the regulatory harmonisation introduced by the Directive 2014/65/EU (MiFID II) in the European Union. In this regard, Italy stands out among other European countries for the particularly high growth in recent years in both the number of certified financial planners and the assets under their management.[2] In view of the growing complexity of financial services and products, technical guidance by qualified financial advisors may prove to be a precious advantage for retail investors to avoid poor decisions. On the other hand, investors are typically only partially informed about the optimal solution to their financial needs (Bolton, Freixas, and Shapiro 2007); this reasonable assumption allows to posit the conflict of interest financial advisors face while selling financial products. These conflicts may be moderated by the reputational cost of misselling and/or misinforming (Inderst and Ottaviani 2009). It is a fact that financial advisors are considered valuable information providers, not only in Italy (Beltratti 2008; Calcagno and Monticone 2015; Calcagno, Giofré, and Urzì-Brancati 2017), but also in other European countries (Lusardi and Mitchell 2011b; Van Rooij, Lusardi, and Alessie 2011) and in the United States (Survey of Consumer Finances, 2004). Coherently with this view, Bolton, Freixas, and Shapiro (2007) point out that 'competition among specialized financial intermediaries can lead to full credible information disclosure, even in the presence of only small reputation costs'.

Financial institutions, particularly private banking institutions, whose clients have often relations with more than one intermediary, face considerable reputational costs for giving misleading advice. Therefore, being more transparent becomes a strategic tool for relationship marketing (Crawford and Sobel 1982; Grönroos 1996; Heffernan et al. 2008; Loewenstein, Cain, and Sah 2011; Assogestioni 2018); financial advisors may be willing to disclose information to differentiate their advisory service and relax price competition. On the other hand, however, some studies (e.g. Lacko and Pappalardo 2004; Cain, Loewenstein, and Moore 2005; Anagol, Cole, and Sarkar 2017) maintain that disclosure can backfire because of information overload or perverse incentive on the advisors' side.

However, acquiring new customers is particularly costly (Roberts-Lombard et al. 2014); it is commonly recognised among both scholars and practitioners that an improvement in the relationship with already acquired customers leads to greater profitability than would do an equivalent effort aimed at attracting new customers (Rust and Zahorik 1993; Barnes and Howlett 1998). These factors, coupled with the recent entry into force of Directive 2014/65/EU (MiFID II), placed the role of financial advisors under the spotlight in the European Union. MiFID II has harmonised the different typologies of financial advisors, their incentives and the level of information to be provided to their clients across Europe. Some of the changes introduced by the directive (e.g. higher transparency on costs and inducements paid to investment firms or financial advisors) are going to affect significantly the strategic importance of a close and stable relationship between advisors and clients (Stolper and Walter 2018). In this changing context, an analysis of financial advisors' educational role, exploited as a strategic tool for the retention of clients, is particularly timely. Thanks to this institutional harmonisation, the results concerning the Italian case can be more directly generalised, at least across Europe.

The main objective of this study is to evaluate whether and to what extent the presence of a financial advisor improves the financial literacy of his/her clients; this phenomenon will be referred to as the 'educational role' of financial advisors. Using a unique dataset, derived from a survey created in collaboration with the European Financial Planning Association (€FPA) and four prominent Italian banks, I make the following contributions to the literature. First, this paper provides original empirical evidence of the educational role of independent advisors enriching the stream of existing literature on the determinants of financial literacy. Moreover, for the first time, to the best of my knowledge, this study deepens the analysis by testing for the different typologies of financial advisors in Europe, highlighting their different incentives and potential degrees of moral hazard. Furthermore, the respondents' financial knowledge is measured using three different financial literacy indexes, computed applying an innovative weighting technique (see section 4.1). Finally, to establish whether the presence of financial advisors plays a role in their clients' degree of financial literacy, I adopt both a static and a dynamic perspective, which cross-sectionally takes into account the length of the relationship between advisors and clients. In this way, I assess the effect of the presence of a financial advisor on her clients' financial literacy over time, virtually regardless of the potential sample selection bias stemming from the complementarity theory.

Ultimately, this approach allows overcoming the bipartition between substitutability and complementarity theories, which characterised the extant literature so far.

To preview the results, the lower the selling incentive of financial advisors, the higher their educational role. In particular, the presence of independent consultants seems to increase in a statistically significant and sizable way the advanced financial literacy of their clients. The other main drivers of the respondents' financial literacy are their willingness to learn (i.e. the personal interest towards economics and finance) and a degree in economics, besides their wealth and being parent and male, as already established in the relevant literature (e.g. Lusardi and Mitchell 2008b). Within the sub-sample of respondents with a financial advisor, the results concerning the length of their relationship suggest that the advisors' educational role tends to grow over time; this result partially alleviates the concerns towards endogeneity, which are directly addressed by a set of causality tests as well.

The paper provides empirical evidence that the presence of financial advisors might constitute a suitable way to convey constant, gradual financial training to investors, which increases their financial literacy, overcoming the quick decay period that traditional one-spot finance courses typically face (e.g. Fernandes, Lynch, and Netemeyer 2014). So, from a policy perspective, this study draws attention to a potentially effective and efficient way to increase investors' financial awareness that does not directly require public resources, as the targeted educational interventions put in place thus far.

The remainder of the paper proceeds as follows: section 2 presents a brief literature review, section 3 focuses on the survey and the sample. The key variables and the empirical methodology used are presented in section 4, whereas section 5 shows the main results and provides some robustness and causality checks. Section 6 concludes.

2. Literature review

The existing empirical literature on the role of financial advisors towards their clients' financial literacy has been particularly heterogeneous, so far.

The conflicting findings in the extant literature may be due to several causes, for instance the national specificity of most studies, the different scales used to measure financial literacy and the different granularity applied to the classification of financial advisors. The national character of the studies[3] hinders the results' comparability, with the exception of a couple of meaningful efforts (e.g. S&P Global FinLit Survey; Global Findex database, OECD/INFE), in which some questions measuring financial literacy[4] are added to national surveys. The different ways in which financial literacy is determined is another relevant factor to be considered; financial literacy is either self-assessed or measured using a quiz that can span from three to over thirty items (Chen and Volpe 1998; Volpe, Kotel, and Chen 2002; Lusardi and Mitchell 2007a, 2007b, 2008a; Servon and Kaestner 2008; Van Rooij, Lusardi, and Alessie 2011). Finally, the heterogeneous results may be partly attributable to the fact that previous studies do not distinguish among the different typologies of advisors, despite this category including professionals with deeply different selling incentives, target clients, remuneration schemes and contractual frameworks (e.g. Calcagno and Monticone (2015) only consider bank-clerks as financial advisors that, as discussed in Section 4.2, may be a limitation).

There are at least three sub-streams within the extant literature that specifically deals with financial advisory and financial literacy.

2.1. Financial advisory and financial literacy – no significant relation

The relevant literature provides conflicting evidence on the relationship between financial advisory and financial literacy. Kramer (2016), for instance, focuses on the demand for and impact of financial advice and finds no relation between objective measures of financial literacy and the presence of a financial advisor; whereas investors with higher confidence in their financial knowledge prove to be less likely to rely on a financial advisor. These results imply that a relation between investors' financial literacy and their propensity to rely on an advisor is not strictly necessary. However, evidence also suggests that people, who tend to overestimate their financial knowledge, are less likely to seek advice, coherently with Kruger and Dunning (1999). According to this theory, it is the investors' confidence towards their own degree of financial literacy, rather than their actual financial knowledge, to drive the decision of relying on financial advisors.

2.2. Financial advisory and financial literacy – the complementarity theory

Another sub-stream of studies provides evidence that financial literacy and financial advisory are complements (Van Rooij, Lusardi, and Alessie 2011; Lusardi and Mitchell 2011b; Collins 2012; Bucher-Koenen and Koenen 2015; Calcagno and Monticone 2015). According to the complementarity theory, investors with high financial literacy are more likely to rely on a financial advisor because of the higher opportunity cost of their time. These individuals are also more aware of the information asymmetry between clients and advisors that may lead to moral hazard and therefore they may induce their consultants to disclose better information (Calcagno and Monticone 2015). In accordance to the complementarity view, but from a perspective coherent with Kramer (2016), other authors (e.g. Kruger and Dunning 1999) provide evidence that less financially-literate people tend to be overconfident about their level of knowledge and therefore they do not seek advice.

2.3. Financial advisory and financial literacy – the substitutability theory

The substitutability theory stems from the latent information asymmetry between advisors and clients. When financial advisors have superior information and financial knowledge, they can improve returns and ensure better diversification among less sophisticated investors, compensating for their poor financial knowledge (Georgarakos and Inderst 2011; Kramer 2012; Hung and Yoong 2013). Moreover, less literate people, who experience higher barriers to access and process financial information, may be less aware of the advisors' selling incentives and therefore rely more heavily on them. Coherently with this view, Stolper (2017) finds that more knowledgeable investors are less likely to follow their advisors' recommendation, because they anticipate the agency conflicts.

2.4. Financial advisory and financial literacy – a comprehensive approach

To establish whether the presence of financial advisors plays a role in their clients' degree of financial literacy, I adopt both a static perspective, which compares the financial literacy levels of individuals who have and who do not have a financial advisor and a more dynamic one that cross-sectionally takes into account the length of their relationship. In this way, I assess the effect of the presence of a financial advisor on her clients' financial literacy over time, virtually regardless of the potential sample selection bias stemming from the complementarity theory. This approach goes beyond the rigid tripartition aforementioned, allowing substitutability and complementarity theories to coexist (see section 5.2 for further discussion).

Drawing on the streams of research aforementioned (e.g. Hackethal, Haliassos, and Jappelli 2012; Calcagno and Monticone 2015; Kramer 2016; Stolper 2017), this study tests whether different typologies of financial advisors exert an educational role towards their clients, to the benefit of their financial literacy; in particular it posits the following hypotheses:

H1: The presence of a financial advisor increases their clients' financial literacy

H2: The more independent the advisor is, the stronger their educational role

3. Data and summary statistics

3.1. The survey

I draw on a unique dataset that includes bank-account holders, both retail and private banking clients, covering all age groups. In order to have a broad geographical coverage and to take into account clients supported by independent advisors, non-independent advisors and bank clerks, the questionnaire was distributed through the European Financial Planning Association (€FPA)[5] and to four of the ten main Italian banks, according to the Mediobanca Leading Italian Companies report (2014).

The banks involved in the project and 3,427 Italian financial advisors registered in €fpa were contacted and briefed on the project; in turn, they sent the link to the questionnaire to their clients or delivered them a hard copy to be filled in and returned in a sealed envelope.[6] The questionnaire was administered mainly on-line, using QuestionPro[TM], as a survey tool and data collection platform, only fully filled in questionnaires were retained (around 23%). A stringent privacy policy statement ensures the respondents' anonymity. A report with specific profiling of the Italian account-holders population, their characteristics and the main drivers identified in order to improve one's financial literacy was offered as a compensation to participants for taking part in the project at the end of the data collection. The sections of the survey used for the purposes of this paper are part of a more comprehensive questionnaire on households, financial literacy and financial behaviour. The first section of the survey collects analytical information on the demographic characteristics of the interviewees (gender, age, schooling, type of degree if any, marital status, number of children if any, region of residence) and their wealth (income, financial and real estate assets). The central part of the survey assesses the respondents' financial literacy using Van Rooij, Lusardi, and Alessie (2011)'s scale, which allows to differentiate between basic and advanced financial literacy. In another part of the survey respondents are asked whether they rely on a financial advisor and, if yes, which typology, how long they have been clients of the current financial firm and of the current advisor. The survey was first tested in a pilot study to refine the instruments and check for comprehension among the respondents.

3.2. Sample and summary statistics

The final sample consists of 552 retail and private banking clients, who fully filled in the questionnaire between September 2014 and February 2015. As the data used in the paper is proprietary, there is no database that perfectly matches the sample; the most suitable comparisons can be made with the following datasets: Overall Italian households (as in, CONSOB annual reports (2015 and 2016), the Bank of Italy Survey on Household Income and Wealth (2015) and the Quinquennial Istat Multipurpose Survey on Households), Italian UC-Survey (as in Calcagno and Monticone 2015) and investors and retail bank clients (as in Kramer 2016).

Table 1 provides an overview of some key statistics for the sample, which is representative of Italian bank account holders. In line with the reference contributions (Van Rooij, Lusardi, and Alessie 2011; Calcagno and Monticone 2015; Kramer 2016), slightly more than half of the sample (54.71%) has a financial advisor and more than 60% of respondents are middle-aged married men.[7] The median income is €32,500, similar to €33,000 reported in UCS (Calcagno and Monticone 2015) and the largest share of respondents report a higher vocational or university degree.

Finally, the geographical breakdown and the occupational statuses reported by the respondents are in line with the Unicredit Customers' Survey (UCS) that has been used by Calcagno and Monticone 2015.

3.3. Financial literacy scores and demographic characteristics

Table 2 reports the differences in terms of average financial literacy scores across demographic variables, Welch and Bonferroni[8] significance tests are used. In line with the most relevant literature, the descriptive statistics show relatively low financial literacy scores among women and respondents with lower education attainment (Lusardi and Mitchell 2008b; Monticone 2010; Van Rooij, Lusardi, and Alessie 2011; Kramer 2016). Over and above the education attainment, among graduates there seems to be a stark difference between the financial literacy level of interviewees with a degree in economics or finance and those with another degree, which confirms that financial knowledge is not widespread even among people with a superior educational attainment (Cavezzali, Gardenal, and Rigoni 2015). As in Monticone (2010), Italian respondents living in north-west Italy display the highest level of financial literacy and their wealth also seems to be a significant determinant of financial literacy scores. Most importantly, the presence of a financial advisor, and in particular of an independent financial advisor, appears to have a significant impact on the clients' literacy, regardless of the index with which it is measured.

Table 1. Summary statistics.

	Mean %	Median	SD
Financial Advisor	54.71	1	0.50
Gender (men percentage)	66.30	1	0.47
Age	43	49	1.34
Married	63.22	1	0.48
Children (nr. of)	1.05	1	1.06
Primary/Secondary ed.	1.45	0	0.12
High School	46.38	0	0.50
College/Above	52.17	1	0.50
Employee	29.71	0	0.46
Manager	16.49	0	0.37
Self-Employed	34.42	0	0.48
Pensioner	8.15	0	0.27
Outside Labour Market	11.23	0	0.32
Income (thousands €s)	36.45	32.50	1.12
North	46.20	0	0.49
Centre	20.65	0	0.41
South and Isles	33.15	0	0.47
Obs. N	*552*		

Notes: The table shows the distribution of the sample ($N = 552$) across demographic characteristics.

Table 2. Financial literacy scores by socio-demographic characteristics.

		Basic F.L.	Advanced F.L.	Overall F.L.
Independent	No	2.89	7.58	10.47
Financial Advisor	Yes	3.15	8.93	12.09
	T-Statistic	−1.83*	−3.17***	−3.13***
Financial Advisor	No	2.61	6.79	9.4
	Yes	3.17	8.43	11.59
	T-Statistic	−6.56***	−6.78***	−7.37***
Gender	Woman	2.74	6.96	9.70
	Man	3.01	8.05	11.06
	T-Statistic	−2.87***	−4.15***	−4.16***
Degree	Non-economic subject	2.74	7.11	9.86
	Economics/finance	3.40	9.31	12.72
	T-Statistic	−7.86***	−9.74***	−10.45***
Area of Residence	North-west	3.02[a]	8.23[b]	11.25[c]
	North-east	2.88	7.35	10.24
	Centre	2.65	6.63	9.29
	South	2.92	7.66	10.57

Table 2 reports the financial literacy scores out of a total of 4 for basic financial literacy, 11 for advanced financial literacy and 15 for overall financial literacy questions. Welch's T-statistics and significance levels are reported; when three or more categories are compared, Bonferroni's correction for mean differences in multiple comparisons is carried out.
*statistical significance at 10% level, **statistical significance at 5% level, ***statistical significance at 1%.
[a]Only the difference between north-west and central Italy is statistically significant. [b]Only the differences between north-west and north-east and north-west and center Italy are statistically significant. [c]Only the differences between north-west and north-east and north-west and center Italy are statistically significant.

4. Key variables and methodology

4.1. Dependent variable: financial literacy

The respondents' financial literacy is the dependent variable in all the empirical models tested; based on Van Rooij, Lusardi, and Alessie (2011), three different typologies of financial literacy – basic, advanced and overall – have been employed (please see the Appendix for the exact wording of the questions). In the previous literature, the financial literacy scores obtained by the respondents are usually either unweighted or weighted by the average percentage of correct answers (e.g. Monticone 2010); in a departure from the literature, I use the average

Table 3. Distribution of financial literacy scores.

	Basic F.L.	Advanced F.L.	Overall F.L.
None correct	1.09%	0.91%	0.54%
At least ¼	98.91%	94.01%	97.11%
At least ½	89.68%	76.62%	78.43%
At least ¾	66.85%	57.06%	55.79%
All correct	36.05%	21.50%	14.13%
Mean correct #	2.9/4	7.68/11	10.60/15
N	552	552	552

The first column of the table reports the percentage of respondents that answered correctly to 0, 1, 2, 3 and 4 questions out of the four measuring basic financial literacy. The second column of the table reports the percentage of respondents that answered correctly to 0, 3, 6, 8 and 11 questions out of the eleven measuring advanced financial literacy. Finally, the last column reports the percentage of respondents that answered correctly to 0, 4, 8, 11 and 15 questions out of the fifteen measuring overall financial literacy. The details of the questions are reported in the Appendix.

percentage of *wrong* answers as weights to compute the basic and advanced financial literacy indexes (BFL and AFL). This technique allows the correct answers to less-commonly-known topics to be weighted more significantly than the correct answers to broadly-known topics. The two indexes, in turn, are linearly combined in an overall financial literacy index (OFL). Finally, the scores are converted in quartiles, for a better comparability across indexes. The empirical results are not particularly sensitive to the weighting technique (see Section 5.3). For the sake of comparability with previous studies, Table 3 provides the scores distribution of *un-weighted* basic, advanced and overall financial literacy indexes.

On average, respondents answered 72.75% of basic financial literacy questions correctly, the percentage decreases to 69% for advanced financial literacy, so overall approximately 70% of the questions assessing financial literacy were answered correctly. These scores are broadly similar to those found in the relevant literature, which adopted the same scales (such as, for example, Van Rooij, Lusardi, and Alessie 2011; Kramer 2016).

4.2. Explanatory variable: Financial Advisory

The extant theoretical and empirical literature shows that financial advice might be biased, particularly when advisors act as mere sellers of financial products (Hackethal, Haliassos, and Jappelli 2012). Coherently with this view, the present study differentiates among different typologies of advisors in an attempt to disentangle their different selling incentives. Devoting time to transfer part of their knowledge to customers is a particularly time-consuming activity, but it is no doubt effective for advisors if they aim to keep a long-term, solid relationship with their clients, especially during a financial downturn (Crawford and Sobel 1982; Marsden, Zick, and Mayer 2011). Moreover, the risk that clients dismiss their advisor and operate autonomously in the financial markets once they reach a satisfying degree of financial knowledge does not represent a concrete threat for financial advisors, as the theoretical financial proficiency helps clients to knowingly understand their advisors' decisions, but does not allow them to independently manage their savings.

For the purposes of this study, and in line with MiFID II, I consider two typologies of consultants: independent (IFA) and non-independent (NIFA) financial advisors. As previously mentioned, I also consider bank clerks, sometimes referred to as restricted financial advisors (RFA), which are professionals not enrolled in the Register of financial advisors held by the Italian financial advisors' supervisor (OCF) and not authorized to conduct door-to-door selling. This tripartition allows disentangling the different selling incentives and moral hazard risk deriving from different remuneration schemes (Shapira and Venezia 2001; Bolton, Freixas, and Shapiro 2007). To this regard, restricted advisors have the strongest 'selling incentive' (Inderst and Ottaviani 2009; Hackethal, Haliassos, and Jappelli 2012). On the other hand, independent consultant are individuals or small/medium-sized companies that are not allowed to receive inducements or retrocession fees and are required to operate in open architecture.[9] To ensure the anonymity of the respondents, I was not allowed to match the respondents with their financial advisors, and therefore I am unable to control for the advisors' financial literacy. To overcome this limitation, only €FPA (European Financial Planning Association) certified advisors have been involved in the project. In order to get the €FPA certifications, a financial advisor needs to pass a test, whose difficulty exceeds by far the one of the questions in the survey.[10] All the financial advisors (both independent and non-independent) involved in the study have therefore a homogeneous, certified minimum level of financial knowledge that is higher than the one required to be considered financially-literate by the Van Rooij et al. scale and that can potentially be transferred to their clients.

4.3. Control variables

Over and above the presence of a financial advisor, the financial literacy measures have been linked to demographic (gender, age, number of children, education, job, area of residence), behavioural (willingness to learn) and financial features (income) of the respondents, used as control variables (see the Appendix for the exact list of control variables, their definitions and correlations). The *willingness to learn* (Elmer 2004) of the respondents is a particularly meaningful characteristic that goes beyond the simple control, but is rarely used in this stream of literature. It is a self-assessed behavioural variable that measures the respondents' personal interest towards financial and economic topics; along with the presence of a financial advisor, this variable seems to explain a significant portion of the respondents' financial literacy (see Section 5).

4.4. Methodology

Table 2 shows the positive and significant relationship between the presence of a financial advisor and the degree of basic, advanced and overall financial literacy displayed by the interviewees. In order to provide empirical support to this qualitative evidence and in accordance to the most recent literature (e.g. Lusardi 2008; Monticone 2010; Calcagno and Monticone 2015; Kramer 2016), a multivariate analysis has been performed. Different specifications of ordered probit models, as exemplified in Equation (1), are employed in order to test hypotheses 1 and 2.

$$Pr(yi = 1) = 1 - \Phi[\beta X_i - u_1]$$
$$Pr(yi = 2) = \Phi[\beta X_i - u_1] - \Phi[\beta X_i - u_2]$$
$$Pr(yi = n) = \Phi[\beta X_i - u_{n-1}] \tag{1}$$

$Pr(y_i = j)$ represents the probability of each financial literacy indexes to fall in the jth percentile of right answers. $\Phi[\cdot]$ is the joint cumulative distribution of the bivariate normal and $u_1, u_2, \ldots, u_n$ are the cutpoints that divide up the probability distribution. In order to be able to interpret the coefficients, the marginal effects of the explanatory variables (see Equation (2)) have been assessed.

$$\Delta Pr(y_i = j) = \Phi[\beta_0 + \beta_1 + \beta_2 X_{2i} + \ldots \beta_k X_{ki}] - \Phi[\beta_0 + \beta_2 X_{2i} \ldots \beta_k X_{ki}] \tag{2}$$

The first specification of the model (see Table 4), tests hypothesis 1 assessing the marginal effect of the presence of financial advisors (both independent and non-independent) on basic (1), advanced (2) and overall (3) financial literacy. Robustness checks of this model have been run (see section 5.3) using OLS models and un-weighted financial literacy indexes, obtaining qualitatively the same results. In order to rule out any possibility for the results to be affected by reverse causality, the baseline model's variables of interest have been instrumented and the model estimated by the Generalized Method of Moments (GMM) (see section 5.4).

The second specification (see Table 5) tests hypothesis 2; it is focused on the sub-sample of respondents supported by a financial advisor and allows differentiating between independent and non-independent consultants. The models are overall significant and correctly specified, according to the ReSET test; the errors reported are clustered at the respondent-level.

The results are strongly consistent among the specifications and provide support that the financial advisors' educational role is positively and strongly significant across all three measures of financial literacy. In particular, independent financial advisors seem to strongly increase the advanced financial literacy of their clients.

Table 4. Financial advisors and financial literacy.

	Basic financial literacy	Advanced financial literacy	Overall financial literacy
	(1)	(2)	(3)
Independent FA	0.195***	0.249***	0.251***
	(0.073)	(0.052)	(0.052)
Non-independent FA	0.140***	0.128***	0.117***
	(0.037)	(0.025)	(0.025)
Gender	0.066*	0.050*	0.031
	(0.057)	(0.026)	(0.026)
Age	−0.014	−0.010	−0.026
	(0.081)	(0.059)	(0.059)
Age squared	0.005	0.006	0.008
	(0.010)	(0.008)	(0.008)
Children	0.025	0.033***	0.041***
	(0.018)	(0.012)	(0.123)
Eco. Degree	0.152***	0.155***	0.167***
	(0.043)	(0.029)	(0.029)
Willingness to learn	0.087***	0.097***	0.098***
	(0.016)	(0.011)	(0.012)
Income	0.012	0.021	0.022*
	(0.018)	(0.013)	(0.013)
Profession controls	Yes	Yes	Yes
Geographical controls	Yes	Yes	Yes
N Obs	552	552	552
Pseudo R^2	0.1060	0.1689	0.1707
ReSET test	Yes	Yes	Yes

Note: The table shows estimates of ordered probit models (marginal effects on conditional probabilities are reported). The financial literacy indexes are weighed by the average number of wrong answers to each questions. Standard errors reported in brackets are clustered at respondent-level. The ReSET test does not reject the null hypothesis for correct model specification.
*statistical significance at 10% level, **statistical significance at 5% level, ***statistical significance at 1%.

5. Results

5.1. Baseline model: financial advisory and financial literacy

Table 4 reports the results of the baseline model that, according to the first hypothesis, assesses the effect of the presence of a financial advisor on basic (column 1), advanced (column 2) and overall (columns 3) financial literacy.

Compared to bank clerks, the presence of a financial advisor seems to increase significantly the conditional probability of being in the highest quartile of the financial literacy distribution. In particular, being assisted by a financial advisor, compared to a bank clerk, increases the chance of being in the top quartile by 19.5, 24.9 and 25.1 percentage points for basic, advanced and overall financial literacy, respectively. These results seem to strongly support hypothesis 1.

Another novel finding in this context is related to the interest in financial and economics subjects; the respondents' willingness to learn proves to have a positive and significant impact on all of the three financial literacy indexes as well.

The demographic characteristics take overall the expected signs. Consistently with the extant literature (Lusardi and Mitchell 2008b; Van Rooij, Lusardi, and Alessie 2011), being male appears to have a higher level of overall financial literacy. Neither the age[11], nor the marital status appear to influence the degree of financial literacy, but interestingly enough the presence of children does, increasing by around 3% the probability of ending up in the highest quartile of the financial literacy scores distribution. The result may have its roots in the 'teachable moments theory' (Havighurst 1953), according to which it is possible or at least more likely to learn a particular topic or task only in specific moments, when either the individual becomes intellectually ready

Table 5. Independent vs non-independent independent financial advisors.

	Basic financial literacy	Advanced financial literacy	Overall financial literacy
	(1)	(2)	(3)
Independent FA	0.048	0.144**	0.158**
	(0.079)	(0.066)	(0.065)
Relationship length	0.020	0.059***	0.063***
	(0.026)	(0.021)	(0.020)
Gender	0.078	0.090**	0.075*
	(0.059)	(0.045)	(0.044)
Age	0.030	0.088	0.071
	(0.098)	(0.085)	(0.084)
Age squared	0.002	−0.012	−0.010
	(0.024)	(0.021)	(0.021)
Children	0.047**	0.039**	0.052***
	(0.024)	(0.019)	(0.019)
Eco. Degree	0.207***	0.135***	0.174***
	(0.062)	(0.049)	(0.048)
Willingness to learn	0.053**	0.069***	0.067***
	(0.024)	(0.019)	(0.020)
Income	0.012	0.029	0.035*
	(0.026)	(0.020)	(0.020)
Profession controls	Yes	Yes	Yes
Geographical controls	Yes	Yes	Yes
N Obs	302	302	302
Pseudo R^2	0.0816	0.1185	0.1302
ReSET test	Yes	Yes	Yes

Note: The table shows estimates of ordered probit models (marginal effects on conditional probabilities are reported). The financial literacy indexes are weighed by the average number of wrong answers to each questions. Standard errors reported in brackets are clustered at respondent-level. The ReSET test does not reject the null hypothesis for correct model specification.
*statistical significance at 10% level, **statistical significance at 5% level, ***statistical significance at 1%.

or the environment requires such capability. Role changes, such as, becoming a parent, may constitute one of those 'teachable moments' that spur an individual to increase their financial awareness, because they perceive their responsibility for conscious financial management to increase. Typically, this is related to saving plans for the children's education (e.g. Lusardi 2008; Lusardi and Mitchell 2011c; Van Rooij, Lusardi, and Alessie 2012). A degree in economics or finance seems to be the real education-related determinant (the coefficient is sizable, always positive and highly significant across the three specifications). The debate on the direction of the causality between personal wealth and financial literacy is still open (Peress 2003; Monticone 2010; Lusardi and Mitchell 2011a; Jappelli and Padula 2013) and the results in Table 4 can only marginally contribute to it, as the impact of the variable Income is statistically significant and positive only for overall financial literacy.

Finally, the geographical controls do not seem to have a strong impact on the degree of financial literacy, consistently with the most recent literature dealing with an Italian sample (Calcagno and Monticone 2015), as well as the five dummy variables that control for the respondents' profession (see Table A2 in the Appendix for the variables construction)[12].

5.2. Different typologies of financial advisors

According to MiFID II, the heterogeneous array of financial consultants has been categorised within the EU into independent (IFA) and non-independent financial advisors (NIFA), so the analysis proceeds focusing on the subsample of respondents with a financial advisor, differentiating between IFAs and NIFAs.

According to the results shown in Table 5, IFAs seem to exert their educational role in a more effective way than NIFAs, particularly with regard to advanced financial literacy. This result provides support to hypothesis

Table 6. Descriptive evidence: age and presence of independent financial advisors.

	Mean presence of IFA	18–34	35–44	45–54	55–64
18–34	0.0239				
35–44	0.0826	0.05818			
45–54	0.0765	0.05214	−0.00604		
55–64	0.0645	0.04013	−0.01805	−0.01204	
> 65	0.243	0.21951***	0.16133***	0.16737***	−0.17939***

Table 6 reports the average presence of independent financial advisors among different age ranges. Bonferroni's test for mean difference is carried out and the F-statistics, with their significance are reported. *statistical significance at 10% level, **statistical significance at 5% level, ***statistical significance at 1% level.

2: the fee-only remuneration scheme of IFAs may provide them with higher incentives to build long-lasting relationships with their clients; as they need to demonstrate that their advice is of added value and worth the fee. Therefore, it is in the advisor's own interest to make sure that her clients fully understand the products they are investing in, the related risks and some portfolio management fundamentals. The educational role of financial advisors is likely to prompt a virtuous circle between client and advisor: with an acceptable degree of financial literacy, the client can knowingly understand and accept the investment choices jointly taken with their advisor (Stolper 2017) and the solidity of their professional relationship would therefore self-reinforce. The positive and significant impact of a degree in economics or finance and the respondents' willingness to learn, together with the number of children, is also confirmed in this second model.

The most significant result in Table 5, though, is the positive, relatively large and significant impact of the length of the relationship between advisor and client. It not only suggests that the longer the client cooperates with her advisor, the more she benefits from their educational role, but it may also be interpreted as an indirect evidence of the causal relationship between advisory and literacy, overcoming the distinction between complementarity and substitutability theories. Even if, according to the complementarity theory, financially knowledgeable clients are more likely to opt for a financial advisor (as in Calcagno and Monticone 2015), still their advanced financial literacy improves over time. Moreover, it is particularly meaningful that the relationship length is not significant for basic financial literacy for which the presence of an IFA does not exert a stronger educational role compared to NIFAs. According to this result, the higher the independency of the advisors, the more technical the information they are going to transfer to their clients is.

The AFL index, in fact, measures the respondents' knowledge regarding financial notions as the definitions of bonds and stocks, the role of the financial markets and secondary markets, the relation between risk, return and interest and bonds' prices, basics of portfolio management and diversification (see the Appendix for the exact wording of the questions).

Referring to BFL, the meaningful difference seems to be made by the presence of an advisor compared to a bank clerk, because the results in Table 4 shows that both IFAs and NIFAs improve their clients' BFL and AFL indexes. In more detail, one can infer from the results in Table 5 that IFAs improve their clients' advanced financial literacy more than their basic one. The BFL index includes very basic concepts that possibly individuals deciding to entrust their savings to such a technical typology of advisors have already had the chance to familiarise with. To support this last consideration, the descriptive statistics in Table 6 show that the presence of an IFA among young people is quite low, as expected, and relatively high among middle age and elderly people, in line with West (2012). It is, then, reasonable to assume that other entities, different from financial advisors, are expected to lay the foundation of investors' basic financial knowledge. Schools and universities, for instance, are more likely to convey the basic financial skills on which people can build more refined levels of financial literacy over the years. IFAs take practical financial choices, talk to their customers about financial asset classes and deal with the basics of portfolio management but do not focus on rather theoretical notions, such as the difference among interest compounding regimes or temporal discount analysis, measured by the BFL index.

5.3. Robustness checks

Table 7 provides two robustness checks of the baseline model, where the dependent variables are the three financial literacy *un-weighted* indexes; columns 1–3 report an ordered probit model, as in the baseline model

Table 7. Robustness checks – the presence of independent financial advisors.

	Basic financial literacy	Advanced financial literacy	Overall financial literacy	Basic financial literacy	Advanced financial literacy	Overall financial literacy
	(1)	(2)	(3)	(4)	(5)	(6)
Independent FA	0.176***	0.199***	0.145***	0.480***	1.938***	2.418***
	(0.063)	(0.052)	(0.038)	(0.162)	(0.477)	(0.583)
Non-independent FA	0.151***	0.095***	0.084***	1.395***	0.989***	1.385***
	(0.033)	(0.023)	(0.018)	(0.089)	(0.227)	(0.280)
Gender	0.006	0.031	0.022	0.015	0.335	0.351
	(0.034)	(0.023)	(0.017)	(0.091)	(0.234)	(0.288)
Age	−0.017	−0.007	−0.033	−0.084	−0.420	−0.503
	(0.058)	(0.040)	(0.039)	(0.194)	(0.492)	(0.619)
Age squared	0.015	0.011	0.007	0.020	0.093	0.113
	(0.015)	(0.011)	(0.005)	(0.025)	(0.065)	(0.081)
Children	0.031**	0.032***	0.026***	0.078**	0.302***	0.379***
	(0.016)	(0.011)	(0.008)	(0.040)	(0.101)	(0.125)
Eco. Degree	0.172***	0.148***	0.120***	0.410***	0.135***	1.785***
	(0.038)	(0.025)	(0.020)	(0.094)	(0.236)	(0.294)
Willingness to learn	0.008***	0.093***	0.048***	0.223***	0.924***	1.147***
	(0.014)	(0.011)	(0.009)	(0.039)	(0.101)	(0.125)
Income	0.015	0.021*	0.015*	0.031	0.176	0.207
	(0.016)	(0.011)	(0.008)	(0.039)	(0.111)	(0.127)
Profession controls	Yes	Yes	Yes	Yes	Yes	Yes
Geographical controls	Yes	Yes	Yes	Yes	Yes	Yes
N. Obs	552	552	552	552	552	552
(pseudo) R^2	0.1042	0.1085	0.1025	0.2437	0.3755	0.3951

Note: The dependent variables in the models are unweighted; columns 1–3 shows ordered probit models, whereas columns 4–6 report OLS models. The standard errors in brackets are clustered at the respondent-level.
*statistical significance at 10% level, **statistical significance at 5% level, ***statistical significance at 1%.

previously presented, whereas columns 4–6 show the results of an OLS model. The results are qualitatively comparable to those presented in Table 4.

5.4. Causality test

The significant impact of the presence of a financial advisor on her clients' financial literacy shown in section 5.1 and 5.2 does not necessarily provide evidence of the direction of the causality between the variables of interest. Coherently with the approach often used in the relevant literature (e.g. Calcagno and Monticone 2015), in order to rule out any possibility for the results to be affected by reverse causality, I resort to the Generalized Method of Moments (GMM). As this model implies a linear relation between dependent and independent variables, the model presented in Table 7, columns 4–6 has been tested. The GMM presented in Table 8 uses the same vector of control variables employed in the baseline model, the variables IFA and NIFA are jointly considered in the dummy variable *Financial advisor* (FA). Both the measures of financial literacy and the variable FA have been instrumented with two exogenous variables each and regressed against each other.

The variable FA has been instrumented with the variables *Distrust in Banking System* and *Fidelity* (see the Appendix for the variables' definition). The two variables are highly and significantly correlated with the presence of a financial advisor, who seems to be perceived as a substitute to restricted advisors and the traditional banking system in general. In contrast, the second instrument indicates that the client had followed the advisor when she moved from a financial institution to another one, as it takes the value of one if the customer has a longer relationship with the advisor, than with the financial institution the consultant currently works for. On the other hand, the measures of financial literacy are instrumented with the respondent's education and a dummy variable that detects the capacity of the respondents to correctly order according to their rating U.S.A, the European Union, Italy and Developing Countries.[13] The education attainment and the ability to assess the correct rating order proxies the respondents' financial knowledge without necessarily correlating with the decision of

Table 8. Causality direction between the presence of a financial advisor and financial literacy.

	First stage dependent: BFL	Second stage dependent: FA	First stage dependent: AFL	Second stage dependent: FA	First stage dependent: OFL	Second stage dependent: FA
FA	1.257*		5.326***		12.008***	
	(0.658)		(1.985)		(4.460)	
Financial literacy		−0.296		−0.132		−0.059
		(0.239)		(0.156)		(0.062)
Controls	Yes	Yes	Yes	Yes	Yes	Yes
N Obs	552	552	552	552	552	552
Hansen J	0.1620	0.0007	2.401	0.4734	1.811	0.325
Hansen J p value	0.6873	0.9789	0.1212	0.4914	0.1783	0.5686

Linear model estimated by GMM. Regressors not reported are the same as in the base-line model (Table 4). Standard errors in brackets are robust to heteroskedasticity. The Hansen'J test for over-identification does not reject the null hypothesis of instruments' validity. *statistical significance at 10% level, **statistical significance at 5% level, ***statistical significance at 1% level.

relying on a financial advisor. The goodness of these instruments is supported by the results of the Hansen's test that does not reject the null hypothesis of instrument validity (see Table 8).

Table 8 shows that, after controlling for the string of variables used in the baseline model, the hypothesis of reverse causality between the presence of a financial advisor and her clients' financial literacy degree is rejected.

6. Conclusive remarks

Using a unique survey carried out on Italian investors, this study provides original evidence on the effect of the presence of financial advisors (independent and non-independent) on the financial literacy degree of their clients. The empirical findings show that the degree of financial literacy is positively and significantly influenced by the presence of a financial advisor and they further suggest that the lower the conflict of interest the advisor faces while choosing between in-house or whole-market financial products, the stronger her educational role becomes. This dynamic finds its rationale in the different incentives the three categories of professional considered (IFAs, NIFAs and RAs) have to build a long-lasting relationship with their clients. The compensation structure varies sensibly among them on a continuum from fee-only of IFAs consultants to flat salary for RAs; reasonably, the more related the wage of the professional is to the customer satisfaction, the stronger will be the incentive to cultivate a solid, transparent, long-lasting relationship.

The analysis carried out in this study is relevant because it addresses timely policy issues and contributes to the literature on the determinants of financial literacy. The world-wide shared concerns about the poor financial literacy of investors might be less worrying if investors' financial literacy can be improved by professional advice, coming from qualified financial advisors. These practitioners may be a proper connecting link between financial information providers and investors; given the constant presence of financial advisors in their clients' life, the meetings between advisors and clients might provide a suitable way to convey constant, gradual financial training to investors. This relation might help to avoid the quick decay period traditional one-spot finance courses face (see e.g. Lusardi 2003; Willis 2008; Fernandes, Lynch, and Netemeyer 2014). According to Fernandes, Lynch, and Netemeyer (2014): '*Even large interventions with many hours of instruction have negligible effects on behaviour 20 months from the time of intervention*'.

From the practitioners' point of view, the findings can be exploited as an important tool of relational marketing (Grönroos 1995) and this awareness may enhance the customer/advisor relationship quality and may also have a positive impact on customer retention. Given their expertise and financial knowledge, financial advisors may become themselves a suitable target for more structured financial education programmes, which would in turn reach the investors *via* the educational role exerted by their advisors. The results also suggest that by reducing the conflicts of interest between intermediaries and investors, financial advisors could spontaneously exert an educational role towards their clients.

Finally, from a policy point of view, encouraging the presence of qualified financial advisory may result in lower expenses for financial education programmes targeted towards retail investors, whose efficacy and decay period have proven to be disappointing.

Notes

1. For a thorough review of the related literature, see Bernheim, DellaVigna, and Laibson (2019).
2. Worldwide, AuM increased by 8% in 2014, the European growth is 1 percentage point higher; this growth is driven in particular by the net inflows in Spain and Italy (BCG Global Asset Management, 2015). According to Assogestioni (Assogestioni, Annual report, 2015), the AuM of the Italian industry stand at €1.584 trillion +20% from 2014, +70% over previous 30 months.
3. Examples include the Italian Survey on Household Income and Wealth; Unicredit Customers' Survey (UCS); the US Health and Retirement Study (HRS); the De Nederlandsche Bank (DNB) Household Survey; Australia and New Zeeland Banking Group; SLPS survey in Japan; ANZ/Retirement Commission Survey of Financial Literacy in New Zealand; Swedish Financial Supervisory Consumer Survey; Beckmann and Stix 2015 in the CEECs; Stolper 2017 in Germany.
4. In these studies, financial literacy is proxied by four questions on Numeracy, Compound Interest, Inflation and Risk.
5. €fpa (or EFPA) is the largest certification body for financial planners and financial advisors in Europe and was the first European financial standards association created for the purpose of increasing professionalism in the European financial services sector.
6. This second method is used in order to avoid the bias found in many Internet surveys, which include only computer users (Stanton and Rogelberg 2001; Volpe, Kotel, and Chen 2002). Around 14% of the overall respondents filled in a hard copy of the questionnaire and delivered it.
7. Most of the respondents are men and married in the reference works by Calcagno and Monticone (2015) and Kramer (2016), as well. Moreover, the Istat annual household surveys shows that men are predominantly heads of household and financial decision makers in around 70% of cases (Istat 2011).
8. Because of the samples sizes' inequality, we use a Welch's Test to perform an ANOVA analysis, Bonferroni correction is used when multiple comparisons are required.
9. 'Open Architecture' is the option offered by an investment firm to let its clients invest not only in that firm's financial products, but also in competing firms' financial products. Open architecture ensures that clients can satisfy their financial needs and that the investment firm can act in each client's best interests by recommending the financial products best suited to that client, even if they aren't proprietary products. Open architecture helps investment firms to avoid the conflict of interest that would exist if the firm only recommended its own products.
10. The Core Competence Framework certified by the EFA and EFP qualifications can be found at the link below. https://www.efpa.es/documento/European-Investment-Practitioner-EIP.pdf.
11. The categorical variable used to control for the respondents' age (see Appendix) does not seem to exert a significant role in explaining their financial literacy; however being over fifty-five year old increases the probability of scoring the highest quartile of the overall financial literacy distribution by approximately 8%; the results are available by the author upon request.
12. The results concerning the variables included in the geographical and professional controls are available by the author upon request.
13. The Developing Countries mentioned in the survey are the MINTs: Mexico, Indonesia, Nigeria and Turkey.

Acknowledgement

This paper was made possible by the cooperation of Assoreti, which contributed to the funding of this research project. Moreover, I thank €FPA, the four anonymous banks and all the advisors which took part in the project and which provided me with the necessary support and data. I also thank the participants in a department seminar at Essex Business School, in Wolpertinger Conference, 2016 and in the 3rd International Workshop of the IFIN for the thoughtful comments.

Disclosure statement

No potential conflict of interest was reported by the author.

References

Anagol, S., S. Cole, and S. Sarkar. 2017. "Understanding the Advice of Commissions-motivated Agents: Evidence from the Indian Life Insurance Market." *Review of Economics and Statistics* 99 (1): 1–15.
Assogestioni. 2018. Annual Report, 2015.
Bank of Italy. 2015. Survey on Household Income and Wealth (SHIW), 2015.
Barnes, J. G., and D. M. Howlett. 1998. "Predictors of Equity in Relationships between Financial Services Providers and Retail Customers." *International Journal of Bank Marketing* 16 (1): 15–23.
Beckmann, E., and H. Stix. 2015. "Foreign Currency Borrowing and Knowledge about Exchange Rate Risk." *Journal of Economic Behavior & Organization* 112: 1–16.
Beltratti, A. 2008. *Crisi Globale, Scelte Individuali—XXVI Rapporto BNL/Centro Einaudi sul Risparmio e sui Risparmiatori in Italia.* Rome, Italy: BNL Edizioni, Guerini e Associati.
Berg, G., and B. Zia. 2017. "Harnessing Emotional Connections to Improve Financial Decisions: Evaluating the Impact of Financial Education in Mainstream Media." *Journal of the European Economic Association* 15 (5): 1025–1055.
Bernheim, B. D., S. DellaVigna, and D. Laibson. 2019. *Handbook of Behavioral Economics-Foundations and Applications 2.* Elsevier.

Bolton, P., X. Freixas, and J. Shapiro. 2007. "Conflicts of Interest, Information Provision, and Competition in the Financial Services Industry." *Journal of Financial Economics* 85 (2): 297–330.

Brown, M., J. Grigsby, W. Van Der Klaauw, J. Wen, and B. Zafar. 2016. "Financial Education and the Debt Behavior of the Young." *The Review of Financial Studies* 29 (9): 2490–2522.

Bruhn, M., L. D. S. Leão, A. Legovini, R. Marchetti, and B. Zia. 2016. "The Impact of High School Financial Education: Evidence from a Large-scale Evaluation in Brazil." *American Economic Journal: Applied Economics* 8 (4): 256–295.

Bucher-Koenen, T., and J. Koenen. 2015. "Do Seemingly Smarter Consumers Get Better Advice?" MEA Discussion Paper.

Bucher-Koenen, T., and M. Ziegelmeyer. 2013. "Once Burned, Twice shy? Financial Literacy and Wealth Losses during the Financial Crisis." *Review of Finance* 18 (6): 2215–2246.

Cai, J., and C. Song. 2017. "Do Disaster Experience and Knowledge Affect Insurance Take-up Decisions?" *Journal of Development Economics* 124 (C): 83–94.

Cain, D. M., G. Loewenstein, and D. A. Moore. 2005. "The Dirt on Coming Clean: Perverse Effects of Disclosing Conflicts of Interest." *The Journal of Legal Studies* 34 (1): 1–25.

Calcagno, R., M. Giofré, and M. C. Urzì-Brancati. 2017. "To Trust is Good, But to Control is Better: How Investors Discipline Financial Advisors' Activity." *Journal of Economic Behavior & Organization* 140: 287–316.

Calcagno, R., and C. Monticone. 2015. "Financial Literacy and the Demand for Financial Advice." *Journal of Banking & Finance* 50: 363–380.

Carpena, F., S. Cole, J. Shapiro, and B. Zia. 2017. "The ABCs of Financial Education: Experimental Evidence on Attitudes, Behavior, and Cognitive Biases." *Management Science* 65 (1): 346–369.

Cavezzali, E., G. Gardenal, and U. Rigoni. 2015. "Risk Taking Behaviour and Diversification Strategies: Do Financial Literacy and Financial Education Play a Role?" *Journal of Financial Management, Markets and Institutions* 3 (1): 121–156.

Chen, H., and R. P. Volpe. 1998. "An Analysis of Personal Financial Literacy among College Students." *Financial Services Review* 7 (2): 107–128.

Collins, J. M. 2012. "Financial Advice: A Substitute for Financial Literacy?" *Financial Services Review* 21 (4): 307.

CONSOB (Commissione Nazionale per le Società e la Borsa). 2015. *Annual Report 2015*. Rome. http://www.consob.it/documents/10194/0/Relazione.

CONSOB (Commissione Nazionale per le Società e la Borsa). 2016. *Annual Report 2016*. Rome. http://www.consob.it/documents/46180/46181/rel2015.pdf/43ade8dd-edf1-443a-8ed8-fd7f72275584.

Crawford, V. P., and J. Sobel. 1982. "Strategic Information Transmission." *Econometrica: Journal of the Econometric Society* 50, 1431–1451.

Drexler, A., G. Fischer, and A. Schoar. 2014. "Keeping it Simple: Financial Literacy and Rules of Thumb." *American Economic Journal: Applied Economics* 6 (2): 1–31.

Elmer, D. 2004. "Willingness to Learn." *Texas Speech Communication Journal* 29 (1): 11–24.

Fernandes, D., J. G. Lynch, Jr., and R. G. Netemeyer. 2014. "Financial Literacy, Financial Education, and Downstream Financial Behaviors." *Management Science* 60 (8): 1861–1883.

Gathergood, J., and J. Weber. 2014. "Self-control, Financial Literacy & the Co-holding Puzzle." *Journal of Economic Behavior & Organization* 107: 455–469.

Georgarakos, D., and R. Inderst. 2011. "Financial Advice and Stock Market Participation." ECB Working Paper.

Grönroos, C. 1995. "Relationship Marketing: The Strategy Continuum." *Journal of the Academy of Marketing Science* 23 (4): 252–254.

Grönroos, C. 1996. "Relationship Marketing: Strategic and Tactical Implications." *Management Decision* 34 (3): 5–14.

Hackethal, A., M. Haliassos, and T. Jappelli. 2012. "Financial Advisors: A Case of Babysitters?" *Journal of Banking & Finance* 36 (2): 509–524.

Havighurst, R. J. 1953. *Human Development and Education*. Retrieved from https://psycnet.apa.org/record/1953-06438-000.

Heffernan, T., G. O'Neill, T. Travaglione, and M. Droulers. 2008. "Relationship Marketing: The Impact of Emotional Intelligence and Trust on Bank Performance." *International Journal of Bank Marketing* 26 (3): 183–199.

Hung, A. A., and J. K. Yoong. 2013. "Asking for Help: Survey and Experimental Evidence on Financial Advice and Behavior Change." In *The Market for Retirement Financial Advice*, edited by O. S. Mitchell and K. Smetters, 182–212. Great Britain: Oxford University Press.

Inderst, R., and M. Ottaviani. 2009. "Misselling Through Agents." *American Economic Review* 99 (3): 883–908.

Istat. 2011. Multipurpose Survey on Households: Aspects of Daily Life. www.istat.it.

Jappelli, T., and M. Padula. 2013. "Investment in Financial Literacy and Saving Decisions." *Journal of Banking & Finance* 37 (8): 2779–2792.

Kramer, M. M. 2012. "Financial Advice and Individual Investor Portfolio Performance." *Financial Management* 41 (2): 395–428.

Kramer, M. M. 2016. "Financial Literacy, Confidence and Financial Advice Seeking." *Journal of Economic Behavior & Organization* 131: 198–217.

Kruger, J., and D. Dunning. 1999. "Unskilled and Unaware of it: How Difficulties in Recognizing One's Own Incompetence Lead to Inflated Self-assessments." *Journal of Personality and Social Psychology* 77 (6): 1121–1134.

Lacko, J. M., and J. K. Pappalardo. 2004. *The Effect of Mortgage Broker Compensation Disclosures on Consumers and Competition: A Controlled Experiment*.

Locke, E. A., and G. P. Latham. 2002. "Building a Practically Useful Theory of Goal Setting and Task Motivation: A 35-year Odyssey." *American Psychologist* 57 (9): 705–717.

Loewenstein, G., D. M. Cain, and S. Sah. 2011. "The Limits of Transparency: Pitfalls and Potential of Disclosing Conflicts of Interest." *American Economic Review* 101 (3): 423–428.

Lusardi, A. 2003. *Saving and the Effectiveness of Financial Education.* http://rider.wharton.upenn.edu/ prc/PRC/WP/WP2003-14.pdf.

Lusardi, A. 2008. *Household Saving Behavior: The Role of Financial Literacy, Information, and Financial Education Programs (No. w13824).* Cambridge: National Bureau of Economic Research.

Lusardi, A., and O. S. Mitchell. 2007a. "Baby Boomer Retirement Security: The Roles of Planning, Financial Literacy, and Housing Wealth." *Journal of Monetary Economics* 54 (1): 205–224.

Lusardi, A., and O. S. Mitchell. 2007b. "Financial Literacy and Retirement Preparedness: Evidence and Implications for Financial Education." *Business Economics* 42 (1): 35–44.

Lusardi, A., and O. S. Mitchell. 2008a. "How Much do People Know about Economics and Finance? Financial Illiteracy and the Importance of Financial Education." *Policy Brief* 5: 1–5.

Lusardi, A., and O. S. Mitchell. 2008b. *Planning and Financial Literacy: How do Women Fare? (No. w13750).* Cambridge: National Bureau of Economic Research.

Lusardi, A., and O. S. Mitchell. 2011a. *Financial Literacy and Planning: Implications for Retirement Wellbeing (No. w17078).* Cambridge: National Bureau of Economic Research.

Lusardi, A., and O. S. Mitchell. 2011b. "Financial Literacy Around the World: An Overview." *Journal of Pension Economics & Finance* 10 (4): 497–508.

Lusardi, A., and O. S. Mitchell. 2011c. "Financial Literacy and Retirement Planning in the United States." *Journal of Pension Economics & Finance* 10 (4): 509–525.

Mandell, L. 2008. "Financial Literacy of High School Students." In *Handbook of Consumer Finance Research*, edited by Jing Jian Xiao, 163–183. New York, NY: Springer.

Marsden, M., C. D. Zick, and R. N. Mayer. 2011. "The Value of Seeking Financial Advice." *Journal of Family and Economic Issues* 32 (4): 625–643.

Mediobanca. 2014. *Le principali società italiane*, October 2014, 16.

Monticone, C. 2010. "How Much does Wealth Matter in the Acquisition of Financial Literacy?" *Journal of Consumer Affairs* 44 (2): 403–422.

OECD. 2016. OECD/INFE International Survey of Adult Financial Literacy Competencies, OECD, Paris. www.oecd.org/finance/ OECD-INFE-International-Survey-of-Adult-Financial-Literacy-Competencies.pdf.

Peress, J. 2003. "Wealth, Information Acquisition, and Portfolio Choice." *The Review of Financial Studies* 17 (3): 879–914.

Roberts-Lombard, M., E. Van Tonder, T. G. Pelser, and J. J. Prinsloo. 2014. "The Relationship between Key Variables and Customer Loyalty Within the Independent Financial Advisor Environment." *The Retail and Marketing Review* 10 (1): 25–42.

Rust, R. T., and A. J. Zahorik. 1993. "Customer Satisfaction, Customer Retention, and Market Share." *Journal of Retailing* 69 (2): 193–215.

Servon, L. J., and R. Kaestner. 2008. "Consumer Financial Literacy and the Impact of Online Banking on the Financial Behavior of Lower-Income Bank Customers." *Journal of Consumer Affairs* 42 (2): 271–305.

Shapira, Z., and I. Venezia. 2001. "Patterns of Behavior of Professionally Managed and Independent Investors." *Journal of Banking & Finance* 25 (8): 1573–1587.

Skimmyhorn, W. 2016. "Assessing Financial Education: Evidence From Boot Camp." *American Economic Journal: Economic Policy* 8 (2): 322–343.

Stanton, J. M., and S. G. Rogelberg. 2001. "Using Internet/Intranet Web Pages to Collect Organizational Research Data." *Organizational Research Methods* 4 (3): 200–217.

Stolper, O. 2017. "It Takes two to Tango: Households' Response to Financial Advice and the Role of Financial Literacy." *Journal of Banking & Finance* 92: 295–310.

Stolper, O. A., and A. Walter. 2017. "Financial Literacy, Financial Advice, and Financial Behavior." *Journal of Business Economics* 87 (5): 581–643.

Stolper, O. A., and A. Walter. 2018. "Birds of a Feather: The Impact of Homophily on the Propensity to Follow Financial Advice." *The Review of Financial Studies* 32 (2): 524–563.

Van Rooij, M., A. Lusardi, and R. Alessie. 2011. "Financial Literacy and Stock Market Participation." *Journal of Financial Economics* 101 (2): 449–472.

Van Rooij, M., A. Lusardi, and R. Alessie. 2012. "Financial Literacy, Retirement Planning and Household Wealth." *The Economic Journal* 122 (560): 449–478.

Volpe, R. P., J. E. Kotel, and H. Chen. 2002. "A Survey of Investment Literacy among Online Investors." *Journal of Financial Counseling and Planning* 13 (1): 1.

West, J. 2012. "Financial Advisor Participation Rates and Low Net Worth Investors." *Journal of Financial Services Marketing* 17 (1): 50–66.

Willis, L. E. 2008. "Against Financial-literacy Education." *Iowa Law Review* 94: 197.

Appendix

Table A1. Financial Literacy Survey Questions Van Rooij, Lusardi, and Alessie 2011; All questions included the options 'All of the above' and 'I don't know'

Basic Financial Literacy	
BFL_1	Suppose you had €100 in a savings account and the interest rate was 2% per year. After 5 years, how much do you think you would have in the account if you left the money to grow? [More than €110; Exactly €110; Less than €110]
BFL_2	Imagine that the interest rate on your savings account was 1% per year and inflation was 2% per year. After one year, how much would you be able to buy with the money in this account? [More than today; Exactly the same; Less than today]
BFL_3	Assume a friend inherits h10,000 today and his sibling inherits h10,000 3 years from now. Who is richer because of the inheritance? [My friend; His sibling; They are equally rich]
BFL_4	Suppose that in the year 2010, your income has doubled and prices of all goods have doubled too. In 2010, how much will you be able to buy with your income? [More than today; The same as today; Less than today]
Advanced Financial Literacy	
AFL_1	Which of the following statements describes the main function of the stock market? [The stock market helps to predict stock earnings; The stock market results in an increase in the prices; The stock market brings people who want to buy with people who wants to sell stocks]
AFL_2	Which of the following statements is correct? If somebody buys the stock of firm B in the stock market [He owns a part of firm B; He has lent money to firm B; He is liable for firm B's debts]
AFL_3	Which of the following statements is correct? [One cannot withdraw money invested in a mutual fund during the first year; Mutual funds can invest in several assets, for example invest in both stocks and bonds; Mutual funds pay a guaranteed rate of return which depends on the past performance]
AFL_4	Which of the following statements is correct? If somebody buys a bond of firm [He owns a part of firm B; He has lent money to firm B; He is liable for firm B's debts]
AFL_5	Consider a long time period (for example 10 or 20 years), which asset normally gives the highest return? [Saving accounts; Bonds; Stocks]
AFL_6	Normally, which asset displays the highest fluctuation over time? [Saving accounts; Bonds; Stocks]
AFL_7	When an investor spreads his money among different assets, does the risk of losing money [Increase; Decrease; Stay the same]
AFL_8	If you buy a 10-year bond, it means you cannot sell it after five years without incurring a major penalty, even with an efficient secondary market. [True; False]
AFL_9	Stocks are normally riskier than bonds [True; False]
AFL_10	Buying a company stock usually provides a safer return than a stock mutual fund [True; False]
AFL_11	If the interest rate falls, what should happen to bond prices? [Rise; Falls; Stay the same]

Table A2. Variables definitions.

Variable	Definition
Dependent variables	
Basic Financial Literacy	Sum of the correct answers to four questions devised to measure BFL, as in Table A1. In the baseline model, the index is expressed in quartiles and each item is weighted by the percentage of medium incorrect answers to the question.
Advanced Financial Literacy	Sum of the correct answers to eleven questions devised to measure AFL, as in Table A1. In the baseline model, the index is expressed in quartiles and each item is weighted by the percentage of medium incorrect answers to the question.
Overall Financial Literacy	Sum of basic and advanced financial literacy indexes, expressed in quartiles.
Explanatory variables	
IFA	Dummy variable taking the value of 1 if the respondent is assisted by an independent financial advisor, 0 otherwise.
NIFA	Dummy variable taking the value of 1 if the respondent is assisted by a non-independent advisor, 0 otherwise.
FA	Dummy variable taking the value of 1 if the respondent is assisted by either an independent or a non-independent financial advisor, 0 otherwise.
RA	Dummy variable taking the value of 1 if the respondent is only assisted by a bank clerk, 0 otherwise.
Rel. Length	Categorical variables controlling for the relationship length between advisor and client [< 6 months; 7 months-1 year; 1–3 years; 3–5 years; > 5 years].
Gender	Dummy variable taking the value of 1 for male 0 for female investors
Age	Five intervals covering from 18 to over 75 years old.
Children	Number of dependent children.
Econ. Degree	Dummy variable taking the value of 1 if the respondents have a degree in economics or finance, 0 otherwise.
Willingness to learn	The self-reported interest towards financial and economics subjects (measured on a Likert scale from 1 -not interested at all- to 5 -extremely interested).
Income	Seven dummy variables controlling for the respondents' gross income [< 25,000; €25,000–50,000; €51,000–80,000; €81,000–15,000; €151,000–205,000; €251,000–500,000; > €500,000].
Geographic controls	Five dummy variables controlling for the respondent living in Northwest, Northeast, Centre and South (including Isles).
Professional controls	Five dummy variables controlling for the respondents' occupation (Employee, Manager, Self-employed, Pensioner and outside the labour market).
Instrumental variables	
Distrust System	Categorical variable controlling for the trust towards the Italian banking system as a whole [Not trustworthy at all; Slightly trustworthy; Neutral; Very trustworthy; Extremely trustworthy].
Fidelity	Dummy variable, which takes the value of 1 if the customer has a longer relationship with the advisor, than with the financial institution the advisor currently works for.
Education	Categorical variable controlling for the respondent's education [elementary/middle school; high school; college or above].
Rating	Dummy variable taking the value of 1 if the respondent assessed the correct rating order of U.S.A., European Union, Italy and Developing Country, 0 otherwise.

Notes: the table provides brief definitions of the variables reported in the descriptive and empirical evidence.

Table A3. Correlation matrix.

	IFA	NIFA	RA	rel. length	gender	age	children	econ.degree	WTL
NIFA	−0.2757*	1							
RA	−0.2678*	−0.8523*	1						
Rel. length	−0.0313	0.0313	.	1					
Gender	−0.0166	0.1224*	−0.1137*	0.0135	1				
Age	0.1194*	0.1125*	−0.1777*	0.3240*	0.0182	1			
Children	−0.0644	0.1843*	−0.1497*	0.2876*	−0.0093	0.2356*	1		
Econ. degree	0.0397	0.0262	−0.0479	−0.0576	0.0366	−0.2527*	−0.0984*	1	
WTL	−0.0593	0.0758	−0.0438	0.055	0.1773*	−0.0531	−0.036	0.2743*	1
Income	0.0295	0.1305*	−0.1469*	0.1963*	0.2583*	0.1872*	0.1824*	0.2069*	0.0629

Note: the table shows the correlations among the regressors of the models aforementioned.
*statistical significance at 5% level.

Financial literacy and fraud detection

Christian Engels, Kamlesh Kumar and Dennis Philip

ABSTRACT
Who is better at detecting fraud? This paper finds that more financially knowledgeable individuals have a higher propensity to detect fraud: a one standard deviation increase in financial knowledge increases fraud detection probabilities by 3 percentage points. The result is not driven by individuals' higher financial product usage and is observed to be moderated by individuals' low subjective well-being, effectively depleting skills to detect fraud. Interestingly, prudent financial behavior relating to basic money management is found to have negligible effects for detecting fraud. The findings attest to the fact that fraud tactics are increasingly complex and it is greater financial knowledge rather than basic money management skills that provide the degree of sophistication necessary to detect fraud. The paper draws policy implications for consumer education programs to go beyond cultivating money management skills, and provide advanced financial knowledge necessary for tackling fraud.

1. Introduction

The 2018 Identity Fraud Study released today [February 6, 2018] by Javelin Strategy & Research, revealed that the number of identity fraud victims increased by eight percent (rising to 16.7 million U.S. consumers) in the last year, a record high since Javelin Strategy & Research began tracking identity fraud in 2003. The study found that despite industry efforts to prevent identity fraud, fraudsters successfully adapted to net 1.3 million more victims in 2017, with the amount stolen rising to $16.8 billion. (Javelin Strategy & Research 2018)

With increased digitalization of financial services and use of plastic payments, recent years have seen an amplification in the volume of fraudulent activities, costing the economy billions of dollars. Particularly on the rise is consumer fraud, which refers to the unauthorized access to another's bank account or payment card details to carry out fraudulent transactions. Noteworthy is the high degree of sophistication with which consumer fraud is committed, such that many fraudulent activities remain undiscovered, with victims being rarely compensated. For instance, authorized push payment frauds, contactless card and card skimming frauds, to name a few, are emergent types of fraud that can continue unhindered for long periods, if detected at all. Banks' fraud detection and verification systems can miss illicit transactions that are designed to appear authentic; therefore, banks place emphasis on their customers to spot and report any fraudulent activities in their accounts.

In this paper, we study the importance of financial literacy – the ability to process economic information and make informed financial decisions (Lusardi and Mitchell 2014) – for fraud detection. We focus specifically on the role of financial knowledge and financial behavior related to prudent money management.[1] Financial knowledge can provide the skills to better disentangle genuine from fraudulent information, make an individual more attentive to fraud risk, reduce their relative ignorance to fraudulent too-good-to-be-true scams, and enable them to cultivate greater effectiveness in detecting fraud. Prudent financial behavior can reduce an individual's exposure to be a target for fraud.

Thus, the paper builds on the growing evidence that there is a strong relationship between financial literacy and economic outcomes. For example, financially literate individuals are observed to be more financially aware of financial products and services (Banerjee et al. 2019), better at engaging in day-to-day financial management activities such as retirement planning and wealth accumulation (Lusardi and Mitchell 2007a, 2007b, 2011; Klapper and Panos 2011), more likely to participate in financial markets (Van Rooij, Lusardi, and Alessie 2011; Yoong 2011; Balloch, Nicolae, and Philip 2015) and better equipped to face macroeconomic shocks such as the financial crisis (Klapper and Panos 2013).

Previous literature on consumer fraud identifies certain risk factors and social contexts associated with victimization. Van Wilsem (2011) observes that people with low self-control run substantially higher victimization risk from internet consumer fraud. DeLiema et al. (2018) find that fraud incidences are non-negligible at older ages as a consequence of poorer financial capability. Studying a sample of survey participants aged 50 or above, the paper documents evidence that older adults may be more susceptible to fraud due to greater asset accumulation and as fraudsters may consider them easier targets due to potential cognitive impairments associated with aging.[2] Financial knowledge can provide the skills required to improve individuals' attentiveness to fraudulent practices, increase their detection capabilities and empower them to deter fraud. In an experimental setup, Anderson (2016) observes that consumer literacy related to understanding various financial marketplaces significantly affect respondents' propensities to accurately identify fraudulent advertisements. Also, Andreou and Philip (2018) find that the financially knowledgeable among the younger generation have a significantly higher propensity of declining an offer to engage in a Ponzi or fraudulent scheme than their peers, after being solicited.

To analyze the relationship between financial literacy and fraud detection, we use information from 5698 US respondents to the National Financial Well-Being Survey (NFWBS), which was fielded in 2016 by the Consumer Financial Protection Bureau (CFPB) and designed to be representative of the adult US population. In addition to granular socio-economic and demographic information, the survey asks respondents whether they have experienced fraud in the past, where someone has, without their permission, used or attempted to use any of their existing accounts, such as a credit or debit card, checking, savings, telephone, online, or insurance account. The NFWBS survey also captures respondents' financial literacy, financial product usage and financial behavior information.

The empirical analysis uncovers a positive and economically meaningful association between financial knowledge and fraud detection: the more financially knowledgeable the respondents, the more fraud they detect. The results corroborate that financial knowledge enhances the financial capability of individuals by being more aware of, and better at recognizing, fraud when it occurs. The significant positive relationship is found to not be driven by more financially knowledgeable individuals more intensively holding financial products and services, and thus exposing themselves to more fraud risk.[3] In fact, we observe that, no matter a low or high number of financial products and services held, the percentage of respondents detecting fraud increases as the level of financial knowledge increases.

Next, we proceed to investigate whether individuals exhibiting prudent financial behavior relating to basic money management are better at detecting fraud. We include in our analysis a battery of information relating to basic financial behaviors that enable individuals to manage their finances better. These include, among others, setting and pursuing financial goals; setting and consulting a budget; whether bills are paid on time; whether statements, bills and receipts are checked for errors; and whether the credit card balance is paid off in full each month. Interestingly, the test results indicate that prudent financial behaviors do not really matter when it comes to the ability to detect fraud. We observe marginal negative significance for the financial behavior dimensions, pursuing financial goals, staying within budget and having a savings habit, such that these prudent financial behaviors marginally reduce the propensity to detect fraud. However, overall we see that the positive effect of financial knowledge in detecting fraud remains the strong influencing factor.

The weak result for financial behavior suggests that efficient management of finances does not directly correlate with greater effectiveness in spotting fraudulent activities. This can be explained by the fact that fraud is becoming increasingly sophisticated and it is not financial behavior but financial knowledge that provides the degree of sophistication necessary to be able to detect consumer fraud. Financial knowledge strengthens one's capacity to recognize fraud risk and also empowers individuals to take necessary steps in detecting fraud when it happens.

We further find that the relationship between financial knowledge and fraud detection can be attenuated when individuals' subjective well-being is low, in effect reducing individuals' capacities to detect fraud due to the high cognitive loads that low well-being imposes. This is in line with previous studies that document a negative relationship between one's capacity to make sensible economic decisions and the impediments to an individual's cognitive function. For example, Mani et al. (2013), Haushofer and Fehr (2014), Deck and Jahedi (2015) and Schilbach, Schofield, and Mullainathan (2016) show that economic decisions worsen with increases in cognitive load.

To empirically test this, we use survey information on three subjective well-being aspects of the individuals, namely, life satisfaction, optimism about the future, and the belief that works yield success. The results identify significant interactions between well-being and financial knowledge in a meaningful way. More specifically, we observe that the greater the life dissatisfaction, the higher the pessimism about the future, and the greater the disagreement that work will yield success in the future, the weaker becomes the relationship between financial knowledge and fraud detection. By contrast, at higher levels of subjective well-being, we observe that financial knowledge emerges as a significant determinant of an individual's abilities to detect fraud. The results indicate that as well-being deteriorates, the beneficial effects of financial knowledge regarding fraud detection tamper off. Overall, the subjective well-being of an individual plays an important moderating role in the relationship between financial knowledge and fraud detection.

Our study has crucial policy implications given the recent interest in the importance of financial literacy for general consumers and retail investors from a behavioral perspective (IOSCO and OECD 2018). As fraud is increasingly sophisticated, policy steps should emphasize consumer education programs to enhance financial knowledge on aspects such as risk and return. If consumers understand how financial products operate, they will be better able to identity and protect themselves from 'too good to be true' offers. Further, training on aspects related to achieving prudent financial behavior must go beyond cultivating money management skills to also include training to detect and deter consumer fraud.

2. Data and variables

2.1. Data sample

We use data from the National Financial Well-Being Survey (NFWBS), fielded by the Consumer Financial Protection Bureau (CFPB) in 2016. The data were weighted to represent the U.S. adult population and key subpopulations. Six thousand three hundred and ninety-four respondents participated in the survey, which forms a representative sample of the adult population from all 50 US states. With the intention of measuring individual-level financial well-being and its determinants, the cross-sectional survey records a rich set of individual and household characteristics at a high level of granularity. The survey captures individual attributes including socio-demographic attributes, namely age, gender, civil-status, ethnicity; socio-economic attributes, namely education, income; and spatial attributes, namely census region and urban-rural linkages. Along with these individual-level attributes, the survey includes important information on financial fraud detection, level of financial knowledge, level of financial product usage, as well as respondents' financial attitudes and behavioral traits. After excluding respondents who did not reveal their information on the various questions that we study in the paper, we are left with a final sample of 5698 individuals for our empirical investigation.

2.2. Variable constructions and descriptive analysis

In order to elicit information on whether the respondent detected attempted or actual fraud, the following survey question was asked:

> In the past 5 years, has someone without your permission used or attempted to use an existing account of yours, such as a credit or debit card, checking, savings, telephone, online, or insurance account?

Table 1. Detection of fraud.

Response	Count	Pct.
Yes	1686	26.37
No	4161	65.08
I don't know	512	8.01
Refused to answer	35	0.55
Total	6394	100

This table reports the distribution (counts and percentages) of responses to the question: *In the past 5 years, has someone without your permission used or attempted to use an existing account of yours, such as a credit or debit card, checking, savings, telephone, online, or insurance account?*

Respondents were offered four choices of answers, namely, 'Yes', 'No', 'I don't know', and 'Refused'. As additional follow-on questions on the specificity and the frequency of the fraud were not asked, we are unable to clearly distinguish the case where the respondent is experiencing more (or less) fraud. A clearer identification of an individual's fraud detection ability requires us to observe the conditional outcome space, where, given the individual is targeted for fraud, he/she is able to or not able to detect it. That is, we require to observe the fraud attempts made. However, in non-experimental data such as surveys, whether or not an individual has been targeted for fraud is unobservable. Thus, we are implicitly assuming that all individuals have a similar probability of being targeted for fraud, and we proceed to study whether, conditional on being targeted, they are able to detect fraud. This assumption is not unreasonable, as fraud victimization has been sharping rising in recent years, with fraudsters randomly hunting for vulnerable individuals on mass to catch those who fall prey to their schemes. Furthermore, large-scale data breaches of corporations holding sensitive customer data have made individuals across the population vulnerable to fraud. Thus, it is likely that the respondents in our representative sample of households have all been subject to fraudulent attempts in the previous five years. Therefore, we interpret the responses to the survey question above as capturing fraud detection.

Table 1 reports the number of responses to the various response categories. We observe that around 26% report that fraud has been detected in their accounts, 65% do not consider that they have been subject to fraud, and a minority 9% of respondents report to be either unaware of fraud or refused to respond to the question. In the empirical analysis, we exclude those respondents who either choose 'I don't know' or have refused to disclose.

Following Knoll and Houts (2012), we measure financial knowledge of respondents using nine survey questions, eliciting their understanding of financial concepts such as long-term returns on investments, stocks vs. bonds vs. savings volatility, benefits of diversification, and the relationship bond prices and interest rates. The actual wordings of the questions and responses choices of the nine questions are reported in Appendix 1. For each individual, a composite score representing their level of financial knowledge is derived from their responses to the nine questions using item response theory (for methodological details, see Knoll and Houts 2012).

Panel A of Table 2 provides a descriptive analysis of the relationship between various levels of financial knowledge and fraud detection. We observe that the proportion of respondents detecting fraud increases with their financial knowledge. For instance, at the lowest financial knowledge score of −2.053, no respondents detect fraud; however, this increases to 36.61% for the case of respondents with the highest financial knowledge score of 1.267.

To measure the financial behavior of respondents, we make use of information from ten questions on money management that capture the financial behaviors relating to their savings habits, their frugality, and how they plan and manage their budgets. The actual wordings of the questions and the Likert response choices are reported in Appendix 2. The questions ask the respondents to rate their financial behaviors in a variety of dimensions such as setting and pursuing financial goals; setting and consulting your budget; whether bills are paid on time; whether statements, bills, and receipts are checked for errors; and whether the credit card balance is paid off in full each month. For each individual, we create a composite score of financial behavior by summing the response choices (which are first mapped to integers) from all ten behavior questions. Panel B of Table 2 reports the descriptive analysis of the relation between the level of financial behavior and fraud detection. Splitting

Table 2. Fraud detection, financial knowledge, financial behavior and financial product usage.

	Fraud detected		No fraud detected	
	Count	Pct.	Count	Pct.
Panel A: Financial knowledge score				
−2.053	0	0.00	6	100.00
−1.900	3	14.29	18	85.71
−1.713	21	25.30	62	74.70
−1.485	38	20.77	145	79.23
−1.215	58	18.77	251	81.23
−0.909	92	17.97	420	82.03
−0.570	178	24.18	558	75.82
−0.188	261	28.00	671	72.00
0.242	372	32.10	787	67.90
0.712	394	34.99	732	65.01
1.267	231	36.61	400	63.39
Panel B: Financial behavior score				
< 33th percentile	457	27.06	1232	72.94
33th to 66th percentile	608	29.64	1443	70.36
> 66th percentile	583	29.78	1375	70.22
Panel C: Traditional financial product usage				
0	27	14.67	157	85.33
1	155	21.12	579	78.88
2	158	24.35	491	75.65
3	236	26.58	652	73.42
4	389	32.18	820	67.82
5	409	33.47	813	66.53
6	213	31.65	460	68.35
7	53	42.40	72	57.60
8	8	57.14	6	42.86
Panel D: Alternative financial product usage				
0	1337	28.93	3284	71.07
1	258	27.74	672	72.26
2	38	33.04	77	66.96
3	12	48.00	13	52.00
4	3	42.86	4	57.14

This table reports the counts and percentages of fraud detection given the different levels of financial knowledge (Panel A), financial behavior (Panel B), and financial product usage (Panels C and D), respectively. Financial knowledge is defined as the composite score derived from nine financial literacy questions. The financial knowledge scores range from −2.053 to 1.267. The financial behavior score is created by summing up the Likert responses (after mapping them to integers) to the financial behavior questions and is then divided into terciles. Traditional and alternative financial product usage is measured as the number of traditional or alternative financial products respondents hold or use, respectively. Traditional and alternative product usage range from 0 to 8 and 0 to 4, respectively.

individuals into terciles according to their financial behavior, we observe that, unlike financial knowledge, fraud detection across the various financial behavior groups are strikingly similar.

We capture individuals' financial product holdings information by the number of traditional and alternative financial products and services they utilize. Traditional financial products refer to savings accounts, life insurance, health insurance, retirement accounts, pensions, non-retirement investments, education savings account, and student or education loans. Alternative financial products refer to payday or cash advance loans, pawn or auto title loans, reloadable cards that are not linked to checking or savings accounts, or using non-banks for international money transfers or for check cashing or purchasing a money order.

Panels C and D of Table 2 report fraud detection rates for different levels of traditional and alternative financial product usage, respectively. We observe that fraud detection increases with the level of financial product usage: 14.67% of respondents utilizing none of the traditional financial products report detecting fraud, in contrast to 57.14% of respondents utilizing all the eight traditional financial products reporting fraud detection. We see a similar trend for the case of alternative financial product usage.

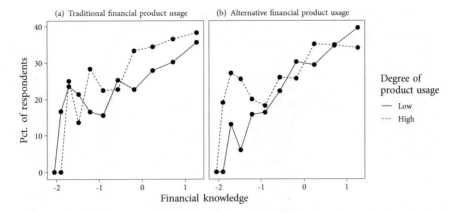

Figure 1. Rates of detected fraud for different levels of financial knowledge, plotted for low and high degrees of financial product usage. The lines indicate the percentage of respondents that detected fraud given their levels of financial knowledge and degrees of product usage. Financial knowledge is defined as the composite score derived from nine financial knowledge questions, which elicit the respondents' understanding of various financial concepts. The financial knowledge composite score ranges from −2.053 to 1.267. Traditional and alternative financial product usage is the number of traditional or alternative products respondents hold, respectively. Low and high product usage is defined as holding fewer or more financial products, respectively, than the median number of financial products held in the sample. (a) Traditional financial product usage. (b) Alternative financial product usage.

Overall, the descriptive analysis in Table 2 indicates that both financial knowledge and financial product usage have a positive relationship with fraud detection. To further investigate the relationship between these two confounding characteristics for fraud detection, Figure 1 provides a visual representation of the percentage of respondents detecting fraud at various levels of financial knowledge, for the case of low and high financial product usage. Panel (a) of Figure 1 plots the case of traditional financial product usage, while Panel (b) plots the case of alternative financial product usage. For both instances, low and high usage is defined as holding fewer or more financial products, respectively, than the median number of financial products held within the sample. Two notable observations emerge. First, we find that the financial knowledge and fraud detection relationship is similar for both low and high financial product usage, and thus the relationship is not driven by the level of financial product utilization. Second, for traditional financial products, we see that individuals with high usage detect slightly more fraud when they possess higher levels of financial knowledge. In contrast, it is the low financial knowledge individuals that detect more fraud when they are also highly utilizing alternative financial products.

Next, we discuss the summary statistics of the individual- and household-level characteristics in our sample. Table 3 reports the distribution of the respondents' age groups, gender, marital status and ethnicity, in addition to their household's income, metropolitan residency status and census region. We observe that our sample is composed of individuals aged 18 to 75 years and older, with variability across all age groups, reflecting the representation of the survey. The distributions of gender, marital status and ethnicity show that the largest groups are male, married and white, respectively. Respondents are heterogeneous with respect to education: only a small fraction (6.14%) report less than high school education, and the remaining with high school (24.83%), some college/associate's degree (30.10%), bachelor's degree (21.02%) or graduate/professional degree (17.90%). Household income exhibits variability; however, the preponderance of households (57.65%) report earnings of $60,000 or more per year. The majority of respondents live in metropolitan areas, approximately evenly spread across the US census regions.

3. Empirical analysis

3.1. Financial knowledge and fraud detection

We test the relationship between financial knowledge and fraud detection in a multivariate setting, accounting for a wide range of socio-economic and demographic attributes of the individuals. More specifically, we estimate

Table 3. Individual and household-level summary statistics.

Demographic attribute	Categories	Count	Pct.
Age	18–24	346	6.07
	25–34	952	16.71
	35–44	742	13.02
	45–54	952	16.70
	55–61	644	11.30
	62–69	944	16.57
	70–74	452	7.93
	75 or older	666	11.69
Gender	Male	3012	52.86
	Female	2686	47.14
Civil status	Married	3480	61.07
	Windowed	325	5.70
	Divorced/Seperated	603	10.58
	Single	969	17.01
	Cohabiting	321	5.63
Ethnicity	White	4097	71.88
	Black	565	9.92
	Other	289	5.07
	Hispanic	748	13.13
Education	Less than high school	350	6.14
	High school	1415	24.83
	Some college/Associate's degree	1715	30.10
	Bachelor's degree	1198	21.02
	Graduate/professional degree	1020	17.90
Income	Less than $20,000	554	9.72
	$20,000 to $29,999	446	7.83
	$30,000 to $39,999	539	9.46
	$40,000 to $49,999	407	7.14
	$50,000 to $59,999	467	8.20
	$60,000 to $74,999	601	10.55
	$75,000 to $99,999	864	15.16
	$100,000 to $149,999	1022	17.94
	$150,000 or more	798	14.00
Residency status	Non-metropolitan	764	13.41
	Metropolitan	4934	86.59
Census region	North-east	1049	18.41
	Midwest	1306	22.92
	South	1998	35.06
	West	1345	23.60
Sample size		5698	

This table reports the sample summary statistics (counts and percentage) of the demographic attributes including age, gender, civil status, ethnicity, education, income, residency status and census region.

the probit regression,

$$fraudDetectProp_i = \beta_0 + \beta_1(finKnow_i) + \beta_2(tradProducts_i)$$
$$+ \beta_3(altProducts_i) + \sum_{k=1}^{K} c_k X_{i,k} + \varepsilon_i \tag{1}$$

for $i = 1, \ldots, N$ respondents. The dependent variable is the latent fraud detection propensity related to the fraud detection indicator variable (taking the value one if the respondent has detected fraud, and zero otherwise) via the probit link function. ε_i is a i.i.d. standard normal error term. *finKnow* denotes financial knowledge score (transformed to z-scores) and is the key explanatory variable of interest. To control for the level of financial product usage, we include *tradProducts* and *altProducts*, which denote the degree of traditional and alternative financial product usage, respectively. Additionally, to account for the heterogeneity in the individual and household characteristics, we include a large set of control variables (denoted X) capturing age, gender, civil status,

Table 4. Financial knowledge and fraud detection.

	(1)	(2)	(3)
Financial knowledge	0.104***	0.090***	0.104***
	(0.03)	(0.03)	(0.03)
Traditional financial product usage		0.064*	0.073**
		(0.03)	(0.03)
Alternative financial product usage			0.109***
			(0.02)
Age	0.036	0.028	0.036
	(0.02)	(0.03)	(0.03)
Female	0.017	0.012	0.019
	(0.04)	(0.04)	(0.04)
Widowed	−0.127	−0.117	−0.119
	(0.10)	(0.10)	(0.10)
Divorced	−0.032	−0.016	−0.017
	(0.07)	(0.07)	(0.07)
Single	−0.227***	−0.201**	−0.193**
	(0.07)	(0.07)	(0.07)
Cohabiting	0.078	0.094	0.088
	(0.10)	(0.10)	(0.10)
White	0.092	0.084	0.100
	(0.10)	(0.10)	(0.10)
Black	0.191	0.186	0.132
	(0.12)	(0.12)	(0.12)
Hispanic	0.206	0.216	0.198
	(0.11)	(0.12)	(0.12)
Education	0.150***	0.139***	0.143***
	(0.03)	(0.03)	(0.03)
Income	0.071**	0.055*	0.069**
	(0.02)	(0.03)	(0.03)
Metropolitan	0.021	0.020	0.019
	(0.06)	(0.06)	(0.06)
North-east	−0.053	−0.061	−0.057
	(0.06)	(0.06)	(0.06)
Midwest	−0.075	−0.084	−0.092
	(0.06)	(0.06)	(0.06)
South	−0.021	−0.025	−0.039
	(0.06)	(0.06)	(0.06)
Constant	−0.630***	−0.623***	−0.628***
	(0.12)	(0.12)	(0.12)
Observations	5698	5698	5698
Pseudo R-squared	0.039	0.041	0.046

This table reports probit regression estimates of financial knowledge, traditional and alternative financial product usage, together with a host of demographic and financial control variables. The dependent variable takes the value of one if the respondent has detected banking fraud in the last five years, and zero otherwise. Financial knowledge is defined as the composite score derived from nine financial knowledge questions. Traditional and alternative financial product usage is defined as the number of traditional and alternative products respondents hold or use, respectively. Definitions of all the variables are reported in the appendices. Robust standard errors are reported in parentheses, and the stars ***, ** and * denote the level of significance at 1%, 5% and 10%, respectively.

ethnicity, education, household income, metro residency status and census region. The definitions of all the control variables is provided in Appendix 5.

Table 4 reports the estimation results. Column (1) presents the baseline results without accounting for the degree of financial product usage, while Columns (2) and (3) additionally include the usage levels of traditional and alternative financial products and services. We observe that the effect of financial knowledge is stable and strongly significant at the 1% level across all the specifications. For the final specification after controlling for financial product usage levels, we estimate the marginal economic significance of financial knowledge by calculating the average marginal effect. We observe that a one standard deviation increase in financial knowledge is associated with a 3 percentage point increase in the probability of fraud detection. The additional number of fraud detection cases due to increased financial literacy will be sizeable, given the high volume of fraudulent activities recorded in recent years. The estimation results show that financial knowledge plays an important role in detecting fraud and the finding holds even after controlling for the individual's level of financial product usage. Further, the coefficients on traditional and alternative financial product usage show significance at the 5% and 1% levels, respectively. The coefficient magnitude for the degree of utilization of traditional financial products is observed to be greater than that of the alternative financial products and services. Although the exact mechanism remains unexplored due to data unavailability, the results support the conjecture that a higher degree of alternative financial product usage exposes individuals to more fraud incidences.

Among the demographic attributes, we observe that education and income play an important role in detecting fraud. Considering the civil-status of respondents, the individuals who are single detect relatively less financial fraud, as compared to the base case of married individuals. None of the spatial characteristics of respondents have a significant impact on the ability to detect financial fraud, suggesting that geographic locations are unimportant in the digital era.

3.2. Financial behavior and fraud detection

In the section, we explore whether the financial behavior of individuals relating to money management plays an important role in detecting fraud. To this end, we make use of a battery of survey questions that capture prudent financial behaviors, including active budgeting, setting and pursuing financial goals, paying bills on time, staying within budget, paying off credit card balances in full each month, checking accounts for errors, frugal spending and saving habits. Additionally, we create a composite financial behavior score for each individual by summing up the response choices from all the financial behavior questions. See Appendix 2 for variables construction and definitions. To empirically test the relationship between financial behavior and fraud detection, we include the financial behavior variables (denoted *finBehav*) as additional regressors in the probit regression,

$$fraudDetectProp_i = \beta_0 + \beta_1(finKnow_i) + \beta_2(tradProducts_i)$$

$$+ \beta_3(altProducts_i) + \beta_4(finBehav_i) + \sum_{k=1}^{K} c_k X_{i,k} + \varepsilon_i \qquad (2)$$

where the dependent variable is the latent fraud detection propensity related to the fraud detection indicator variable (taking the value one if the respondent has detected fraud, and zero otherwise) via the probit link function. Further, we include all the individual- and household-level control variables as in Equation (1).

Table 5 reports the estimation results. Columns (1) to (11) present the results for the financial behaviors added individually as regressors, while Column (12) shows the results for the financial behavior composite score variable. Interestingly, we observe that except for the financial behavior variables *Stayed within budget* and *Saving habit*, which are marginally significant at the 5% and 10% levels, respectively, none of the other financial behavior variables is significant. The test results indicate that prudent financial behavior relating to basic money management does not substantially matter when it comes to the ability to detect fraud. As found previously, the positive effect of financial knowledge in detecting fraud remains a strong influencing factor.

We conduct additional analysis to understand how financial behavior and financial knowledge interact in relation to detecting fraud. For instance, if individuals with the highest financial behavior, defined as individuals reporting fullest compliance with the respective prudent behavior, do not detect fraud when they also possess high financial knowledge, it may indicate that high prudence in financial behavior is preventing individuals from being targeted. On the other hand, if financially knowledgeable individuals with the highest financial behavior are still detecting fraud, the evidence indicates less of a case of prudent financial behavior reducing being targeted for fraud. We test this premise in the data by considering individuals who have indicated the highest Likert response to the various financial behavior questions, and sorting them further into high and low financial knowledge. High (low) financially knowledgeable individuals are those with a financial knowledge score higher (smaller) than the sample average.

Table 5. Financial knowledge, financial behavior and fraud detection.

	(1)	(2)	(3)	(4)	(5)	(6)	(7)	(8)	(9)	(10)	(11)	(12)
Financial knowledge	0.104***	0.104***	0.104***	0.105***	0.102***	0.104***	0.107***	0.104***	0.104***	0.102***	0.106***	0.105***
	(0.03)	(0.03)	(0.03)	(0.03)	(0.03)	(0.03)	(0.03)	(0.03)	(0.03)	(0.03)	(0.03)	(0.03)
Traditional financial product usage	0.073**	0.073**	0.072**	0.076**	0.076**	0.072**	0.077**	0.071**	0.072**	0.073**	0.082**	0.076**
	(0.03)	(0.03)	(0.03)	(0.03)	(0.03)	(0.03)	(0.03)	(0.03)	(0.03)	(0.03)	(0.03)	(0.03)
Alternative financial product usage	0.109***	0.109***	0.108***	0.109***	0.109***	0.109***	0.106***	0.109***	0.109***	0.109***	0.107***	0.108***
	(0.02)	(0.02)	(0.02)	(0.02)	(0.02)	(0.02)	(0.02)	(0.02)	(0.02)	(0.02)	(0.02)	(0.02)
Active budgeting 1		0.003										
		(0.02)										
Active budgeting 2			0.020									
			(0.02)									
Set financial goals				−0.027								
				(0.02)								
Pursue financial goals					−0.040							
					(0.02)							
Bills paid on time						0.007						
						(0.02)						
Stayed within budget							−0.051*					
							(0.02)					
Paid off CC balance								0.014				
								(0.02)				
Check accounts for errors									0.010			
									(0.02)			
Frugal spending										0.016		
										(0.02)		
Saving habit											−0.049*	
											(0.02)	
Financial behavior score												−0.018
												(0.02)

(continued).

Table 5. Continued.

	(1)	(2)	(3)	(4)	(5)	(6)	(7)	(8)	(9)	(10)	(11)	(12)
Age	0.036	0.036	0.037	0.034	0.038	0.035	0.044	0.034	0.034	0.036	0.037	0.038
	(0.03)	(0.03)	(0.03)	(0.03)	(0.03)	(0.03)	(0.03)	(0.03)	(0.03)	(0.03)	(0.03)	(0.03)
Female	0.019	0.018	0.019	0.019	0.015	0.019	0.019	0.019	0.018	0.018	0.018	0.019
	(0.04)	(0.04)	(0.04)	(0.04)	(0.04)	(0.04)	(0.04)	(0.04)	(0.04)	(0.04)	(0.04)	(0.04)
Widowed	-0.119	-0.120	-0.121	-0.121	-0.120	-0.120	-0.123	-0.120	-0.120	-0.120	-0.124	-0.120
	(0.10)	(0.10)	(0.10)	(0.10)	(0.10)	(0.10)	(0.10)	(0.10)	(0.10)	(0.10)	(0.10)	(0.10)
Divorced	-0.017	-0.017	-0.017	-0.018	-0.020	-0.017	-0.021	-0.014	-0.016	-0.016	-0.020	-0.020
	(0.07)	(0.07)	(0.07)	(0.07)	(0.07)	(0.07)	(0.07)	(0.07)	(0.07)	(0.07)	(0.07)	(0.07)
Single	-0.193**	-0.193**	-0.190**	-0.198**	-0.198**	-0.192**	-0.192**	-0.193**	-0.192**	-0.189**	-0.196**	-0.197**
	(0.07)	(0.07)	(0.07)	(0.07)	(0.07)	(0.07)	(0.07)	(0.07)	(0.07)	(0.07)	(0.07)	(0.07)
Cohabiting	0.088	0.088	0.089	0.085	0.082	0.089	0.088	0.089	0.089	0.089	0.084	0.085
	(0.10)	(0.10)	(0.10)	(0.10)	(0.10)	(0.10)	(0.10)	(0.10)	(0.10)	(0.10)	(0.10)	(0.10)
White	0.100	0.100	0.101	0.102	0.098	0.100	0.100	0.099	0.100	0.100	0.097	0.099
	(0.10)	(0.10)	(0.10)	(0.10)	(0.10)	(0.10)	(0.10)	(0.10)	(0.10)	(0.10)	(0.10)	(0.10)
Black	0.132	0.132	0.129	0.139	0.140	0.135	0.125	0.136	0.134	0.134	0.134	0.131
	(0.12)	(0.12)	(0.12)	(0.12)	(0.12)	(0.12)	(0.12)	(0.12)	(0.12)	(0.12)	(0.12)	(0.12)
Hispanic	0.198	0.197	0.195	0.205	0.209	0.197	0.208	0.196	0.198	0.198	0.206	0.202
	(0.12)	(0.12)	(0.12)	(0.12)	(0.12)	(0.12)	(0.12)	(0.12)	(0.12)	(0.12)	(0.12)	(0.12)
Education	0.143***	0.143***	0.143***	0.143***	0.144***	0.143***	0.144***	0.142***	0.143***	0.142***	0.145***	0.143***
	(0.03)	(0.03)	(0.03)	(0.03)	(0.03)	(0.03)	(0.03)	(0.03)	(0.03)	(0.03)	(0.03)	(0.03)
Income	0.069**	0.069**	0.070**	0.070**	0.070**	0.069***	0.070**	0.067**	0.070***	0.071**	0.076**	0.069**
	(0.03)	(0.03)	(0.03)	(0.03)	(0.03)	(0.03)	(0.03)	(0.03)	(0.03)	(0.03)	(0.03)	(0.03)
Metropolitan	0.019	0.018	0.018	0.020	0.021	0.019	0.020	0.017	0.018	0.019	0.021	0.020
	(0.06)	(0.06)	(0.06)	(0.06)	(0.06)	(0.06)	(0.06)	(0.06)	(0.06)	(0.06)	(0.06)	(0.06)
North-east	-0.057	-0.057	-0.055	-0.060	-0.060	-0.057	-0.060	-0.057	-0.058	-0.056	-0.060	-0.059
	(0.06)	(0.06)	(0.06)	(0.06)	(0.06)	(0.06)	(0.06)	(0.06)	(0.06)	(0.06)	(0.06)	(0.06)
Midwest	-0.092	-0.091	-0.090	-0.094	-0.092	-0.091	-0.095	-0.091	-0.091	-0.091	-0.095	-0.093
	(0.06)	(0.06)	(0.06)	(0.06)	(0.06)	(0.06)	(0.06)	(0.06)	(0.06)	(0.06)	(0.06)	(0.06)
South	-0.039	-0.039	-0.040	-0.038	-0.036	-0.039	-0.040	-0.039	-0.040	-0.039	-0.036	-0.039
	(0.06)	(0.06)	(0.06)	(0.06)	(0.06)	(0.06)	(0.06)	(0.06)	(0.06)	(0.06)	(0.06)	(0.06)
Constant	-0.628***	-0.628***	-0.628***	-0.630***	-0.629***	-0.628***	-0.629***	-0.627***	-0.628***	-0.629***	-0.628***	-0.628***
	(0.12)	(0.12)	(0.12)	(0.12)	(0.12)	(0.12)	(0.12)	(0.12)	(0.12)	(0.12)	(0.12)	(0.12)
Observations	5698	5698	5698	5698	5698	5698	5698	5698	5698	5698	5698	5698
Pseudo R-squared	0.046	0.046	0.046	0.047	0.047	0.046	0.047	0.046	0.046	0.046	0.047	0.046

This table reports probit regression estimates of financial knowledge, financial behavior and financial product usage, together with a host of demographic and financial control variables. The dependent variable takes the value of one if the respondent has detected banking fraud in the last five years, and zero otherwise. Financial knowledge is defined as the composite score derived from nine financial knowledge questions. The construction of the financial behavior variables used in Columns (1) to (11) are described in Appendix 2. In Column (12), the composite financial behavior score is used, which is created by summing up the responses to the financial behavior questions. Traditional and alternative financial product usage is defined as the number of traditional and alternative financial products respondents hold or use, respectively. Definitions of all variables are reported in the appendices. Robust standard errors are reported in parentheses, and the stars ***, **, and * denote the level of significance at 1%, 5% and 10%, respectively.

Table 6. Fraud detection and the interaction of financial knowledge and financial behavior.

	Active budgeting 1 (1)	Active budgeting 2 (2)	Set financial goals (3)	Pursue financial goals (4)
FB = 0 × FK = 1	0.197***	0.187***	0.188***	0.199***
	(0.05)	(0.05)	(0.05)	(0.05)
FB = 1 × FK = 0	0.068	0.006	−0.027	−0.006
	(0.07)	(0.08)	(0.08)	(0.10)
FB = 1 × FK = 1	0.237***	0.229***	0.193**	0.127
	(0.07)	(0.08)	(0.08)	(0.09)
Product usage variables	Yes	Yes	Yes	Yes
Individual and household-level controls	Yes	Yes	Yes	Yes
Observations	5698	5698	5698	5698
Pseudo R-squared	0.046	0.046	0.046	0.046

	Bills paid on time (5)	Stayed within budget (6)	Paid off CC balance (7)	Check accounts for errors (8)
FB = 0 × FK = 1	0.161*	0.195***	0.231***	0.232***
	(0.09)	(0.05)	(0.06)	(0.07)
FB = 1 × FK = 0	−0.040	−0.102	−0.000	−0.026
	(0.07)	(0.07)	(0.07)	(0.06)
FB = 1 × FK = 1	0.165**	0.086	0.147**	0.131**
	(0.07)	(0.07)	(0.06)	(0.06)
Product usage variables	Yes	Yes	Yes	Yes
Individual and household-level controls	Yes	Yes	Yes	Yes
Observations	5698	5698	5698	5698
Pseudo R-squared	0.046	0.047	0.047	0.047

	Saving habit (9)	Frugal spending (10)	Overall (11)
FB = 0 × FK = 1	0.188***	0.129**	0.211***
	(0.05)	(0.06)	(0.06)
FB = 1 × FK = 0	−0.085	−0.038	−0.025
	(0.07)	(0.06)	(0.06)
FB = 1 × FK = 1	0.131*	0.227***	0.149**
	(0.07)	(0.06)	(0.06)
Product usage variables	Yes	Yes	Yes
Individual and household-level controls	Yes	Yes	Yes
Observations	5698	5698	5698
Pseudo R-squared	0.047	0.047	0.046

This table reports probit regression estimates of the interaction of financial knowledge and financial behavior. The dependent variable takes the value of one if the respondent has detected banking fraud in the previous five years, and zero otherwise. The variable FK takes the value of one if the respondent's financial knowledge score is greater than the sample average, and zero otherwise. The variable FB captures the highest self-reported prudence in financial behavior and takes the value of one if the respondent chooses the highest Likert response to the ten financial behavior questions, and zero otherwise. Columns (1) to (10) reports the results for the ten financial behaviors. Column (11) aggregates information from all the other columns and FB takes the value of one if the respondent self-reports highest prudence in the number of financial behaviors above the average number in the sample, and zero otherwise. Product usage variables comprise information on the number of traditional and alternative financial products respondents hold or use, respectively. Definitions of all variables are reported in the appendices. Robust standard errors are reported in parentheses, and the stars ***, ** and * denote the level of significance at 1%, 5% and 10%, respectively.

Table 6 reports the probit estimation results for the probability of fraud detection. For brevity, we report only the coefficients of interest. Columns (1) to (10) present results for the various financial behaviors considered separately and Column (11) aggregates information from all the financial behaviors to construct an overall highest financial behavior indicator variable, which takes the value of one for individuals reporting highest prudence in the number of financial behaviors above the average number in the sample, and zero otherwise.

We find that the estimates for the interaction of the highest self-reported financial behaviors with financial knowledge are significant only for the case of high financial knowledge, while it remains not significant when financial knowledge is low. The results indicate that individuals with the highest self-reported financial behavior detect fraud only when their financial knowledge is also high. The findings suggest that financial behavior related to money management skills is insufficient when it comes to preventing fraud; however financially knowledge provides the sophistication necessary for detecting fraud.

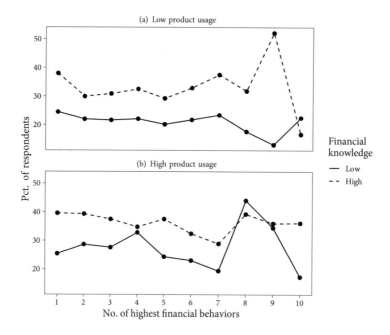

Figure 2. Rates of detected fraud given number of highest self-reported financial behaviors. The different lines indicate the percentage of respondents that detected fraud given their number of highest self-reported financial behaviors, split by low and high financial knowledge. A given financial behavior is defined as high if the respondent chooses the highest Likert response to the corresponding financial behavior question, and low otherwise. All financial behaviors considered are listed in Appendix 2. Respondents' financial knowledge is defined as high if it is greater than the sample average, and low otherwise. The different panels show the corresponding lines for low and high degrees of financial product usage, which comprises both traditional and alternative financial product usage, defined as the number of traditional or alternative products respondents hold, respectively. Low and high product usage is defined as holding fewer or more financial products, respectively, than the median number of financial products held in the sample.

To confirm the findings further, we plot in Figure 2 the percentage of respondents detecting fraud, given the number of self-reported highest financial behaviors, and examine separately those with low and high financial knowledge and low and high financial product usage. It can be seen that fraud detection rates are remarkably similar for any number of highest financial behaviors. However, there is an upward shift in detection rates for high financial knowledge individuals. Similar patterns are observed both for low as well as high product usage.

Overall, the results suggest that efficient management of money through good financial behavior is inadequate when it comes to spotting fraud. The result attests to the fact that consumer fraud is complex, and its incidences are unexpected. Thus a certain degree of financial sophistication through financial knowledge is necessary to detect fraud when it occurs.

3.3. Limits to financial knowledge and fraud detection

The findings so far establish a strong association between financial knowledge and fraud detection. Financially knowledgeable individuals have the skills to better detect fraud when it occurs. This relationship, however, may be weaker for individuals who possess a low cognitive assessment of their life or lower subjective well-being. That is, individuals with lower (higher) levels of subjective well-being will generally be less (more) attentive to their general well-being needs and have less (more) cognitive capacity to detect fraud. We test this premise in the data. To measure subjective well-being, we utilize three statements in the survey that invite Likert responses capturing respondents' subjective well-being:

(1) *I am satisfied with my life*
(2) *I am optimistic about my future*
(3) *If I work hard today, I will be more successful in the future*

Responses to all the statements are measured on a 7-point Likert scale. We accordingly map the responses to integers from 1 to 7, where the higher the integer, the higher the degree of disagreement with the statement. To estimate the effect of financial knowledge on fraud detection probabilities, given the different levels of subjective well-being, we specify a probit regression with interaction effects,

$$fraudDetectProp_i = \beta_0 + \sum_{l=1}^{L} \beta_{1,l}(wellBeing_{i,l} \times finKnow_i)$$

$$+ \beta_2(tradProducts_i) + \beta_3(altProducts_i) + \sum_{k=1}^{K} c_k X_{i,k} + \varepsilon_i \qquad (3)$$

for respondents $i = 1, \ldots, N$. The dependent variable is the latent fraud detection propensity related to the fraud detection indicator variable (taking the value one if the respondent has detected fraud, and zero otherwise) via the probit link function. As independent variables, we include the interaction between financial knowledge ($finKnow$) and the various levels of well-being ($wellBeing$), specified by the integer values for the Statements (1) to (3) shown above. We also include all individual- and household-level control variables in the regression specifications.

Table 7 reports the estimation results. Columns (1) to (3) report the results for the three subjective well-being statements. We observe that the interactions between financial knowledge and well-being levels 1 to 3 are statistically insignificant. However, for levels 4 and above, which relates to greater well-being, the financial knowledge coefficient estimates start to show significance. The results indicate that low subjective well-being weakens the positive relationship between financial knowledge and individual propensities to detect fraud, while at higher levels of subjective well-being we observe that financial knowledge emerges as a significant determinant of an individual's abilities to detect fraud. Interestingly, however, we also observe that at very high levels of subjective well-being the relationship between financial knowledge and fraud detection breaks down. In this case, individuals appear too positive and optimistic to engage in effective fraud detection; as such, when it comes to detecting fraud it pays not being overly optimistic. Overall, subjective well-being of an individual plays an important moderating role in the relationship between financial knowledge and fraud detection.

3.4. Robustness analysis – instrumental variable approach

In estimating the effect of financial knowledge on the likelihood of detecting fraud, a potential source of concern might be a bias due to omitted variables influencing both financial knowledge and fraud detection. One such variable can be the respondents' digital literacy, which prior research has found to affect human capital accumulation and potentially financial literacy. For example, Servon and Kaestner (2008) find evidence of a possible link between digital literacy and financial knowledge. Also, Lee (2018) argues that digital media literacy can help people better understand 'issues of misinformation and privacy, cyber crimes such as phishing and other types of fraud' (465).

To test that the results concerning the relationship between financial knowledge and fraud detection are not driven by unobserved factors, we employ an instrumental variable approach. We instrument financial knowledge by an indicator variable that takes the value of one if the parent who raised the respondent attended graduate school, and zero otherwise. Graduate school degrees in the U.S. encompass master's degrees and PhD or other doctoral degrees, such as doctorates from medical and law schools. We argue that graduate parent as an instrument satisfies both the relevance and exclusion restrictions. First, individuals with graduate education, on average, earn higher incomes and acquire more wealth, subsequently investing in the acquisition of advanced financial knowledge. Over time, graduate parents will pass on their knowledge to their children, increasing also the children's financial knowledge. We thus expect a strong correlation between the respondents' parent having attended graduate school and their financial knowledge. Second, having a graduate parent will be, arguably, orthogonal to the respondents' fraud detection propensities, after controlling for various socio-economic and demographic characteristics. As the digital revolution is a recent phenomenon, the parents' graduate education will not entail the acquisition of digital literacy skills that can be readily passed onto their children. Moreover,

Table 7. Financial knowledge, subjective well-being and fraud detection.

	(1)	(2)	(3)
1 × Financial knowledge	−0.007	−0.031	0.093
	(0.13)	(0.15)	(0.13)
2 × Financial knowledge	−0.001	0.003	−0.162
	(0.14)	(0.13)	(0.15)
3 × Financial knowledge	−0.011	0.068	0.066
	(0.09)	(0.10)	(0.11)
4 × Financial knowledge	0.095	0.081	0.117
	(0.07)	(0.07)	(0.06)
5 × Financial knowledge	0.149**	0.127**	0.111*
	(0.05)	(0.05)	(0.05)
6 × Financial knowledge	0.122**	0.161***	0.138**
	(0.04)	(0.04)	(0.04)
7 × Financial knowledge	0.096*	0.076	0.097*
	(0.04)	(0.04)	(0.04)
Financial behavior score	−0.018	−0.019	−0.018
	(0.02)	(0.02)	(0.02)
Traditional financial product usage	0.077**	0.076**	0.075**
	(0.03)	(0.03)	(0.03)
Alternative financial product usage	0.107***	0.107***	0.107***
	(0.02)	(0.02)	(0.02)
Age	0.037	0.038	0.038
	(0.03)	(0.03)	(0.03)
Female	0.022	0.022	0.020
	(0.04)	(0.04)	(0.04)
Widowed	−0.120	−0.122	−0.122
	(0.10)	(0.10)	(0.10)
Divorced	−0.022	−0.024	−0.021
	(0.07)	(0.07)	(0.07)
Single	−0.197**	−0.195**	−0.195**
	(0.07)	(0.07)	(0.07)
Cohabiting	0.087	0.086	0.084
	(0.10)	(0.10)	(0.10)
White	0.105	0.100	0.100
	(0.10)	(0.10)	(0.10)
Black	0.129	0.131	0.128
	(0.12)	(0.12)	(0.12)
Hispanic	0.212	0.207	0.203
	(0.11)	(0.11)	(0.12)
Education	0.145***	0.145***	0.146***
	(0.03)	(0.03)	(0.03)
Income	0.068**	0.068**	0.067**
	(0.03)	(0.03)	(0.03)
Metropolitan	0.021	0.020	0.019
	(0.06)	(0.06)	(0.06)
North-east	−0.060	−0.062	−0.059
	(0.06)	(0.06)	(0.06)
Midwest	−0.092	−0.096	−0.094
	(0.06)	(0.06)	(0.06)
South	−0.039	−0.043	−0.041
	(0.06)	(0.06)	(0.06)
Constant	−0.638***	−0.634***	−0.628***
	(0.12)	(0.12)	(0.12)
Observations	5698	5698	5698
Pseudo R-squared	0.047	0.047	0.047

This table reports the probit regression estimates of financial knowledge interacted with levels of well-being, controlling for financial behavior and financial product usage, in addition to a host of financial and demographic variables. The dependent variable takes the value of one if the respondent has detected banking fraud in the last five years, and zero otherwise. Columns (1) to (3) report results for the three well-being statements, *I am satisfied with my life*, *I am optimistic about my future* and *If I work hard today, I will be more successful in the future*, respectively. The higher the integer value for the level of well-being, the higher the degree of agreement to the statement. Financial knowledge is defined as the composite score derived from nine financial knowledge questions. Definitions of all variables are reported in the appendices. Robust errors are reported in parentheses, and the stars ***, ** and * denote the level of significance at 1%, 5% and 10%, respectively.

we find in our analysis above that prudent financial behaviors, which can be effectively fostered by a parent with graduate education, are insignificant for fraud detection, thus also ruling out these indirect effects. Therefore, graduate parent, as an instrumental variable, extracts the exogenous part of the residual variation in fraud detection, identifying all relevant parameters.

Given that our outcome variable of interest is the fraud detection indicator variable, the standard two-stage least squares estimator is likely to be inappropriate. We therefore estimate a probit model in which we instrument financial knowledge in a Limited Information Maximum Likelihood (LIML) framework. The regression setup is a recursive set of equations with the dependent variables fraud detection (*fraudDetect*) and financial knowledge (*finKnow*), in which the endogenous variable, financial knowledge, appears on the right-hand side of the fraud detection equation:

$$fraudDetectProp_i = \beta_0 + \beta_1(finKnow_i) + \sum_{k=1}^{K} \gamma_k X_{i,K} + \varepsilon_{i,1} \tag{4}$$

$$finKnow_i = \alpha_0 + \alpha_1(graduateParent_i) + \sum_{k=1}^{K} \delta_k X_{i,K} + \varepsilon_{i,2} \tag{5}$$

$$(\varepsilon_{i,1}\ \varepsilon_{i,2})' \sim \mathcal{N}(0, \Sigma) \tag{6}$$

$$\text{where}\quad \Sigma = \begin{pmatrix} 1 & \sigma_2\rho \\ \sigma_2\rho & \sigma_2^2 \end{pmatrix} \tag{7}$$

where the error terms $\varepsilon_{i,1}$ and $\varepsilon_{i,2}$ for fraud detection and financial knowledge equations, respectively, are related in a Seemingly-Unrelated Regression specification. More specifically, Equations (6) and (7) show that they are assumed to be jointly drawn from a multivariate normal distribution with a mean vector of zeros and a covariance matrix Σ. The standard deviation σ_1 is standardized to unity to identify the probit equation. The correlation term ρ captures possible endogeneity of financial knowledge for fraud detection, a testable quantity. If the above identifying assumptions are satisfied, an estimate of β_1 yields the causal effect of financial knowledge on fraud detection.

Table 8 reports the estimation results. Column (1) reports the first-stage estimates relating to financial knowledge (Equation (5)), while Column (2) reports the second-stage estimates relating to fraud detection (Equation (4)). In Column (1), we observe that the graduate parent instrumental variable is significant at the 1% level, with a coefficient estimate of 0.162. The Kleibergen–Paap rk LM test indicates that we reject at the 1% level that the instrument relevance assumption is not satisfied. Overall, the use of graduate parent as an instrument provides a strong first-stage result, satisfying the instrumental variable relevance assumption.

The second-stage estimates in Column (2) show that the causal effect of financial knowledge on fraud detection is 0.564, with weak significance (*p*-value of 7%). Importantly, in contrast to the probit estimates in Table 4, we observe that the IV estimate of financial knowledge on fraud detection is approximately five times larger in magnitude. This is possibly a result driven by the subset of the population captured by the instrument. That is, respondents with a graduate parent may have significantly higher advanced financial knowledge than the rest of the population. Further, in addressing the initial concern of omitted variable bias, the Wald test of exogeneity finds no significant correlation between the errors of Equations (6) and (7) ($H_0 : \rho = 0$), indicating that we cannot reject exogeneity of financial knowledge for fraud detection.

4. Conclusion

We study the role of financial literacy, measured through the dimensions of financial knowledge and financial behavior, for fraud detection. Consumer fraud is becoming increasingly complex such that detecting fraud requires a great deal of sophistication. As automated fraud detection systems do not always recognize fraudulent activities, banks place emphasis on their customers spotting and reporting fraudulent transactions in their accounts.

Table 8. Financial knowledge and fraud detection: instrumental variables approach.

	Financial knowledge (1)	Detected fraud (2)
Graduate parents	0.162***	
	(0.04)	
Financial knowledge		0.564*
		(0.31)
Traditional financial product usage	0.215***	−0.034
	(0.02)	(0.08)
Alternative financial product usage	−0.080***	0.138***
	(0.01)	(0.03)
Age	0.156***	−0.038
	(0.02)	(0.06)
Female	−0.332***	0.173
	(0.03)	(0.11)
Widowed	−0.024	−0.100
	(0.05)	(0.10)
Divorced	0.040	−0.034
	(0.04)	(0.07)
Single	0.045	−0.202***
	(0.04)	(0.06)
Cohabiting	−0.120**	0.138
	(0.06)	(0.10)
White	0.108*	0.043
	(0.06)	(0.11)
Black	−0.342***	0.287*
	(0.07)	(0.15)
Hispanic	−0.136*	0.250**
	(0.07)	(0.12)
Education	0.138***	0.062
	(0.02)	(0.07)
Income	0.160***	−0.014
	(0.02)	(0.07)
Metropolitan	−0.014	0.021
	(0.04)	(0.06)
North-east	−0.108***	0.001
	(0.04)	(0.07)
Midwest	−0.024	−0.069
	(0.04)	(0.06)
South	−0.054	−0.010
	(0.04)	(0.06)
Constant	0.153**	−0.666***
	(0.08)	(0.12)
Observations	5698	5698
R-squared	0.361	–
Kleibergen–Paap rk LM test	17.564***	–
Wald test of exogeneity		1.70
P-value		0.192

This table reports the results for the instrumental variable (IV) probit regression. Column (1) reports the first stage of IV regression, where the dependent variable is the financial knowledge score of respondents. Column (2) reports the second stage of IV regression, where the dependent variable takes the value of one if the respondent has detected banking fraud in the last five years, and zero otherwise. We use graduate parent as an IV for financial knowledge, which takes the value of one if either of the respondent's parents is a graduate, and zero otherwise. Definitions of all the variables are reported in the appendices. Robust standard errors are reported in parentheses, and the stars ***, ** and * denote the level of significance at 1%, 5% and 10%, respectively.

We study whether financially literate individuals, through greater financial knowledge and prudent financial behavior, will be more capable of assessing fraud risk and be better equipped to spot fraud incidences. Using a representative sample of US residents, we investigate this relationship and find strong evidence for the case of financial knowledge but not for prudent financial behaviors related to basic money management. More specifically, the results indicate that the more financially knowledgeable an individual, the greater is the fraud detection.

This corroborates the conjecture that, with financial knowledge, individuals become more skilled in detecting fraud when it occurs. Financial knowledge provides the financial sophistication necessary to detect fraud.

Prudent financial behaviors related to money management, however, do not systematically matter when it comes to the ability to detect fraud. We proxy for prudence in financial behavior by measuring money management behaviors such as setting and pursuing financial goals; setting and consulting a budget; whether bills are paid on time; whether statements, bills and receipts are checked for errors; and whether the credit card balance is paid off in full each month. The weak result for financial behavior suggests that efficient management of finances does not directly correlate with greater effectiveness in spotting fraudulent behavior, and that it is indeed financial knowledge that provides the degree of sophistication necessary to be able to detect fraud.

We observe that the positive effect of financial knowledge in detecting fraud remains a strong influencing factor, even after accounting for the individuals' usage levels in traditional and alternative financial products and services. Further, we find that subjective well-being plays an important moderating role in the relationship between financial knowledge and fraud detection. Lower levels of subjective well-being can reduce attention to fraud occurrences due to greater cognitive loads, and thus attenuating the relationship between financial knowledge and fraud detection.

Our study has important policy implications considering the recent interest in the role of financial literacy for general consumers and retail investors from a behavioral perspective. The findings suggest policy steps that emphasize consumer education programs to enhance financial knowledge to help consumers detect fraud.

Notes

1. Financial knowledge refers to one's understanding of important financial concepts such as long-term returns on investments, stocks vs. bonds vs. savings volatility, benefits of diversification, and the relationship bond prices and interest rates, among others. For each individual, a composite score representing their level of financial knowledge is derived from the number of accurate responses to the various survey questions. On the other hand, financial behavior is captured from questions on money management relating to their savings habits, their frugality, and how they plan and manage their budgets. The survey questions in this regard ask respondents to rate their financial behaviors in a wide variety of dimensions such as setting and pursuing financial goals; setting and consulting your budget; whether bills are paid on time; whether statements, bills, and receipts are checked for errors; and whether the credit card balance is paid off in full each month, among others.
2. For a review of the literature surrounding fraud victimization, refer to Financial Fraud Research Center (2012, 2013).
3. We capture individuals financial product holdings information by the number of traditional and alternative financial products and services they utilize. Traditional financial products refer to savings accounts, life insurance, health insurance, retirement accounts, pensions, non-retirement investments, education savings account, and student or education loans. Alternative financial products refer to payday or cash advance loans, pawn or auto title loans, reloadable cards that are not linked to checking or savings accounts, or using non-banks for international money transfers or for check cashing or purchasing a money order.

Disclosure statement

No potential conflict of interest was reported by the authors.

References

Anderson, K. B. 2016. "Mass-Market Consumer Fraud: Who is Most Susceptible to Becoming a Victim?" FTC Bureau of Economics No. 332. https://papers.ssrn.com/sol3/papers.cfm?abstract id = 2841286.

Andreou, P., and D. Philip. 2018. "Financial Knowledge Among University Students and Implications for Personal Debt and Fraudulent Investments." *Cyprus Economic Policy Review* 12 (2): 3–23.

Balloch, A., A. Nicolae, and D. Philip. 2015. "Stock Market Literacy, Trust, and Participation." *Review of Finance* 19 (5): 1925–1963.

Banerjee, A., I. Hasan, K. Kumar, and D. Philip. 2019. "The Power of a Financially Literate Woman." SSRN Working Paper.

Deck, C., and S. Jahedi. 2015. "The Effect of Cognitive Load on Economic Decision Making: A Survey and New Experiments." *European Economic Review* 78 (Supplement C): 97–119.

DeLiema, M., M. Deevy, A. Lusardi, and O. S. Mitchell. 2018. "Financial Fraud Among Older Americans: Evidence and Implications." NBER Working Paper No. 24803. https://www.nber.org/papers/w24803.

Financial Fraud Research Center. 2012. "Scams, Schemes & Swindles: A Review of Consumer Financial Fraud Research." http://longevity.stanford.edu/2012/11/19/scams-schemes-and-swindles-a-review-of-consumer-financial-fraud-research/.

Financial Fraud Research Center. 2013. "The Scope of the Problem: An Overview of Fraud Prevalence Measurement." http://longevity.stanford.edu/2013/11/14/the-scope-of-the-problem-an-overview-of-fraud-prevalence-measurement/.

Fujiwara, T., and I. Kawachi. 2009. "Is Education Causally Related to Better Health? A Twin Fixed-Effect Study in the USA." *International Journal of Epidemiology* 38 (5): 1310–1322.

Haushofer, J., and E. Fehr. 2014. "On the Psychology of Poverty." *Science* 344 (6186): 862–867.

IOSCO and OECD. 2018. "The Application of Behavioural Insights to Financial Literacy and Investor Education Programmes and Initiatives." http://www.oecd.org/finance/The-Application-of-Behavioural-Insights-to-Financial-Literacy-and-Investor-Education-Programmes-and-Initiatives.pdf.

Javelin Strategy & Research. 2018. "Identity Fraud Hits all Time High with 16.7 Million U.S. Victims in 2017 [Press Release]. https://www.javelinstrategy.com/press-release/identity-fraud-hits-all-time-high-167-million-us-victims-2017-according-new-javelin.

Klapper, L., and G. A. Panos. 2011. "Financial Literacy and Retirement Planning: The Russian Case." *Journal of Pension Economics and Finance* 10 (4): 599–618.

Klapper, L., and G. A. Panos. 2013. "Financial Literacy and Its Consequences: Evidence from Russia During the Financial Crisis." *Journal of Banking & Finance* 37 (10): 3904–3923.

Knoll, M. A., and C. R. Houts. 2012. "The Financial Knowledge Scale: An Application of Item Response Theory to the Assessment of Financial Literacy." *Journal of Consumer Affairs* 46 (3): 381–410.

Lee, N. M. 2018. "Fake News, Phishing, and Fraud: A Call for Research on Digital Media Literacy Education Beyond the Classroom." *Communication Education* 67 (4): 460–466.

Lusardi, A., and O. S. Mitchell. 2007a. "Baby Boomer Retirement Security: The Roles of Planning, Financial Literacy, and Housing Wealth." *Journal of Monetary Economics* 54 (1): 205–224.

Lusardi, A., and O. S. Mitchell. 2007b. "Financial Literacy and Retirement Preparedness: Evidence and Implications for Financial Education." *Business Economics* 42 (1): 35–44.

Lusardi, A., and O. S. Mitchell. 2011. "Financial Literacy and Planning: Implications for Retirement Wellbeing." NBER Working Paper No. 17078. https://www.nber.org/papers/w17078.

Lusardi, A., and O. S. Mitchell. 2014. "The Economic Importance of Financial Literacy: Theory and Evidence." *Journal of Economic Literature* 52 (1): 5–44.

Mani, A., S. Mullainathan, E. Shafir, and J. Zhao. 2013. "Poverty Impedes Cognitive Function." *Science* 341 (6149): 976–980.

Schilbach, F., H. Schofield, and S. Mullainathan. 2016. "The Psychological Lives of the Poor." *American Economic Review* 106 (5): 435–440.

Servon, L. J., and R. Kaestner. 2008. "Consumer Financial Literacy and the Impact of Online Banking on the Financial Behavior of Lower-Income Bank Customers." *Journal of Consumer Affairs* 42 (2): 271–305.

Van Rooij, M., A. Lusardi, and R. Alessie. 2011. "Financial Literacy and Stock Market Participation." *Journal of Financial Economics* 101 (2): 449–472.

Van Wilsem, J. 2011. "Bought It, But Never Got it' Assessing Risk Factors for Online Consumer Fraud Victimization." *European Sociological Review* 29 (2): 168–178.

Yoong, J.2011. "Financial Illiteracy and Stock Market Participation: Evidence from the RAND American Life Panel." In *Financial Literacy: Implications for Retirement Security and the Financial Marketplace*, edited by O. S. Mitchell and A. Lusardi, 76–97. Oxford: Oxford University Press.

Appendix 1. Wordings of financial knowledge questions

No.	Topic	Question	Responses
1	Understanding of long-term returns on investment	Considering a long time period (for example 10 or 20 years), which asset described below normally gives the highest return?	a. Savings accounts b. Bonds c. Stocks
2	Understanding of stocks vs bond vs savings volatility	Normally, which asset described below displays the highest fluctuations over time?	a. Savings accounts b. Bonds c. Stocks
3	Understanding of benefits of diversification	When an investor spreads his or her money among different assets, does the risk of losing a lot of money increase, decrease or stay the same?	a. Increase b. Decrease c. Stay the same
4	Understanding of possibility of stock market losses	Do you think the following statement is true or false? 'If you were to invest $1000 in a stock mutual fund, it would be possible to have less than $1000 when you withdraw your money.'	a. True b. False
5	Understanding of life insurance	Do you think the following statement is true or false? '"Whole life" insurance has a savings feature, while "term" insurance does not.'	a. True b. False
6	Understanding of possibility of housing market losses	Do you think the following statement is true or false? 'Housing prices in the US can never go down.'	a. True b. False
7	Understanding of credit card minimum payments	Suppose you owe $3000 on your credit card. You pay a minimum payment of $30 each month. At an Annual Percentage Rate of 12% (or 1% per month), how many years would it take to eliminate your credit card debt if you made no additional new charges?	a. Less than 5 years b. Between 5 and 10 years c. Between 10 and 15 years d. Never, you will continue to be in debt
8	Understanding of relationship of bonds and interest rates	If interest rates rise, what will typically happen to bond prices?	a. They will rise b. They will fall c. They will stay the same d. There is no relationship between bond prices and the interest rate
9	Understanding of mortgage term length on total interest paid	Do you think the following statement is true or false? 'A 15-year mortgage typically requires higher monthly payments than a 30-year mortgage, but the total interest paid over the life of the loan will be less.'	a. True b. False

Appendix 2. Wordings of financial behavior questions

No.	Variable Label	Question and Responses	Variable Construction
Panel A: To what extent do you agree or disagree with each of the following statements?			
1	Active budgeting 1	I consult my budget to see how much money I have left a. Strongly disagree b. Disagree c. Neither agree nor disagree d. Agree e. Strongly agree	Variables in Panel A take values 1-5, corresponding to the response choices a–e, respectively, and then transformed to z-scores.
2	Active budgeting 2	I actively consider the steps I need to take to stick to my budget a. Strongly disagree b. Disagree c. Neither agree nor disagree d. Agree e. Strongly agree	
3	Set financial goals	I set financial goals for what I want to achieve with my money a. Strongly disagree b. Disagree c. Neither agree nor disagree d. Agree e. Strongly agree	
4	Pursue financial goals	I prepare a clear plan of action with detailed steps to achieve my financial goals a. Strongly disagree b. Disagree c. Neither agree nor disagree d. Agree e. Strongly agree	
Panel B: Please indicate how often you have engaged in the following activities in the past six months			
5	Bills paid on time	Paid all your bills on time a. Not applicable b. Never c. Seldom d. Sometimes e. Often f. Always	Variables in Panel B take values 1-5, corresponding to the response choices b-f, respectively, and then trans-formed to z-scores.
6	Stayed within budget	Stayed within your budget or spending plan a. Not applicable b. Never c. Seldom d. Sometimes e. Often f. Always	
7	Paid off CC balance	Paid off credit card balance in full each month a. Not applicable b. Never c. Seldom d. Sometimes e. Often f. Always	

(continued).

Appendix 2. Continued.

No.	Variable Label	Question and Responses	Variable Construction
8	Check accounts for errors	Checked your statements, bills and receipts to make sure there were no errors a. Not applicable b. Never c. Seldom d. Sometimes e. Often f. Always	

Panel C: To what extent do you agree or disagree with the following statements:

No.	Variable Label	Question and Responses	Variable Construction
9	Saving habit	Putting money into savings is a habit for me a. Strongly disagree b. Disagree c. Disagree slightly d. Agree slightly e. Agree f. Strongly agree	Variables in Panel C take values 1-6, corresponding to the response choices a-f, respectively, and then trans-formed to z-scores.
10	Frugal spending	If I can re-use an item I already have, there's no sense in buying something new a. Strongly disagree b. Disagree c. Disagree slightly d. Agree slightly e. Agree f. Strongly agree	

Appendix 3. Wordings of financial product usage questions

Variable Label	Product Name	Variable Construction
Traditional financial product usage	Which of the following financial products and services do you currently have? a. Checking or Savings Account at a bank or credit union b. Life Insurance c. Health Insurance d. Retirement Account (such as a 401k or IRA) e. Pension f. Non-Retirement Investments (such as stocks, bonds or mutual funds) g. Education Savings Account (such as 529 or Coverdale) h. Student/Education Loan (for yourself or someone else)	Product usage score is the number of formal financial services the respondents utilize and then transformed to z-score.
Alternative financial product usage	Which of the following, if any, have you used in the past 12 months? a. Payday Loan or Cash Advance Loan b. Pawn Loan or Auto Title Loan[a]. c. A re-loadable card that is not linked with a checking or savings account[b] d. A place other than a bank or credit union to give or send money to relatives or friends outside the U.S e. A place other than a bank or credit union to cash a check or purchase a money order	Product usage score is the number of infor-mal financial services the respondents utilize and then transformed to z-score.

[a] Auto title loan is a small loan for a short period of time (usually 30 days) where you give the lender your auto title.

[b] These cards may have logos such as MasterCard, VISA, Discover or American Express and you can keep adding money onto this card and use it to make purchases and pay bills anywhere credit cards are accepted or withdraw the cash from an ATM. This does not include phone cards, gift cards for a particular store or service or cards that you cannot add more funds onto.

Appendix 4. Wordings of subjective well-being questions

Variable Label	Question and Responses	Variable Construction
	Please indicate the degree to which you agree or disagree with each of the following statements:	
Life satisfaction	I am satisfied with my life a. Strongly disagree ⋮ g. Strongly agree	Variables in Panel B take values 1-7, corresponding to the response choices a-g, respectively.
Optimism about future	I am optimistic about my future a. Strongly disagree ⋮ g. Strongly agree	
Work yield success	If I work hard today, I will be more successful in the future a. Strongly disagree ⋮ g. Strongly agree	

Appendix 5. Individual and household-level control variable definitions

Variable name	Variable definition
Age	The survey captures age of respondents in seven non-overlapping age brackets, between 18 and 74, and the eighth age bracket captures respondents older than 75. The variable 'Age' for a respondent is equal to the midpoint age of the age bracket the respondents belong to. For respondents in the eighth age bracket, the variable takes values equal to the lower limit of the age bracket. The variable is then transformed to z-score.
Female	It takes the value of one if respondent is female, and zero otherwise.
Widowed	It takes the value of one if the respondent has reported their civil status as widow, and zero otherwise.
Married	It takes the value of one if the respondent has reported their civil status as married, and zero otherwise.
Divorced	It takes the value of one if the respondent has reported their civil status as divorced, and zero otherwise.
Single	It takes the value of one if the respondent has reported their civil status as single, and zero otherwise.
Cohabiting	It takes the value of one if the respondent has reported their civil status as cohabiting, and zero otherwise.
Black	It takes the value of one if the respondent has reported their ethnicity as black, and zero otherwise.
Hispanic	It takes the value of one if the respondent has reported their ethnicity as hispanic, and zero otherwise.
Other	It takes the value of one if the respondent has reported their ethnicity as other than white, black or hispanic, and zero otherwise.
Education	The survey captures the education level of respondents, classified into five categories. The variable 'Education' takes values equal to the minimum number of schooling years required to attain the degree. To map the academic degrees to number of schooling years, we adapt the mapping in Fujiwara and Kawachi (2009). The variable is then transformed to z-score.
Income	The survey captures the income level of respondents, classified into nine non-overlapping income brackets and the ninth income bracket captures income of $150,000 or above. The variable 'Income' for a respondent is equal to the midpoint income of the income bracket the respondents belong to. For respondents in the lower most income bracket, the variable takes values equal to the upper limit of the income bracket. Similarly, for the upper most income bracket, the variable takes values equal to the lower limit of the income bracket. The variable is then transformed to z-score.
Metropolitan	It takes the value of one if the respondent resides in a metropolitan residency area, and zero otherwise.
North-east	It takes the value of one if the respondent resides in the north-east census region, and zero otherwise.
Mid-west	It takes the value of one if the respondent resides in the mid-west census region, and zero otherwise.
South	It takes the value of one if the respondent resides in the south census region, and zero otherwise.

Index

Note: Figures are indicated by italics and tables by bold type. Endnotes are indicated by the page number followed by "n" and the endnote number e.g., 57n50 refers to endnote 50 on page 57.

For Product Safety Concerns and Information please contact our
EU representative GPSR@taylorandfrancis.com Taylor & Francis
Verlag GmbH, Kaufingerstraße 24, 80331 München, Germany